God, Me and Being Very Old

Stories and Spirituality in Later Life

God,
Me and
Being Very Old

Stories and Spirituality in Later Life

Edited by

Keith Albans and Malcolm Johnson

scm press

Published in 2013 by SCM Press
Editorial office
3rd Floor, Invicta House,
108–114 Golden Lane
London EC1Y 0TG

SCM Press is an imprint of Hymns Ancient & Modern Ltd
(a registered charity)
13A Hellesdon Park Road, Norwich, Norfolk NR6 5DR, UK
www.scmpress.co.uk

The extract from 'I Look Out Over the Timeless Sea' by R. S. Thomas
is from *Collected Later Poems 1988–2000*, Bloodaxe, 2004.
Used by permission.

British Library Cataloguing in Publication Data

A catalogue record for this book is available
from the British Library

978-0-334-04945-6

Typeset by Manila Typesetting Company
Printed and bound by
ScandBook AB, Sweden

Contents

Foreword

This book is not about old age. Old age is a scientific or sociological construct that people feel the need to define and describe in biological or financial terms, expressing its needs and opportunities and often its cost to society. There is something of that in the book, but essentially this book is about *old people*, known and loved or lost and bemused. Some of the old people featured in this book have grown old imperceptibly, slipping from one stage of life into the next, gradually changing roles and responsibilities. Some have been catapulted into old age by accident or disease; they have woken up one day and been told they need extra care because they are old. And they have found themselves, by their choice or by that of their relatives or carers, in residential care, dementia care or nursing homes run by Methodist Homes.

That has been their good fortune.

I have more reason to be grateful for Methodist Homes than many who will read this book. My mother-in-law spent the last years of her life in a fairly happy state of dementia in MHA, and my husband was magnificently cared for after significant brain damage left him needing more physical care than I could give.

At the heart of this book lie the stories and songs of people whose lives began in the years between 1908 and 1938. Their stories reflect years of hardship and austerity, of deep fulfilment and of disappointment, of lovers lost or married, of work done and families raised. Many remember more vividly their childhood years as their own years increase and recall their parents and the influences of the time. Many are able to rest in the faith that has sustained them all their life and others feel the need to explore what life really means as the time to die draws closer.

The authors of the book reflect on the experience of knowing and caring for people in Methodist Homes. In particular the chaplains, appointed to each home as the 'hopeful presence' for the residents, their families and staff, have carefully researched and offered stories for us in the voices of the people themselves. This is authentic research and comes to us with integrity. We hear the struggles and delights of the faith journeys of real people and the impact these have on those with whom they share their daily life. They will have their impact on us too as we read them.

For some, entry into residential care is a traumatic experience of loss; for others, it offers a grateful release from anxiety and fear. When did this journey into old age start? The seeds of our ageing have been there from birth. As someone said, 'If a thing is old, it is a sign that it was fit to live.' The songs that our hearts sing are likely to be the same that have sustained us in our lives – though we may be singing them in a different key! The ability to embrace ageing with serenity is not easy for everyone and some need careful help to enable them to let go of the lives they have known without feeling they are falling into a vacuum of nothingness.

It is the contention of this book that autumn and winter of the seasons of our lives can be some of the most fruitful. Many old people discover the joys of freedom from responsibility so they can wear purple and act outrageously! Others fulfil a calling to be of service to others, and we find many of the volunteers are old themselves while still active. Many would echo the words on the tombstone of Winifred Holtby, 'God give me work until my life shall end and life until my work is done.' But some of those whose physical frailty needs the care of others discover a life of the spirit that has been waiting for the opportunity to develop. The freshness of old memory gives new chance for regrets and hurts to be healed and forgiven, and for joys and delights to be lived again. And the religious faith that kept hope alive, or that had been shelved in the day-to-day struggles of existence, springs afresh at the expectation of meeting the mystery of death.

It is also the hope of the authors of this book that those reading it will be prompted to review the good experiences and tools for living well that they currently enjoy and build up the resources of faith and love that will last into the experience of ageing. The book is also offered to churches and religious groups that may be looking for ways to encourage conversation around the issues of living and dying well.

The poet R. S. Thomas wrote:

I look out over the timeless sea
over the head of one, calendar
to time's passing, who is now open
at the last month, her hair wintry.

Am I catalyst of her mettle that,
at my approach, her grimace of pain
turns into a smile? What it is saying is:
'Over love's depths only the surface is wrinkled.'

It is the privilege of those who work with old people to catch glimpses of the way God is at work and sometimes to assist him.

KATHLEEN RICHARDSON
June 2013

The Contributors

The Editors

Keith Albans is a Methodist minister with almost 30 years' experience in a variety of settings. Prior to ordination, he read Chemistry at Oxford University, took a PhD in Chemical Entomology at Southampton University, and a BD at Manchester University.

In 2001, Keith was appointed as Senior Chaplain and then Director of Chaplaincy and Spirituality at Methodist Homes (MHA). In this role, he has particular responsibility for working to support the spiritual needs of older people in care homes, housing schemes and community services, in collaboration with local chaplains, building relationships between MHA and local churches and faith communities and looking to share experience and expertise with churches and community groups.

As well as developing a general understanding of the spiritual aspects of ageing, Keith has a particular interest in end-of-life issues, and has produced a training programme to support staff in becoming active accompanists to older people as they embark on their final lap of life.

Keith is married to Helen and they have two adult children. His interests include walking, running and singing as well as following many sports in general and cricket in particular. He is a member of the Board of Trustees of the National Council for Palliative Care.

Malcolm Johnson is currently Visiting Professor of Gerontology and End of Life Care at the University of Bath, and has been Professor of Health and Social Policy at the University of Bristol (now Emeritus) since 1995. From 1984 to 1995 he was Professor of Health and Social Welfare and first Dean of the School of Health and Social Welfare at the Open University.

His research and academic interests include the social aspects of health and illness, biographical studies, death and dying, and his major specialism, ageing and the lifespan. Of his 11 books and over 160 monographs, chapters and articles, more than half relate to ageing. He is a former Secretary of the BSA Medical Sociology Group and of the British Society of Gerontology, and Founding Editor of the international journal *Ageing and Society*. He is Director of the International Institute on Health and Ageing. An elected Academician of the Academy of Social Sciences (AcSS), he is also a Fellow of the Royal Society of Arts, a Fellow of the Gerontological Society of America and a Founding Fellow of the British Society of Gerontology. His direct involvement in the care of older people includes serving as a member of the Board of Methodist Homes since 2006. Married to Christine, he is an active member of the United Reformed Church.

The Contributors

Margaret Goodall grew up in a small village where her world revolved around extended family and the Methodist chapel at the end of the road where the singing was important. When very young, and sitting through a long sermon, a favourite distraction was to count how many in the congregation she was related to! Being surrounded by grandparents and great aunts and uncles, as well as younger family members, gave an appreciation of the value of all ages. This may have been strengthened because her first love was music, especially playing the piano, and older relatives had the time to sit and listen to her play and later on to hold her three boys while she did.

Margaret's working life began as a teacher, but all aspects of life seemed to come together when she was ordained as a Methodist minister. By chance, she became chaplain to MHA's first dementia care home and began a steep learning curve that led to her becoming an MHA Chaplaincy Advisor and completing doctoral studies. This has enabled her to offer reflections on her research and experience to groups as well as to contribute articles in books and journals.

In her free time she still enjoys music, being a member of three choirs, and loves to encourage plants to flourish in her garden – sometimes too well!

Albert Jewell – Living now in Leeds, the Revd Dr Albert Jewell has served the Methodist Church for over 50 years in a variety of pastoral, educational and ecumenical contexts. His last position was as Pastoral Director and Senior Chaplain of Methodist Homes (MHA). He has written and edited a number of books on ageing, the most recent being *Spirituality and Personhood in Dementia* (2011). An executive committee member of the Christian Council on Ageing, he edits their six-monthly Dementia Newsletter. He is a Visiting Research Fellow of Glyndŵr University.

Lawrence Moore is the Director of the Windermere Centre – one of the United Reformed Church's Resource Centres for Learning that resources the URC for mission 'through hospitality and theological adventure'.

A systematic theologian and biblical scholar by training, Lawrence grew up in Zimbabwe (formerly Rhodesia). He served in political and military intelligence during the Independence war. It was while doing research into South African political theology that the penny dropped and he realized that he had been on the wrong side, involved in deeply unchristlike actions while being a keen young Christian.

This particular journey has left him with a deep passion for helping the Christian Church to realize that it is frequently part of that from which the world needs saving, rather than sign and symbol of the Kingdom of God.

The phenomenon of the ageing population has particular visibility in the United Reformed Church, which has a disproportionately high age profile. The journey into the Fourth Age throws up new questions to face about what it means to be human, and for what a lifetime pilgrimage of faith is coming to mean and involve. Lawrence is deeply concerned to discover what the gospel and the Church have to offer and learn – and, very particularly, what it means for the Church to be very old in order to discover what it means to be young.

Ann Morisy is from Liverpool but now lives in South London. Ann is a lay member of the Church of England. Her working life has been predominantly within the field of social responsibility, culminating in directing the Commission on Urban Life and Faith as a follow-up to the report *Faith in the City*. Ann is the author of a number of books on mission and social action including a consideration of intergenerational fairness – from the perspective of a baby-boomer.

Ann has been a keen student of ageing for almost 30 years – it began as a theoretical interest – but has become more and more personal. Ann is an associate of PSALM – a pan London organization that 'takes ageing and faith seriously'. Her contributions draw on up-to-date research and thinking alongside gospel insights and are always down to earth, engaging and frequently light-hearted.

Andrew Norris works as a full-time Chaplaincy Adviser for MHA where he recruits and supports the chaplains attached to each of the organization's residential services. He is an ordained Anglican priest based in Somerset where he was involved in parish ministry for 20 years. Prior to this, he worked for both Health and Social Services as a Clinical Psychologist specializing in the care of older people. He has written and contributed to several books on the subject of 'Reminiscence' and 'Group Work with the Elderly'. Andrew is married to Alison, who is also an Anglican priest. They met at university in St Andrews, in a psychiatric hospital as volunteers 'entertaining' the long-term patients. It was in this city that Andrew also met Alison's Great Aunt Maggie, through whose stories of wisdom and experience he learnt the joy of being alongside older people. Andrew and Alison have three children, and Andrew includes among his hobbies and interests dog walking, cooking, music and working as a radio presenter and DJ. He also has a deep interest in gaining theological insights about the nature of humanity from studying numerous episodes of *Star Trek*.

Joanna Walker is the Bishop's Adviser on Adult Education in the Diocese of Guildford, where she has worked since 2005, developing activities such as an annual summer school for lay people and other discipleship learning opportunities. Previously Jo worked as a lecturer in the Department of Educational Studies at Surrey University, for an educational charity called Life Academy, and in health education. Her first job as a social science graduate was with Age Concern England (now AgeUK).

She has a long-standing interest in older adults and the nature of later life and has recently started part-time doctoral studies on ageing and spirituality at Southampton University. She has published two books on retirement education and articles and book chapters on various aspects of learning in later life. She chaired the Association for Education and Ageing from 2005 to 2012 and is associate editor of its *International Journal of Education and Ageing*.

She hopes to combine her interests and experience in adult learning, ageing and spirituality in order to produce useful research on the faith and spirituality of older people. As a mid-lifer, she views this period of life as formational and wishes to promote its spiritual, life-enhancing potential.

James Woodward – After reading theology at Kings College London, James Woodward worked as a nursing auxiliary at St Christopher's Hospice with Dame Ciciley Saunders, making a particular study of the pastoral care of patients with motor neurone disease.

Alongside parish ministry in County Durham and work as a Bishop's Chaplain in Oxford, his expertise in pastoral theology led to pioneering work in the Church's response to HIV and AIDS and to a doctoral thesis on the role and identity of hospital chaplains while serving as lead Chaplain at the Queen Elizabeth Hospital Birmingham.

As priest-in-charge of Middleton and Wishaw and Bishop's Adviser in Health and Social Care, James developed a robust theological critique of health policy, serving as a lay member of the Royal College of Anaesthetists and non-executive Director of Solihull Primary Care Trust. His *Blackwell Reader in Practical Theology* remains a core textbook in pastoral and practical theology.

Master of The Lady Katherine Leveson Foundation at Temple Balsall from 1998 to 2009, James stimulated significant conversation around the theological issues of ageing and innovative practice in the spiritual care of older people and intergenerational community, including a ground-breaking book, *Valuing Age*.

Alongside his responsibilities for fabric and fundraising as Canon Steward of St George's Windsor Castle, James works alongside colleagues in St George's House in convening diverse consultations on pastoral, ethical and theological issues, drawing participants from a wide range of faith communities, statutory and voluntary organizations, nationally and internationally. For further information, see www.jameswoodward.info.

The Chaplains

Karen Balmer works as chaplain at an MHA housing scheme. She also works as Spiritual Care Lead in a Mental Health Trust. Her great love is walking mountains and walking her delightful cats (who follow her around the block each night).

Judith Briggs is an elder in a local Baptist church and is chaplain at two MHA sites. Judith recently graduated in theology after a career in horticulture. She has three grown-up children and enjoys gardens and travel.

Simon Goddard is a Baptist minister and a chaplain at an MHA care home. He is involved regionally and nationally in the Fresh Expressions movement, and is a trained mission consultant. He enjoys supporting Reading FC and watching *West Wing*.

Birgitte Grace is chaplain to an MHA nursing and residential home and housing with care scheme. Birgitte is married to Philip and has two children, Jacob and Esther, and they all worship at an Anglican church.

John Grundy is a URC lay leader at a church in north Liverpool and chaplain to three MHA housing with care schemes. John also serves on synod and national URC committees and in his free time enjoys cooking, classic comedy films and gadgets.

John Lansley is a (supposedly) retired Methodist minister and chaplain to an MHA scheme which has recently changed from being a traditional care home to an independent living with care scheme. Prior to entering the ministry, he taught at Liverpool University and claims to be one of the first generation of ageing gerontologists.

Andy Metcalf managed international exhibition and event companies before becoming a full-time MHA chaplain working in three care homes. His interests are in restoring ancient buildings and visiting pre-historic sites in Britain on holiday while walking his two dogs.

Anne Rusbridge is a Methodist minister now working as an MHA chaplain. She is married with three children and enjoying the experience of being a grandparent. In her free time, Anne enjoys reading, sewing and papercrafts.

Becki Stennett is a local preacher in the Methodist church and lay chaplain at an MHA residential care home. She graduated with an MA in theology and religion and enjoys being a Rainbow and Guide leader, reading and watching films with her hubby.

Sue Stilwell is an ordained priest in the Church of England, working as a self-supporting curate in two parishes and a chaplain in an MHA care home offering dementia and nursing care. Sue has recently been caring for her late sister who had MND (motor neurone disease).

Gail Wall is chaplain at an MHA housing with care scheme, and a young families worker at the Methodist/URC Church in the same town. Gail gained a certificate in theology and is a worship leader at her church. Her hobbies include swimming, walking, cycling and enjoying her five grandchildren.

Maddy Whittle has been chaplain in an MHA residential home for four years. She is a Methodist local preacher and retired junior school teacher. She also sings in a women's harmony group. Her interests include music, quizzes and travel.

Acknowledgements

We wish to offer our warmest thanks to all who have assisted in the preparation and development of this book.

To Albert Jewell for beginning the MHA work on spirituality.

To Andrew Norris and Margaret Goodall for their extensive work in helping to fashion the book, their expert contribution to the editing process and especially their engagement with the chaplains.

To the older people in MHA homes and schemes and what we learn from listening to them.

To the chaplains who live in close contact with older people as they live out the later stages of their lives.

To Roger Davies, CEO of MHA, for his own spiritual values and his encouragement of this project.

To Natalie Watson, Senior Commissioning Editor at SCM Press, for her willingness to see the distinctive character of the practices of accompanying older people.

To Hazel Twynham and Cath McIntosh, who have supported the editors throughout the two years of preparation and given the enterprise humour and good order.

To Fiona Dix, who provided swift and expert copy-editing skills on the final manuscript.

We especially thank our wives, Helen Albans (who also proofread much of the text) and Christine Johnson, for living patiently with our preoccupation with this book and for sharing in our belief that serving older people well matters a great deal.

Editors' Introduction

According to the Chinese proverb, 'Even the longest journey starts with a single step', so, by implication, that journey must end in a similar fashion. Human beings seem fascinated by the beginnings and endings of epic journeys – spacecraft blasting off and landing, round-the-world yachts returning, or simply the elite runners and the stragglers finishing a marathon – and at the climax of such expeditions journalists are there with the inevitable questioning as to how the participant managed to make it to the end. Exhaustion usually prevents a particularly insightful answer.

Similar interest is shown towards those living into extreme old age. At her one hundred and tenth birthday party, Charlotte was asked by the radio interviewer what her secret of living so long was. With typical forthrightness she replied, 'If I told you, it wouldn't be a secret!'

In this book we are seeking to listen to the voices of some of the oldest old in order to discover the extent to which their religious faith has helped them meet the challenges of life and, in particular, the final lap of the journey. In so doing, our hope is that we will be better able to support the spiritual needs of the growing number of very old people in our society, and gain insights which may help to light the path of others who are following in their wake.

The context out of which the particular older voices in this book come is quite specific. Each is a resident in a care home or an independent living with care scheme operated by Methodist Homes (MHA). For almost 20 years MHA has been at the forefront of developing work in the UK on the spirituality of ageing and end-of-life care, and some of those most closely involved are among the authors. The particular role that care homes play in supporting dependent older people is often ignored or, sadly, only makes the headlines when something goes wrong. Within MHA there is a particular emphasis on addressing an individual's spiritual needs alongside their physical needs and this has its focus in the work of chaplains. This diverse group of people, ordained and lay, are the ones who listen to the stories that the residents relate and who thus become aware of some of the challenges of belief and self-belief in old age. Chaplains are there for everyone, residents and their families, irrespective of an individual's religious faith or lack of it.

If that is the specific context out of which this book has arisen, our belief is that it speaks to a much wider audience. One of the recurring features of the care and support of the oldest old is the tendency to adopt an approach that, while professing to be person-centred, concentrates on their conditions and ailments and ignores their stories and personalities. For those who have problems with verbal communication, through stroke or dementia, this can be particularly distressing and is one of the prime causes for an astonishing disregard for the pastoral and spiritual support for people in the so-called Fourth Age – the oldest old whose voices we are trying to hear. This book addresses the universal needs of the very old, but it draws its strength from a fusion of innovative thinking and a managed development of practice.

We are all too aware that living into the Fourth Age can be both a pleasure and a pain.

Reviewing one's life, as we all do frequently, and more so as we get older, inevitably produces a mixture of emotions, feelings and reactions. As human beings we are the accumulation of our life experience. What we have lived, observed, thought, felt and done is the essence of our personhood. Our journey along the life path is unique, even if it has been shared with others who have lived in the same places, lived in the same houses, been to the same schools, experienced the same world and local events, gone through the stages from childhood to now; loved some people and disliked and been hurt by others, been sometimes lucky and also suffered hurtful losses. The distinctive nature of our journey is our personal biography. The story of our lives is a detailed narrative that we have constructed from millions of recollections, to form an account of who we are. As we have gone through life we have been mentally writing this story, adding to it new features and editing out others.

Curiously, we very rarely get the opportunity to tell more than episodes and tales, while what might be considered the whole life story remains for most people an unrevealed secret. Many individuals will have heard fragments and stories of special note. Some of our family members and close friends may have heard these noteworthy tales more times than they would have liked. But unless we have been in extended therapy, it is likely that even our closest kin have never heard the whole. There are two sides to this – lack of opportunity and an inbuilt restraint, which makes us reluctant to expose the totality of ourselves to another person. We will come to the reluctance later. As for the opportunities, in a world of busy-ness and schedules, there are few people with whom we would feel comfortable enough to relate our story, who would have the several hours it would take even to make a good start.

Being listened to, without constant interruption, by a non-judgemental listener is a rare and special opportunity. Having your life recollections heard with engaged interest and your inter-pretations of what they mean to you taken seriously is a particular privilege. Enabling others to know how to be such a listener is central to our purposes. What we have attempted to create here is a volume that provides, on the one hand, a handbook of sound practice for those who wish to work with older people to value themselves and the life they have lived and to set that against their faith and beliefs, and, on the other hand, a guide to chaplains and other spiritual supporters that offers a series of contextual chap-ters to explore what underpins our approach.

The main structure of the book is in three parts. The first four chapters offer a general overview of the contemporary issues around ageing, looking in particular at the growth in the number of those living into extreme old age, their stories and spiritual needs and the extent to which the churches in the UK have responded. The second part is made up of the voices of 15 older people in conversation with a chaplain who has offered both an account of the story told and their own reflection on its significance. The final part gathers together a series of practitioners who bring their own particular insight and expertise into dialogue with the older people's stories.

Names and locations in the stories have been changed so as to preserve anonymity, and, for the same reason, there is no reference to which of the chaplains is involved in the writing of any particular story. Bible references within the stories have come primarily from an individual's memory and are not therefore referenced to a particular version.

PART I

An Introduction to the Contribution, Care and Support of Older People Living in their Fourth Age

I

The Changing Face of Ageing and Old Age in Twenty-First-Century Britain

MALCOLM JOHNSON

The essential elements of the great demographic revolution that has seen life expectancy double over the past 150 years are well known and often repeated. They are usually accompanied by headlines that employ terms such as 'burden', 'challenge', 'adverse dependency ratios' and many others that portray the added years as simply more old age and more cost to the young and the tax-payer.

This book is about the stories of some of those whose lives have been part of this revolution, stories that should generate very different headlines.

Changing demography, changing old age

In a special bulletin on ageing in 2010, the Office of National Statistics (ONS) published a summary update (ONS, 2010). It reports that during the previous 25 years the percentage of the population aged 65 and over increased from 15 per cent in 1984 to 16 per cent in 2009, an increase of 1.7 million people in this age group. Over the same period, the percentage of the population aged under 16 decreased from 21 per cent to 19 per cent. This ageing of the population is projected to continue. By 2034, 23 per cent of the population is projected to be aged 65 and over, compared with 18 per cent aged under 16.

The fastest population increase has been in the number of those aged 85 and over, the 'oldest old'. In 1984, there were around 660,000 people in the UK aged 85 and over. Since then the numbers have more than doubled, reaching 1.4 million in 2009. By 2034 the number of people aged 85 and over is projected to be 2.5 times larger than in 2009, reaching 3.5 million and accounting for 5 per cent of the total population. The ONS bulletin highlights the fact that life expectancy at birth in the UK has reached its highest level on record for both males and females, 77.7 years at birth for males and 81.9 years at birth for females (2007–09).

Spectacular reductions in premature death are at the root of the demographic revolution. Dramatic declines in infant and perinatal mortality, maternal deaths in childbirth, deaths of children from infectious diseases and of adult workers from the hazards of heavy industry and unsafe workplaces, together with better nutrition and healthier housing, have all been key factors. On top of that are the benefits of modern medicine and surgery. As Michael Marmot demonstrates, these life bonuses are not equally distributed across the population, but are markedly skewed by social class, occupation, locality, income, education and lifestyle (Marmot et al., 2003; Marmot, 2004). The evidence is strong in support of the view that the life you have lived will determine your old age. Those journeys, both physical and experiential, are profoundly present in your body, self-image and spiritual reflection.

The benefits of a rapidly growing, healthy and capable ageing population are less well understood. Even less appreciated are the years of very late life, which can present even the most resilient with profiles of chronic illnesses which make their lives, and those who care for and support them, arduous, undignified, painful and all too often disregarded. However, there is a much more positive view of these developments that celebrates the dramatic reduction in premature deaths, the added years of healthy life, the greatly improved physical environment in which we live and work, the greater prosperity of modern societies, the democratization of learning and communication, and the greater equality among people of different races, religions and backgrounds.

This stream of largely unpredicted changes has appeared within the lifetimes of those who are now the oldest old. For them, rapid modernization has provided challenges of a considerable variety. Among the fastest growing sector of the populations of developed societies are those over 90, many of whose lives began during the First World War. They probably experienced childhood in sibling groups of around ten children, in times of poverty, overcrowding and disease, with an education that ended at 13 when employment in manual work began. They also lived through the gruelling interwar years when there was still a pervasive sense of threat from rival nations, economic stagnation, high unemployment, repeated epidemics of communicable diseases and extensive malnutrition in urban centres.

Despite these hardships, increasing numbers are surviving into very old age. The latest official figures show a continuing upward trend:

> Life expectancy continues to increase for both males and females in England and Wales with improvements in the recent decades mainly due to improvements in mortality at older ages. This has resulted in increasing numbers of people aged 90 and over in the population. In 2011 there were estimated to be 440,290 people aged 90 and over living in England and Wales, 0.8% of the total population (Figure 1). Although they still account for only a very small proportion of the population, over the last thirty years the number of those aged 90 and over has almost tripled. Between 2002 and 2011 alone, there was a 26% increase. (ONS, 2013a)

As can be seen in Figure 2, the UK rates are typical of the developed world.

Figure 1: Population aged 90 and over, 1981–2011 England and Wales

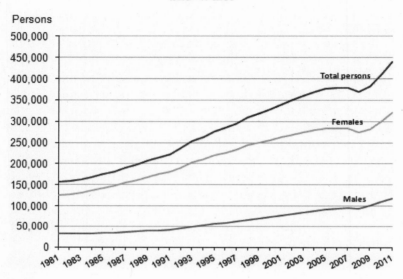

Figure 2: International comparison – number of persons aged 90 and over per 100,000

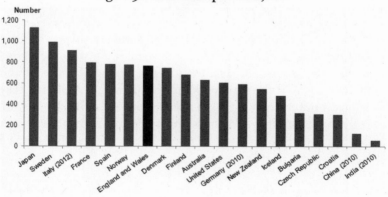

Source for Figures 1 and 2: ONS Statistical bulletin: Estimates of the Very Old (including Centenarians), 2002–11, England and Wales, released 21 March 2013.

Emergence of the Third and Fourth Ages

Ages and stages of human life have been a feature of the writings of moralists, theologians and novelists since the late Middle Ages. During the intervening centuries the calibrations of what was perceived as a good life have varied from age to age and from world-view to world-view. Thomas Cole (1992) maps the history of such ideologies of how life should be lived and the virtues that were essential to each stage. Wonderful images of the life cycle were presented, as models of the good and Christian life became popular inspirational pictures mounted in the houses of the devout and successful. Some were depicted as circles of life; others as bridges, where those who journeyed through life became more disfigured and sick as they encountered the vicissitudes of living. Bunyan's *Pilgrim's Progress* is the best known of the moral literary form, where he separates the progress of spiritual development from physical ageing.

Yet for all the theological models, the one that persisted in the public mind throughout the twentieth century was Shakespeare's 'seven ages of man', as depicted at the end of the monologue 'All the world's a stage' in *As You Like It*:

> . . . Last scene of all,
> That ends this strange eventful history,
> Is second childishness and mere oblivion,
> Sans teeth, sans eyes, sans taste, sans everything.

This graphic imagery helped to sustain the deeply negative conception of late life which Robert Butler railed against in his 1975 Pulitzer Prize-winning book, *Why Survive? Being Old in America*. It is worth rereading Butler's sketch of the clichés, stereotypes and myths he believed were held by many:

> An older person thinks and moves slowly. He does not think as he used to or as creatively. He is bound to himself and to his past and can no longer change or grow. He can neither learn well nor would he wish to. Tied to his personal traditions and

growing conservatism, he dislikes innovations and is not dis-
posed to new ideas . . . He enters a second childhood, caught up
in increasing egocentricity and demanding more from his environment than he is willing to give to it . . . He becomes irritable
and cantankerous, yet shallow and enfeebled . . . He is aimless
and wandering of mind, reminiscing and garrulous . . . He is
often stricken by diseases which, in turn, restrict his movement,
his enjoyment of food . . . He has lost his desire and capacity for
sex. His body shrinks and so too does the flow of blood to his
brain . . . Feeble, uninteresting, he awaits his death, a burden to
society, to his family and to himself. (Butler, 1975, pp. 6–7)

Butler's exposé of these widely held, baseless and pejorative views,
which were reflected in the poorest services and the lowest expectations of any sector of the population, stirred his nation and
was noted in the developed nations of Europe. Butler became the
standard-bearer for both a better informed and a more humane
approach to old age. He invented the term 'ageism' (Butler, 1980)
and articulated the pattern of prejudices based on age that operate against the interests of older people. His book can be seen as a
turning point; but when he died in 2010 the transformation into
an age-blind world remained sadly incomplete.

However, our understanding of the nature and character of old
age has changed a good deal over recent decades. As we have seen,
even by the 1980s better nutrition, less hazardous working conditions, better housing and improved medical care had produced a
rapidly growing retired section of the population who were living
longer and doing so more healthily than any previous cohort. The
benefits of a rapidly growing, healthy and capable population are
self-evident, yet the concepts of a 'Third Age' and a 'Fourth Age',
with their individual and collective characteristics, are still only
partly understood.

The identification of the Third Age as a definable new stage in
the life course was probably the creation of the French professor
Pierre Vellas, when founding the first *Université du Troisième Âge*
(U3A) in Toulouse in 1973. But it was the Cambridge historian,
philosopher and demographer Peter Laslett, a co-founder of the

University of the Third Age in Britain, who fully articulated the new four-stage pattern of the lifespan in his book *A Fresh Map of Life* (Laslett, 1989). There he draws the Third Age out of the history of population change and the emergence of retirement. Following a lengthy analysis, Laslett defines the two stages of old age as:

- The Third Age of Personal Achievement
- The Fourth Age of Dependence and Decrepitude. (p. 152)

Today we would see Laslett's use of the term decrepitude as archaic and an inappropriate description.

Laslett is adamant that neither of these stages is a chronological age. The Third Age is defined by the exit of the individual from the employed workforce into a period freed for personal fulfilment, so some will never reach the Third Age because necessity requires them to continue in economic labour. Others, through ill health, early retirement, redundancy or simply by choice (for those with enough resources) will enter it in their fifties or even earlier. Some may, because of serious illness, move straight into the Fourth Age. Those who reach the Third Age in good functional health are among the first to experience a period of active life beyond work; a marked change from the regime for most retired workers of the past. As Young and Schuller (1991) put it in their book *Life After Work*:

> The watch or clock that employers traditionally handed over to their retiring workers was a deceit. It symbolised the gift of the time that was now to be their own, rather than the employers'. But the new owner was going to wear out long before the watch.

While there is still much to be done to improve opportunities for the active old (sometimes called the young-old), this chapter and this book focus on the very old, for whom the Third Age has become seriously inhibited by disabling illnesses, which steal their ability to be independent persons. Now in the Fourth Age, they are on the final lap. This group, who need and deserve personal and dignified care, are even less well understood and are not always afforded the nuanced arrangements of support: where good provision is made it is directed overwhelmingly towards their physical ailments and discomforts. Yet the inner life of older people is profoundly important, though it is largely unseen and rarely nurtured. The Fourth Age is still subject to the neglect and stereotyping about which Butler was so angry four decades ago.

Parameters of the Fourth Age

In England, around 470,000 people die each year. Eighty per cent of all deaths are of people over 65. Two-thirds of deaths are of people over 75; one-third is 85+. In simple terms this means that at any one time there is an annual cohort of approaching 315,000 people over 75, plus another group of 65,000 65–75-year-olds, who are on the final lap of life. These 380,000 are destined to die, each year, from degenerative diseases that make their health frail for a long period before death. Heart disease, cancers, organ system failures (liver, kidney, heart, respiration), along with strokes and dementia, account for the overwhelming majority of these deaths – around 90 per cent.

What we know about the living circumstances of these increasingly frail older people is that two-thirds of those aged over 75 are women (with an even greater proportion in the higher age groups) and that two-thirds of that group of women live alone: widowed, divorced or never married.

As an overlay to the cluster of chronic illnesses that will bring their lives to an end they will typically suffer severe visual impairment. Of the 1 million 'blind' people in the UK, 90 per cent are late onset sufferers, principally of the irremediable condition macular degeneration. Similar proportions are severely hard of hearing.

Dementia is essentially a condition of old age, the incidence of which rises steeply with age; it affects women more than men. Among the over-80s around 30 per cent suffer from dementia (Peters, 2001). The Berlin Ageing Study shows that, with or without a diagnosis of dementia, there is a high probability that intelligence and cognitive functioning show decline during old age (Baltes et al., 1999). As Margaret Baltes puts it (Baltes, 1998):

[E]ven though the onset time and regulation of decline may differ across psychological domains, all domains will eventually exhibit some type of dysfunctionality and this may take the form of a cascade of decline. The Fourth Age would thus be characterised by a functional breakdown of the psychological system and less desirable psychological profiles (e.g. loss of positive wellbeing, psychological dependence on others, poor memory and impaired reasoning).

In Chapter 10 of this book, Margaret Goodall writes about accompanying people with dementia and how it affects their lives, their sense of self and their beliefs.

Depression is the epidemic condition of old age, although only 15–20 per cent of sufferers receive any treatment (Anderson and Krishnamoorthy, 2012). It affects women twice as frequently as men and multiplies the impact of co-morbid conditions such as angina, asthma, diabetes and dementia.

The prevalence of incontinence is less well documented but studies show levels of over one-third of older people in the later stages of life (Crome et al., 2001). It increases with age and most rapidly in the eighth decade. As well as being distressing and uncomfortable, incontinence is frequently precipitated by other medical conditions, such as stroke and diabetes (Harari, 2012).

As these debilitating conditions come in clusters, rather than on their own, they produce patterns of illness that make everyday life a struggle for the very old and a challenge for their carers.

Differing pathways in the Fourth Age

The highly respected American epidemiologists Joanne Lynn and David Adamson (2003), having analysed huge Medicare datasets, have concluded: 'One useful way of envisioning care for elderly people who are sick enough to die, follows from classifying them into three groups, using the trajectory of decline over time that is characteristic of each major type of disease or disability.'

Lynn and Adamson observe that each trajectory corresponds to a different rhythm and set of priorities in care (2008, p. 9):

1 *Trajectory One: Short period of evident decline – typical of cancer.*
   Most patients with malignancies maintain comfort and functioning for a substantial period. However, once the illness becomes overwhelming, the patient's status usually declines quite rapidly in the final weeks and days preceding death.

2 *Trajectory Two: Long-term limitations with intermittent exacerbations and sudden dying – typical of organ system failure.*
   Patients in this category often live for a relatively long time and may have only minor limitations in everyday life. From time to time, some physiological stress overwhelms the body's reserves and leads to a worsening of serious symptoms. Patients survive a few such episodes but then die from a complication or exacerbation, often rather suddenly. [For such patients] on-going disease management, advance-care planning, and [the provision of] mobilizing services to the home are key to optimal care.

3 *Trajectory Three: Prolonged dwindling – typical of dementia, disabling stroke, and frailty.*
   Those who escape cancer and organ system failure are likely to die at older ages of either neurological failure (such as Alzheimer's or other dementia) or generalized frailty of multiple body systems. [This large group of patients require] supportive services at home, like meals on wheels, home help, regular nursing and then skilled palliative nursing. For many, care homes where round-the-clock care, every day, is standard and necessary become the best option.

In developing these trajectories Lynn and Adamson investigated the extensive datasets held by the American Department of Health and Human Services about the claims made against the national system of healthcare support for poorer people, known as Medicare. From the analyses of records of claimants, the course of their illnesses and the treatment they received, it became evident that about 20 per cent fitted the short period of decline they labelled Trajectory One. A further 20 per cent fell into Trajectory Two, who largely suffered organ system failures. Another fifth experienced sudden deaths and consequently required no treatment.

By far the largest group is the 60 per cent who needed most help and fell into Trajectory Three. Those in this group were inelegantly but tellingly labelled 'prolonged dwindling'. Their experience of the extended last lap of life is often painful and depressing. It is typically exhausting for their (often elderly) carers. It goes on for too long. Confined to the house, and with little to stimulate them, these older people deserve spiritual as well as functional care. This greatly disabled group are also given detailed attention in Lynn et al. (2008).

Is the Fourth Age a black hole?

The research and interpretations I have presented so far look pretty gloomy. Living with a mix of chronic and disabling conditions when you know life is coming rapidly to its end is not a state to be desired. To counter the worst consequences, a person needs supportive connections (e.g. associations, churches, clubs, volunteering), younger friends (with the capacity to conduct reciprocal relationships), autonomy, self-esteem, social interaction and stimulation.

For many in the UK and around the developed world, illness, aloneness, failing faculties, daily handfuls of medication and an unwanted dependence on family and a changing army of briefly visiting strangers is their unenviable lot. The ones who get a better deal are often those with caring family nearby, better education or more money.

Avoiding the black hole

As this book powerfully illustrates, there are enough Fourth-Agers living positive fulfilling lives, within the constraints of their reduced capabilities, for us to be in no doubt that the black hole can be avoided.

An important feature of the good Fourth Age is to be able to reflect on the life lived, with satisfaction and a sense of worthiness. This is an essentially *spiritual* enterprise, which is recognized by a small section of the gerontological community – but is currently given little place in public policy for older people.

The greatest desire of all but a few of the oldest old is to have regular, reliable human contact, which both meets the shortcomings in their health condition in practical ways and also makes them feel valued, still connected with the world they no longer see, and able to have the pleasure of human warmth. Yet our support services (with the partial exception of those for cancer sufferers) are mainly instrumental, rationed, low skill, standardized and based on the most rudimentary assessments of need.

Around the time that Robert Butler's book challenged the prejudices of ageism (Butler, 1975), I was looking for ways of presenting the needs and experiences of older people to health and social care professionals. I struggled to engage their imaginations with fresh understandings of oldness. It was not that they were peculiarly insensitive or lacking in human feeling for others, yet in their professional lives they colluded with the prevailing paradox: speaking in respectful tones of the wisdom and beneficence of old age, but in policy and practice treating old people with neglect, inferior medicine, woeful housing, residential homes often resembling the workhouse, and with scant attention to their mental or spiritual health.

The metaphor of the long-distance runner presented itself to me. We the professionals are like the people in the stadium as the marathon runners enter the gates for their final lap. Exhausted and bruised by the exertions of the first 26 miles, these valiant human beings, hot and battered, remain determined to reach the finishing line. Some of them stumble and fall. We rush out to wash their wounds and take them away from the arena to a place of safety. But as we tend to their wounds no one asks about how they ran the race. All we see is the weary person in need of care and attention.

So often, this storied version of how we were treating older people hit the spot. Its brevity, drama and characterization were far enough away from everyday life, but sufficiently telling, to cause acute discomfort and reflection. Frequently it provoked indignation. Yet the strength of the imagery stayed with many listeners, who in turn used it with others.

In the ensuing, decades, societies across the world have developed more humane, whole-person approaches to elders. There is much to be proud of in the greater recognition of the proper needs of those we call old. A still growing array of opportunities and services now exist, specifically for those who have lived beyond full-time employment, which reflect their desire to be entertained and educated as well as to support others. Grandparenting is seen as an important gift between generations (Harper, 2005), providing family care to children and the opportunity for work and leisure to their parents. Retired volunteers provide the committed workforce of many charities (and churches) and in turn are supporters of travel, music, theatre and the arts.

So there is much progress to be seen, despite increasing episodes of public hand-wringing about the availability and quality of health and social care for those who are old and sick, physically or mentally. Medical conditions that brought the lives of earlier generations to a premature end are now curable or remediable. In addition, there is increasing access to health information, as Liz Lloyd has highlighted, drawing attention to the way individuals manage their own health. She writes:

> The capacity of biomedicine to drown out 'lay' voices in defining health . . . has almost hidden . . . the growing availability of information about health conditions and diseases . . . so that people living with these conditions can develop a level of expertise that can exceed that of their general practitioner. (2012, p. 29)

In a fuller investigation of the way older people are actively engaging with their own health, Higgs and Rees Jones (2009) focused on the ways in which a more educated older population has shifted the boundaries in relationships between doctors and patients.

This is significant since, as we have discussed, many who survive into late old age must live with a variety of chronic conditions for which there are no cures, only symptom management.

In social care for older people there are deep public concerns about assistance to those living at home and in care homes. Media coverage is predominantly about failures and lapses, but the story of remarkable family caring is under-reported. The UK 2011 Census (ONS, 2013b) shows that 5.8 million people in England and Wales provide unpaid care on a regular basis; up by 600,000 since 2001. Of these, around 1.4 million, that is, almost a quarter, provide in excess of 50 hours unpaid care a week. The extensive growth of supported housing, based on social housing models, enables many to maintain their independence in purpose-built dwellings. By the same token, the transformation of care homes for older people is remarkable. In startling contrast to published accounts of a relatively few examples of inadequate standards, care homes now offer more personal space, in buildings of hugely better design, with more dignity, better trained staff, far better food and a person-centred approach.

Spirituality and belief in the Fourth Age

As we have shown, we know a good deal about demography and epidemiology, which tell us that the Fourth Age is the fastest growing and most frail sector of our population. We have still fully to embrace the reality of the new old age; we still treat those in the last stage of their long lives with the poorest services of any age group. Fortunately there are imaginative initiatives and centres of excellent care to demonstrate how supporting Fourth-Agers should be done. But the largest and least visible gap is in our understanding of the profound emotional and spiritual needs of those who, having experienced the loss of loved ones and of independence, must now face their own death.

This phenomenon of the Fourth Age brings with it another set of barely observed phenomena. A long-lived life can be the source of pleasurable recollection and deepening of faith. The true wisdom of old age, which grows out of experience and the refinement of judgement about people, human values and the living out of belief, is powerful. Having 'run the race' well can be a profound pleasure, yet this gift of assurance and completion is not available to all. For many, the losses of people and capabilities that may define the Fourth Age produce spiritual distress and biographical pain (Johnson, 2013). As they face finitude and the advancing of life's end, many find that frequent periods of life review cause them profound distress. Religious faith provides great sustenance for some, while for others its weakening can lead to anxiety and the amplification of depression.

Methodist Homes (MHA) is a major provider of care homes and supported living where the spiritual needs of residents are a priority. In each of its facilities it uses its not-for-profit status to add valuable additional services. In each of its residential communities, alongside the carefully personalized activities and the trained volunteers, there are chaplains. These chaplains are there principally to address the inner lives and well-being of residents, and also to support staff and families. Here we simply note that one important area of the lives of very old people is given due prominence, in a wider world that has yet to address spiritual health and concerns.

There has been progress and it should be acknowledged, but there is still a gulf to be crossed as big as the one Robert Butler uncovered half a lifetime ago. This book aims to provide insights from the spiritual lives of some of the oldest old, and some knowledge, experience and guidance about how to engage with them. In a world where the oldest old are the most rapidly increasing sector of society, these matters deserve serious and sensitive attention.

In conclusion

In this chapter we have encountered some of the inescapable realities that attend many in the Fourth Age. In the following chapter Keith Albans looks at the later stages of life as a journey of differing strands, which emerge in the stories older people tell. He identifies the themes of the whole volume. Our intention is to explore the possibility of enhancing those lives by using the profoundly human gift of listening and listening well, with purpose.

The rest of this book looks to the ways in which the giving and receiving of well-directed accompanying can provide older people with the opportunity to tell their stories, safely, to listeners who will avoid being judgemental or directional. The power of telling stories and being attentively heard is well known. But for those at the far end of life there are ground rules and good practice that have been tried and tested. As Andrew Norris outlines in Chapter 12, the essential principles of chaplaincy can aid very old people in seeing themselves and their lives as being of real worth, enabling them to look beyond the struggles of the Fourth Age.

References

Anderson, D. and Krishnamoorthy, A., 2012, 'Depression', in Gosney, M., Harper, A. and Conroy, S. (eds), *Oxford Desk Reference: Geriatric Medicine*, Oxford: Oxford University Press, pp. 272–4.

Baltes, M. M., 1998, 'The psychology of the oldest-old: the fourth age', *Current Opinion in Psychiatry* 11:4, pp. 411–15.

Baltes, P. B., Staudinger, U. M. and Lindenberger, U., 1999, 'Lifespan psychology: theory and application to intellectual functioning', *Annual Review of Psychology* 50, pp. 471–507.

Butler, R. N., 1975, *Why Survive? Being Old in America*, New York: Harper & Row.

Butler, R. N., 1980, 'Ageism: a foreword', *Journal of Social Issues* 362:2, pp. 8–11.

Cole, T. R., 1992, *The Journey of Life: A Cultural History of Aging in America*, Cambridge: Cambridge University Press.

Crome, P., Smith, A. E., Withnall, A. and Lyons, R. A., 2001, 'Urinary and faecal incontinence: prevalence and status', *Reviews in Clinical Gerontology* 11:2, pp. 109–13.

Harari, H., 2012, 'Faecal incontinence in older people', in Gosney, M., Harper, A. and Conroy, S. (eds), *Oxford Desk Reference: Geriatric Medicine*, Oxford: Oxford University Press, pp. 318–22.

Harper, S., 2005, 'Understanding grandparenthood', in Johnson, M. L., Bengtson, V. L., Coleman, P. G. and Kirkwood, T. B. L. (eds), *The Cambridge Handbook of Age and Ageing*, Cambridge: Cambridge University Press, pp. 422–8.

Higgs, P. and Rees Jones, I., 2009, *Medical Sociology and Old Age*, London: Routledge.

Johnson, M. L., 2013, 'Biography and generation: spirituality and biographical pain at the end of life in old age', in Silverstein, M. and Giarrusso, R. (eds), *Kinship and Cohort in an Aging Society: From Generation to Generation*, Baltimore, MD: Johns Hopkins University Press, pp. 176–90.

Laslett, P., 1989, *A Fresh Map of Life: The Emergence of the Third Age*, London: Weidenfeld & Nicolson.

Lloyd, L., 2012, *Health and Care in Ageing Societies*, Bristol: Policy Press.

Lynn, J. and Adamson, D. M., 2003, *Living Well at the End of Life: Adapting Health Care to Serious Chronic Illness in Old Age*, Santa Monica, CA: Rand Health.

Lynn, J., Lynch Schuster, J., Wilkinson, A. and Noyes Simon, L., 2008, *Improving Care for the End of Life: A Sourcebook for Healthcare Managers and Clinicians*, 2nd edn, Oxford: Oxford University Press.

Marmot, M., 2004, *Status Syndrome*, London: Bloomsbury.

Marmot, M., Banks, J., Blundell, R., Lessof, C. and Nazroo, J. (eds), 2003, *Health, Wealth and Lifestyles of the Older Population in England: The 2002 English Longitudinal Study of Ageing*, London: Institute of Fiscal Studies.

ONS, 2010, *Statistical Bulletin: Focus on Older People, Older People's Day, 2010*, http://www.ons.gov.uk/ons/rel/mortality-ageing/focus-on-older-people/older-people-s-day-2010/focus-on-older-people.pdf.

ONS, 2013a, *Statistical Bulletin: Estimates of the Very Old (including Centenarians), 2002–2011, England and Wales*, http://www.ons.gov.uk/ons/rel/mortality-ageing/estimates-of-the-very-old--including-centenarians-/2002---2011/stb-evo.html.

ONS, 2013b, *2011 Census Analysis: Unpaid care in England and Wales, 2011 and comparison with 2001*, http://www.ons.gov.uk/ons/rel/census/2011-census-analysis/provision-of-unpaid-care-in-england-and-wales--2011/art-provision-of-unpaid-care.html.

Peters, R., 2001, 'The prevention of dementia', *Journal of Cardiovascular Risk* 8, pp. 253–6, quoted in Stephan, B. and Brayne, C., 2008, 'Prevalence and projections of dementia', in Downs, M. and Bowers, B. (eds), 2008, *Excellence in Dementia Care: Research into Practice*, New York: McGraw-Hill, pp. 9–34.

Young, M. and Schuller, T., 1991, *Life After Work: The Arrival of the Ageless Society*, London: HarperCollins, p. 18.

2

Supporting and Learning from the Oldest Old: The Spiritual Journey of Ageing

KEITH ALBANS

Sitting down to Sunday lunch in a care home, I found myself sharing a table with the manager and a couple of residents, one of whom I knew to be the eldest member of their community. 'Ask him to guess what you've asked for for your hundred-and-fifth birthday!' suggested the manager. Fortunately her retort, 'I don't know what all the fuss is about,' saved me from the dilemma of guessing, and so I asked her to tell me herself. With a broad smile she announced, 'I've asked for a Kindle! I read a lot, they're light, and even if I don't get a lot of use of it, someone else will when I'm gone!' Although I was separated in age from this woman by almost half a century, it struck me that she was in a place where, should I live that long, I would want to be: still active and engaged with this world and those who matter to me, but sitting lightly to it and fully accepting of my mortality.

As Director of Chaplaincy and Spirituality at Methodist Homes (MHA), I am in the privileged position of meeting many representatives of the oldest old, and often remind our staff and our chaplains that they are in one of the few jobs that offers them the opportunity to work with their own future. But in reality that privilege is shared by others, particularly family members and those offering pastoral support in community and residential settings. And it is that double focus – of being both an accompanist to and a learner from those in extreme old age – that we are seeking to explore in this book. As Rabbi Zalman Schachter-Shalomi puts it, in describing what he calls 'the December years':

> I want you to understand what it is like . . . so that when you work with people, you do not give them the kind of false hope when you tell them to buck up, be strong and so on . . . What I now need is for you to understand who I am, what I am and recognize that you, too, will someday be in this same situation if God helps you to extend your lifespan. (2011, p. 244)

Who are the oldest old?

In speaking of 'the December years' Schachter-Shalomi points to two of the defining experiences of this group of elders. First, they are those with many miles on the clock and for whom the vast majority of their lifespan is in the past. Second, their current life is being lived with a view of the finishing line, which is looming out of the future and towards the present. But in reality this is simply the final phase of the two ticking clocks that mark out all of our lives: one counting up from birth and acknowledged annually with each birthday, and the other counting down towards zero, which by its very nature does so in a hidden and covert way.

In an ageing society, it is remarkable just how large a span of life is contained in the category of those defined as old. Entering the so-called 'SAGA generation' at 55, we are still only halfway towards the age of 110, which is where we are likely to find Britain's oldest man and woman. And it is no less remarkable that, at the time of writing, the oldest man, Ralph Tarrant (110), is described as living independently in his own flat and still able to shop and cook on his own, while the oldest woman, Grace Jones (113), is described as having recently given evidence in court, leading to the conviction of the man who had burgled her house (Holmes, 2013). So even if we narrow down the age range of those about whom we are writing, we must be clear that we are not looking at a homogeneous group with a common experience of ageing; and equally, if we follow the general pattern of defining the oldest old as those aged 85 and over, we are still talking about a cohort covering a quarter of a century of life and one that can, therefore, include both parent and offspring.

Making sense of the journey

As the literature on spirituality and ageing has expanded over the past 20 years, there has been a considerable degree of unanimity among the authors, irrespective of their religious or cultural background. The one area of greatest diversity has been the attempt to define spirituality. However, I am content here to follow what has become the majority hypothesis, as expressed by Koenig et al. when they define spirituality as 'the personal quest for understanding answers to ultimate questions about life, about meaning, and about relationship to the sacred or transcendent, which may (or may not) lead to or arise from the development of religious rituals and the formation of community' (2001, p .18). However, it must be added that some fight shy of the term spirituality precisely because it is so often used in connection with religious faith and practice. Alyson Peberdy suggests one way out of that conundrum when she writes, 'Perhaps it may help to see spirituality as a search for meaning, and religion as a particular expression of that (one that usually involves God-language)' (1993, p. 219).

These parameters have given rise to some significant signposts that allow us to begin to try and speak about the journey we are exploring. First, and perhaps most importantly, there is the issue of whether or not exploring the experience of ageing through the lens of spirituality gives rise to a fundamentally different core narrative. Kenneth Howse, for one, offers an image that suggests it does:

> We think of human powers and capabilities as following a parabolic trajectory through the life course: eventually they stop climbing upwards and take a downward turn. If there is a dimension of life which stands apart from this pattern of change, it is the spiritual dimension. (1999, p. 64)

This is a significant claim, both for older people themselves and for those who accompany them. The expectation that no new experience of growth or development will occur in late life is a common feature of the narratives of ageing with which many individuals approach their own old age, while the Shakespearian notion of a seventh age 'sans everything' leads to an expectation of complete decline. But Howse's contention is confirmed by many, not least by those whose stories form part of this book. For some older people, the experience of entering a care home or a retirement living facility can enable them to reconnect with a worshipping community, albeit an informal one that only engages in an occasional hymn-sing or a rather minimalist service of Holy Communion. That alone can be enough to reawaken an important aspect of their personality and provide something that has been missing while frailty and isolation at home have prevented them attending their local church and cut them off from a vital part of their way of making sense of who they are.

A second signpost emerging from the literature is the connection between ageing, spirituality and the concepts of meaning and purpose in life. Paul Tournier expressed it in terms of an existential question: 'How can the person who has seen a meaning in life also see a meaning in old age, which seems to him to be a diminution, an amputation, a stifling of life?' (1983, p. 190). Tournier's question points us to two related aspects, namely the extent to which the experience of entering extreme old age affects our sense of who we are, and the issue of whether the ways in which we spend our time enhance or diminish our appreciation of life.

Traditionally, ageing tends to be described in terms of multiple losses, and for some of the oldest old it is the sum total of all those losses that can be catastrophic and lead to significant experiences of depression. In an online interview, 'How can I maintain my sense of self?' (Almost Home, 2008), Susan McFadden highlights some of the ways in which ageing can contribute to the loss of self. She cites the experience of being treated as a generic old person, which can lead to people feeling ignored or no longer of value. McFadden also draws attention to the fact that while many elders have a sense of self that is built up from the past and has to do with how they feel on the inside, it is also affected by the presence or absence of external support. This last point is of huge importance to anyone with a formal or informal relationship with an older person, and particularly significant for those working in residential care homes. It is also worth noting that these are issues for consideration by all of us regarding our own experience of ageing, because if Paul Tournier's question does have an answer, it lies in how we define our sense of self earlier in life, not in extreme old age.

The third signpost that the literature offers us to try and make sense of the ageing journey is the idea that the different stages of our life are marked by tasks or priorities, and that this is as true of late life as it is in the stages which precede it. These ideas are expounded most clearly in the work of Erik and Joan Erikson, particularly in the former's last book, *The Life Cycle Completed* (Erikson, 1982), which was reissued in 1997 after his death, in an extended version, with new chapters added by his widow.

Erikson suggests that there are eight significant stages on the journey of life that lead towards maturity, each of which involves a struggle that must be resolved. The seventh stage, which relates to mid-life, is focused, according to Erikson, on a struggle between what he calls 'generativity' and stagnation. The former is made up of a real concern both for younger generations and for the future of the world, while the latter is typified by a withdrawal from that. He identifies the struggle of the eighth stage, which relates to late life, as being between 'integrity', which he understands in terms of wholeness and pulling everything together, and despair. In the busyness of earlier life, much has to be left 'on hold' and so Erikson believes that only in old age is there the time and space to achieve such integrity. However, for some older people, this is not attempted or achieved because of a feeling that life is not worth living, and a sense of despair and worthlessness takes over, often leading to depression.

The outline of this eighth stage is reminiscent of Kierkegaard's famous dictum: 'Life can only be understood backwards; but it must be lived forwards' (Kierkegaard, 1996, p. 161). For many older people, the process of sifting through memories and accrued paraphernalia is a helpful one, which moves them through a time of de-cluttering and review towards the acceptance of ageing and some of the limitations it might bring. The stories in the next part of this book offer several illustrations of people for whom this experience is real, but it is clearly not something everyone experiences.

Extending Erikson's eight stages of life, his widow Joan Erikson has written of a further ninth stage in our human development. She draws on the work of the Scandinavian gerontologist Lars Tornstam, who has coined the term 'gerotranscendence', which speaks of the possibility in old age of going above or beyond the limitations and the self-absorption that can dominate the stories of ageing, and experiencing 'a new feeling of cosmic communion with the spirit of the universe, a redefinition of time, space, life and death, and a redefinition of the self' (Tornstam, 1993). For people of faith this is an interesting and thought-provoking concept, not least because while the language used is redolent of religious experience, it also points beyond the confines of religion to a wider realm of spirituality. In analysing his research based on a group of older Methodist people in Leeds (Hawley and Jewell, 2009), Albert Jewell writes:

> Certainly, growing old can make some people appear more selfish but . . . gerotranscendence did indeed grow with increasing years in the people taking part. Around three-quarters reported that they could accept the changes brought by ageing, that they were becoming less interested in material things and, most encouragingly, that they found new spiritual gifts to explore in their old age. As one person interviewed put it: 'My family are still there but they are not my purpose. My purpose is to continue unfolding the gifts I have been given – and that will continue as long as I live.' (p. 31)

There can, therefore, be little doubt that anyone seeking to support or learn from the oldest old has to take seriously the spiritual aspects of ageing. For not only do the signposts I have identified point to stages and tasks of ageing that help to make sense of the experience of growing older, they also help to articulate a narrative of ageing that runs counter to many of the stories that we usually tell and that tend to colour our expectations of becoming very old.

How was the trip?

In looking to concentrate on the testimonies of the very old, it must be acknowledged that irrespective of how people try to make sense of their story of ageing, the journey itself will have been wildly different for each individual. This is a vital truth as, in recent years, people have begun to speak and write of the emerging new narrative of ageing. Thus it is just as deceitful to construct an over-optimistic way of speaking of old age as it is to assume that being old equates with being frail or decrepit. In her recent book, Susan Jacoby claims that 'The reality evaded by propagandists for the new old age is that we all are capable of ageing successfully – until we aren't' (2012, p. xiii). Jacoby also coins the term 'emotional correctness', wherein the word 'old' is seen as an expression of prejudice rather than a factual description of a stage of life (2012, p. 5). Nevertheless, we have to acknowledge that many people's journey into very old age is marked by reasonable health and active participation in wider society and, if it happens at all, their time of restriction and frailty is relatively short. The new narrative of ageing has to have a 'both, and' quality rather than simply an 'either, or' if it is to command any credibility, and in listening to the stories many older people tell, their acceptance of the inevitability of some age-related limitation enables them to speak in relatively positive terms. This is also coloured by the sense of surprise that many elders feel at having survived so long and far in excess of what average life expectancy was when they were born. As time passes this aspect will inevitably change, as long life becomes an ever-increasing likelihood, but for now the sense of being surprised by age will remain, particularly as a man in the UK reaching 85 in 2013 can on average expect to live for another 6.3 years, while a woman reaching the same age has an average life-expectancy of a further 7.1 years (Office for National Statistics, 2011).

Landmarks along the way

As a research chemist, I was always taught the importance of a control sample in any experimental process, for it gave a way of comparing a result with what would have happened if nothing had been done. Life, of course, is not like that, and we arrive at any point with no way of knowing whether we might have reached the same place by any number of other routes. This is particularly true of the very old, and, as a consequence, when listening to their accounts it is possible to come to all kinds of conclusions about what their needs are or how best they might be supported. Nearly 20 years ago, Harold Koenig (1994, pp. 283ff.) listed up to 14 spiritual needs of physically ill elders, and similar lists of varying lengths have been produced in the intervening years.

However, as we will see in Chapter 4, a more helpful approach lies in the growing discipline of storytelling, and in particular its application in both reminiscence work with older people and in narrative gerontology. Elizabeth MacKinlay offers a broad overview of both developments in her book *Spiritual Growth and Care in the Fourth Age of Life*, where she highlights the contribution of Faith Gibson (2006) in particular. Here we see the ways in which, for both the storyteller and the listener, the process of sharing enables connections to be made between the three temporal dimensions of past, present and future. And it is the dynamic interplay between these dimensions that gives the stories of older people their particular richness, and offers helpful direction to those who accompany or support them. The question of identity – 'Who am I now?' – is tied up with so much of a person's past identity, occupation, joys and sorrows, and their present and future well-being will be determined, at least in part, by the extent to which they have begun to redefine themselves in the light of the past. But well-being will also be affected as much by the ways in which an individual is willing to entertain the possibility of a future where new things can yet be experienced, as it will by the signs that someone has begun to accept the reality of death.

Before exploring five key landmarks that tend to emerge from the stories of the oldest old, it is worth introducing one motif that has become a recurring theme in much writing about the spirituality of later life. It is the idea of 'harvest', which Edith Sitwell introduces in 'Eurydice': 'Love is not changed by Death, and nothing is lost and all in the end is harvest' (Sitwell, 1957, pp. 267–70). The importance of this idea is that it is in itself a two-sided notion that affirms both the positive and negative aspects of ageing. People speak of old age as the autumn of life, and a simple exercise in word association underlines its ambiguity. Autumn is the time of endings: the days shortening and the trees shedding their leaves as nature battens down the hatches for winter; but it is equally the season of bright vivid colours and the season for harvesting the fruits of the earth. Autumn is the crowning point of the year, and in the midst of the dying back, the whole purpose of the year becomes obvious.

Little wonder then that this theme has entered the vocabulary of ageing. Jenny Goodman suggests:

The experience of our latter years [should be shifted] from 'everybody expecting me just to wind down and disintegrate' to a place of joyful, conscious ripening, with a revitalising sense of focus and self-worth: a place from which to harvest the fruits of a lifetime. (1999, pp. 65–6)

In a similar vein, Philip Newell writes:

Old age is repeatedly devalued into an inferior state of being, regarded as a decline or fall from the fullness of life. We have forgotten the fruit that an old tree can bear, yielding an abundance that will far outweigh the crops of the young. (1999, p. 76)

This idea can be seen in each of the following landmarks on the journey into extreme old age.

Diminishment

A significant factor in the experience of ageing, which informs both Goodman and Newell, is the very real sense in which the world of the oldest old can become increasingly small. For someone moving into a care home this is a physical reality, as everything they possess has to be contained within a single bedsitting room. Depending on circumstances, such a move may involve leaving behind the house where marriage and family life have been spent, and with it the accrued set of 'stuff' which no longer has a use, and for which there is no longer any room. This can be a sudden wrench, which all the positive talk about downsizing does little to soothe.

For others, the experience of diminishment may simply be that, as travelling or walking become more difficult, their sense of the space in which they live becomes more limited, and with it comes a feeling that their impact upon the world is reduced. This is not always a sudden experience; but it can be one that creeps up gradually as the generations move relentlessly on. Parenting and grandparenting are active and time-consuming roles, whereas that of great-grandparent is usually much less so. It is hardly surprising, then, that people's sense of who they are and what their purpose is can be undermined by the passing of the years.

Kenneth Howse's comment about the parabolic nature of life (see page 22) speaks of this experience of diminishment as the natural progression into old age. His claim that the spiritual dimension of life stands against this pattern is both a promise and a challenge. If the promise is to the older person, the challenge is to those who accompany them, to find ways within the experience of diminishment of discovering a new purpose or rekindling an old one. The daily routine of 'always being done to' and the feeling of being 'a burden' – tolerated rather than being loved and accepted – can gnaw away at anyone's sense of self. Facilitating true participation in community, with a role appropriate to a person's ability, is vital to helping them to discover or even rediscover a purpose in living. Likewise, the visitor to the care home, whether family member or not, brings a sense of connection to the outside world, a connection that, while no longer physically possible, is nonetheless of immeasurable spiritual significance to many. When such connections are made across the generations, the possibility of older people giving as well as receiving can also be life-affirming.

For those with religious faith, this sense of connection has yet another dimension, and Howse's assertion of the possibility of spiritual growth in older age is another counterblast to the experience of diminishment. The role played by those who help to facilitate acts of worship, prayer, fellowship and Bible study in our care homes is therefore of vital importance, not simply for the residents but for families and staff too.

Contemplation

According to the Eden Alternative programme, the three main plagues affecting those older people living in care homes are loneliness, helplessness and boredom (Eden Alternative, 2013). The feeling of being left high and dry, with little to do except wait for the next meal, is hardly conducive to a state of well-being, but is sadly a familiar experience for many older people. Goodman's image of 'being left just to wind down and disintegrate' is a perfect summary of such an existence, just as her aspiration for 'a place of joyful, conscious ripening, with a revitalising sense of focus and self-worth' is an obvious antidote.

Most famous classical symphonies include a passage towards the end that recapitulates the principal themes around which the piece has been built. The experience of contemplation in later life is in many ways an opportunity and an invitation to do the same, but one that can require help and encouragement. Tom Gordon from the Iona Community has used the motif of an older person's photograph album in a delightful piece that explores this experience (Gordon, 2008):

Do you know, can I make you understand
that what you see – and like, it seems – is but the final page,
the most recent image in the album of my life?
Because, you see, you've started at the last page.
For that's where the album of my life lay open
when you came along, open there for you to gaze upon.
I'm glad you like that page.

But do you know, can I make you understand that this is not
it all?
There's more than this to see and know and learn about.
So, take some time to turn the pages of the album of my life.
Turn back the pages now with me.
Gaze upon the images you didn't know were there, and look
and learn.

It is a very common experience for us to gauge an older person by
how they present now, and for many young carers this is under-
standable. But as Gordon reminds us, a little time taken to turn
back the pages, to listen to the stories and to reconnect with the
person before us is a great way of valuing the individual and helping them to re-evaluate their current worth.

For those who practise a religious faith, contemplation can have
a further meaning that can help retain this sense of self-worth.
In Chapter 10, Margaret Goodall explores the particular significance that this can have for those living with dementia, but it is
by no means limited to them. In the Christian tradition, the shape
of worship is designed to focus on the transformative nature of
faith and to remember ourselves as made in the image of God and
loved by God.

Legacy

In common parlance the notion of legacy has come to mean that
which someone leaves to family and friends in their will. And this
aspect can be a cause of difficulty to many older people when
what they had hoped to leave becomes used up in paying for their
care and support in later life. It can also become a cause of friction
between the generations and there are even signs of it taking on a
political significance in a time of ageing and austerity.

From a spiritual point of view, legacy has much more to do
with the motif of harvest and the question of what impact we
have made on those around us and how, if at all, we might be
remembered after our death.

It is one of the recurring sadnesses of contemporary life that only at a person's funeral do we discover some vital fact about their story that would have completely altered our connection with them if only we had known it sooner. It is equally sad if someone is made to feel inadequate because they have not lived a heroic life of great achievement and endeavour and are unable to appreciate the ways in which they have affected others for good.

For anyone who is alongside older people, whether as formal or informal carers, family or friends, the willingness to help identify and harvest the legacy is a great gift to offer, and can be of immeasurable benefit to both the older person and to yourself. And in the current generation this can be particularly important to those who describe themselves as 'I was only a housewife'.

In many of our care homes, when a resident dies there is an opportunity for those who are left to reflect together and share something of what that person has meant to them. It is just as moving when someone speaks of how the person annoyed them as it is when someone else describes their friendship or the kindnesses received, and such occasions are almost always marked by a happy mixture of laughter and tears. All in the end really can be harvest.

Finitude

It is said that one of the perils of youth is a tendency to think that you are indestructible. For the very old the opposite is true and the last years are often lived in an ongoing dialogue with the inevitability of death. For some this gives way to depression and morbid feelings, but, for others it can be liberating, giving rise to a feeling that there is nothing to lose and that each day is a rather unexpected gift.

Fred Kaan poses a relevant question in one of his hymns: 'Were the world to end tomorrow, would we still be planting trees?' (1989, no. 16). Described as a hymn on 'not giving up', it offers an insight into how people live with this experience of finitude. For someone very old, planting a tree can be seen as rather pointless, or as an expression of their understanding that life will go on without them – indeed the tree may be part of their legacy to the next generations. A more familiar experience is watching those in extreme old age plant bulbs in the autumn, again something that could be read as an act of defiance and a desire to still be around come springtime, or simply as an act of hope that there will be a spring irrespective of whether they are still there to enjoy it.

For family and friends, accompanying those coming to terms with this experience of finitude can be frustrating and bewildering. One day they are unwilling to entertain the possibility of making plans for something in the future because 'they may not still be here', but the next day the same person will be fussing as to what you want for a Christmas or birthday present. The acknowledgement of finitude involves recognizing the interplay between the linear nature of time, the cyclical nature of the seasons and the anticipation of the eternity beyond death – irrespective of whether that final element carries the humanistic notion of non-existence or the religious promise of eternal life.

Completion

The final landmark on the journey of the oldest old is the sense of completion that can come in the final days and hours before death. For while any dying leaves behind much that is incomplete and involves family and other carers in tidying up and, indeed, in all kinds of new beginnings, for the dying person themselves, the metaphor of approaching the finishing line is apt. St Paul, in his letter to the church at Philippi, uses precisely this image in describing his attitude to the rest of his life: 'I press towards the finishing line, to win the heavenly prize to which God has called me in Christ Jesus' (Phil. 3.14).

In writing about factors that make up a so-called good death, MacKinlay includes in her list, 'to feel the time is right – sense of life completion' (2012, p. 53). In Chapter 13 of an earlier volume, she focuses on those living in aged care facilities, both residents and staff, and highlights the ways openness in talking about dying and death can help older people experience this sense of completion (MacKinlay, 2006). This is an important truth for society as a whole, one which was specifically highlighted in the National End of Life Care Strategy (Department of Health, 2008) and has featured in the work of the Dying Matters Coalition and other similar organizations (see, for example, www.dyingmatters.org, www.finalfling.com and www.goodlifedeathgrief.org.uk). It is interesting that Nolan (2012), writing out of his experience of working with dying patients in healthcare chaplaincy, develops a model of spiritual care as 'presence' and describes the role of the chaplain as 'hopeful presence'. Once again this highlights the important role that is available to those of us who accompany older people in their last years, in being present and finding opportunity for meaningful conversations as the finishing line approaches. In Methodist Homes we have developed 'The Final Lap', a training programme for staff in all of our homes, which has the express purpose of facilitating open communication with older people and giving staff in particular the confidence to remain fully present when residents wish to discuss their hopes and fears around dying (MHA Care Group, 2006).

Concluding comments

Understanding more fully the spiritual needs of the oldest members of society is a vital component of offering them better support and care. And although it is still a relatively new field, there is a growing body of recorded experience and academic reflection, both of which serve to help and guide us in our efforts. But more than that, the voices of today's oldest old can help the next generations to reflect on our own ageing and, perhaps, reassess our priorities and values. The stories in Part 2 give voice to a testimony of age that must inform the emerging narratives of ageing and be held in creative tension with them.

References

Almost Home, 2008, 'How can I maintain my sense of self?', http://www.almosthomeoutreach.org/node/118.

Department of Health, 2008, *End of Life Care Strategy: Promoting High Quality Care for All Adults at the End of Life*, London: Department of Health.

Eden Alternative, 2013, http://www.eden-alternative.co.uk/.

Erikson, E. H. and Erikson, J. M., 1982, extended 1997, *The Life Cycle Completed*, New York: W. W. Norton.

Gibson, F., 2004, *The Past in the Present: Using Reminiscence in Health and Social Care*, Maryland: Health Professions Press, cited in MacKinlay, E., 2006, *Spiritual Growth and Care in the Fourth Age of Life*, London and Philadelphia, PA: Jessica Kingsley Publishers, pp. 81–95.

Goodman, J., 1999, 'Harvesting a lifetime', in Jewell, A. (ed.), *Spirituality and Ageing*, London: Jessica Kingsley Publishers, pp. 65–70.

Gordon, T., 2008, 'The photo album of my life', in Paynter, N. and Boothroyd, H. (eds), *Holy Ground*, Glasgow: Wild Goose Publications, pp. 147–50.

Hawley, G. and Jewell, A., 2009, *Crying in the Wilderness: Giving Voice to Older People in the Church*, Derby: Methodist Homes.

Holmes, A., 2013, *Oldest in Britain*, http://oldestinbritain.nfshost.com/.

Howse, K., 1999, *Religion, Spirituality and Older People*, London: Centre for Policy on Ageing.

Jacoby, S., 2012, *Never Say Die: The Myth and Marketing of the New Old Age*, New York: Vintage Books.

Kaan, F. H., 1989, *Planting Trees and Sowing Seeds*, Oxford: Oxford University Press.

Kierkegaard, S., 1996, *Papers and Journals*, trans. Hannay, A., London: Penguin.

Koenig, H. G., 1994, *Aging and God: Spiritual Pathways to Mental Health in Midlife and Later Years*, New York: Haworth Pastoral Press.

Koenig, H. G., McCullough, M. E. and Larson, D. B., 2001, *Handbook of Religion and Health*. New York: Oxford University Press.

MacKinlay, E., 2006, *Spiritual Growth and Care in the Fourth Age of Life*, London and Philadelphia, PA: Jessica Kingsley Publishers, pp. 197ff.

MacKinlay, E., 2012, *Palliative Care, Ageing and Spirituality: A Guide for Older People, Carers and Families*, London and Philadelphia, PA: Jessica Kingsley Publishers.

MHA Care Group, 2006, *The Final Lap*, Derby.

Newell, J. P., 1999, *One Foot in Eden: A Celtic View of the Stages of Life*, Mahwah, NJ: Paulist Press.

Nolan, S., 2012, *Spiritual Care at the End of Life: The Chaplain as 'Hopeful Presence'*, London: Jessica Kingsley Publishers.

Office for National Statistics, 2011, 'Period and cohort life expectancy tables, 2010-based', http://www.ons.gov.uk/ons/publications/re-reference-tables.html?edition=tcm%3A77-227587.

Peberdy, A., 1993, 'Spiritual care of dying people', in Dickenson, D. and Johnson, M. L. (eds), *Death, Dying and Bereavement*, London: Sage, p. 219.

Schachter-Shalomi, Z., 2011, 'The December years of life', *The Journal of Transpersonal Psychology* 43:2, pp. 239–45.

Sitwell, E., 1957, *Collected Poems*, 4th edn, London: Duckworth.

Tornstam, L., 1993, 'Gerotranscendence: a theoretical and empirical exploration', in Thomas, L. E. and Eisenhandler, S. A. (eds), *Aging and the Religious Dimension*, Westport, CT: Greenwood Publishing Group, cited in Erikson, E. H. and Erikson, J. M., 1997, *The Life Cycle Completed*, New York: W. W. Norton, pp. 123–4.

Tournier, P., 1983, *Learn to Grow Old*, Louisville, KY: Westminster/ John Knox Press.

3

The Churches and Older People: Gift or Burden?

ALBERT JEWELL

What do the demographics tell us?

In his closing address at the 2002 Second International Conference on Spirituality and Ageing, and under the heading 'Geriatric Burden or Elderly Blessing?', David Jenkins, the former Bishop of Durham, called upon participants to facilitate 'a momentum for tackling the economic, political and humane issues arising out of the increasing proportion of the "aged" or the "ageing" in the community' (Jenkins, 2002, p. 197). Clearly, Jenkins' approach was societal rather than ecclesiastical.

If older people in churches and wider society, especially the very old, are to be regarded as either 'gift' or 'burden', I suggest that this presents a challenge: how far are churches affirming the gift and/or bearing the burden? It is important, therefore, to establish the size of this challenge.

From a statistical point of view the main information source has been the findings of the Christian Research organization, which has conducted periodic church attendance reviews in England. The figures from 1998 for the main Christian denominations (Brierley, 2000) were updated in 2005 as shown in Table 1 (the earlier figures where available appearing in brackets).

From these figures it is clear that in all churches, with the exception of the Pentecostal and Orthodox, both the proportion of church attenders aged over 65 and the average age of congregations have increased, and are likely to have increased

Table 1

Denomination	% aged 65+	% aged 85+	Average age
Church of England	35 (29)	3	49 (46)
Baptist	25 (23)	3	43 (41)
Roman Catholic	29 (22)	2	44 (42)
Methodist	47 (38)	5	55 (49)
New Churches	8 (7)	1	34 (32)
Orthodox	20 (23)	0	40 (41)
Pentecostal	10 (10)	1	33 (33)
United Reformed Church	47 (38)	6	55 (49)

further since 2005. The 'New Churches' (comprising, among others, New Frontiers, Pioneer, Vineyard and Ichthus) and the Baptists have shown only a small increase, whereas the Methodist and URC denominations have shown by far the greatest increases.

It is informative to relate these figures to the wider demographic data reported in Chapter 1. Whereas in the population at large the percentage of people aged 65 and over in 2011 was 16.4 per cent, in the Church of England the 2005 figure is more than twice that, and within the Methodist and URC denominations almost three times as great. In the wider community the number of 'very old' (i.e. those over 85) has risen from 1 per cent in 1985 to 2 per cent in 2010; in half the churches (excluding the Roman Catholic, Pentecostal, Orthodox and New Churches) the figure is at least 50 per cent higher, and in the case of Methodist and URC Churches again around three times greater. Indeed, demographic data collected for the first time within British Methodism for the year 2011–12 revealed that 17 per cent were estimated as being over 81 years of age.

Interestingly, if the figures reported in 2005 for the 45–64 age group (i.e. those soon to be added to the 65+ age group) are examined, it would appear that almost all denominations are likely to face a comparable challenge: a similar gift to enjoy and/ or burden to bear.

What progress has been made?

In order to discover what progress, if any, has been made within the churches in meeting this demographic challenge, it will be helpful to establish some of the major benchmarks against which this progress can be measured, and these can be summarized under two headings: reports and research.

Reports

It will be appreciated that space does not permit a comprehensive survey; for example, the valuable Age Concern publication *Spirituality: Roots and Routes* (Burke, 2007) is omitted, because it specifically concentrates on what might be termed 'secular spirituality' and is not directed towards the churches. Moreover, the following summaries are necessarily abbreviated and fuller information can be obtained from the websites of the organizations concerned.

The earliest ecumenical response is to be found in the Christian Council on Ageing (CCOA),[1] which was established in 1985. Its declared purpose is to be an active Christian voice on issues that relate to older people in the Church and society, and in particular to explore the potential and vocation of Christians in later years within their local church and the wider community. CCOA seeks to fulfil its purpose through publications and conferences and has established a dedicated Dementia Network that has promoted project work and produces an informative newsletter twice a year.

Within the various denominations, the *Ageing* report (Church of England, 1990), from the then Church of England Synod Board for Social Responsibility, was of particular significance. It set out challenges to policy-makers, opportunities for the churches, and an appraisal of the contribution of faith in relation to ageing. In

1 www.ccoa.org.uk.

evaluating the Church's own ministry towards older people, the working party 'found many stories of love, service and concern, but also examples of contributions and needs of older people being ignored' (p. 136). Two of its conclusions are of special note: first, the need for churches to recognize the centrality of prayer and spirituality in their work with older people; second, 'to affirm the value of older people to the whole life of the Church – in its worship, work and witness. The Church is an all-age community, where each stage of faith has its own authority' (p. 138).

Among other denominations, the URC, at its General Assembly in 1998, endorsed a report entitled *Respecting the Gift of Years* (Appleton, 1998), which it believed would enable the Church to regard older people more appreciatively; enable older people themselves, whether members of the Church or not, to regard themselves more positively; and affirm the contributions made by older people.

The URC has more recently produced a pastoral resource, *Matters of Life and Death: Reflections upon Ageing and Spirituality for Churches and Individuals* (Ball, 2010), which encourages those in the pre- and post-retirement periods of life to reflect spiritually and practically, devoting a specific section to death preparation and giving clear information about wills, probate and lasting power of attorney.

In neither the Church of England nor the URC is there much evidence that these ground-breaking reports filtered down effectively into local church communities or were firmed up into policies to ensure a lasting effect, though some dioceses have appointed officers or advisers with a special concern for older people within their social responsibility, education or pastoral care departments. Significantly, neither report is readily available today.

In 1998 the Pontifical Council for the Laity's *The Dignity of Older People and their Mission in the Church and in the World*[2] was circulated throughout the Roman Catholic Church. It has five main sections:

---

2 www.vatican.va/roman_curia/pontifical_councils/laity/documents/rc_pc_laity_doc_05021999_older-people_en.html.

- *The meaning and value of old age.* Older people are to be respected as a gift whose special 'charisms' should be affirmed: disinterestedness, memory, experience/wisdom, interdependence and a more complete vision of life that emphasizes 'being' over 'having'.
- *Older people in the Bible.* The point is made that nowadays death has 'lost its sacred character, its sense of fulfilment'.
- *Older people's problems.* These are summarized as: marginalization and consequential loneliness; the wish to stay in their own homes with appropriate support; loss of educational and employment opportunities; and the desire to participate in civil life and voluntary work.
- *The Church and older people.* The 'Third Age' is seen as 'particularly conducive to transcendental value'. The Church should counter the fatalism to which older people may be prone and due recognition should be given to 'the apostolate of older people among people of their own age group' and to the way they hold fast the faith in difficult times.
- *Pastoral guidelines.* Churches should promote the integration of older people into the Christian community, ensuring their continued participation in its sacramental life, providing spiritual support especially to those in care homes, administering the sacrament of the sick and dying, and promoting intergenerational solidarity.

The Pontifical communication also recommended that 'the dioceses should set up their own diocesan offices for the ministry to older people, and that parishes should be encouraged to develop spiritual, community and recreational activities for this age group'. Progress has again been difficult to plot. However, more recently Caritas Social Action Network (CSAN) has given a focus to dementia, producing a DVD, *It's Still ME, Lord* (Bano, 2009), and one example of a local initiative in parishes is 'Growing Old Gracefully', a joint project currently being developed by the Leeds and Hallam Roman Catholic dioceses.

Most recently the Church of England Education Division and the Methodist Council have worked in parallel producing internal unpublished reports (entitled respectively 'Going on Growing' and 'Third Age Discipleship'). These emphasize the need to address the continued learning and spiritual development of older people, to encourage them to make sense of their life experience and to value the gifts and graces that they have to offer, rather than regarding them as largely the recipients of pastoral care. Both reports draw attention to the Cliff College course entitled 'Diploma in Third Age Mission and Ministry', which was recently validated by Manchester University, but has attracted few students to date. The reports also note the need to provide user-friendly learning resources for the training of ministers and for local churches out of the numerous reports and books that have been produced concerning 'Third Age discipleship'. It has yet to be seen how far the governing Church of England and Methodist authorities are willing to endorse and implement the recommendations of these reports.

Research

A report commissioned by the secular Centre for Policy on Ageing, *Religion, Spirituality and Older People* (Howse, 1999), gave considerable emphasis to the role and contribution of churches both in terms of pastoral care and in relation to public policy. Longitudinal research carried out by Professor Peter Coleman and colleagues with a sample of people over 65 from Christian backgrounds, of whom 65 per cent regarded themselves as C of E, showed that after 20 years 37 per cent of those surviving reported that religion meant less to them than earlier in their lives (Coleman et al., 2007). Coleman believed that this might indicate that neglect of their social, psychological and spiritual needs by churches could have left them more vulnerable in advanced old age.

In the late 1990s the ecumenical Sir Halley Stewart Age Awareness Project, administered by MHA, produced a number of resources for churches and for use in ministerial training, culminating in *Older People and the Church* (Jewell, 2001). This sought to investigate why some older people evidently felt marginalized or neglected in churches.

The findings of this research project were that, although many participants expressed satisfaction in their relationship with, and support by, their church, a significant number did not. The main reasons for their dissatisfaction were, on the one hand, a lack of sensitivity towards the changed circumstances of older people and a consequent overlooking of their pastoral and fellowship needs, and, on the other hand, escalating changes in worship styles and an assumption that older people were untroubled in their faith. Above all, older people resented being simply taken for granted.

In a book also titled *Older People and the Church*, Knox (2002) presented the findings of his PhD research based upon interviews with church leaders and members in ten denominations in the Coventry area. Knox found that churches were affected by ageist attitudes rather than contesting them. Some church leaders were frustrated by their older members and, while professing enthusiasm for their elders as a great resource, were ambivalent about how this might be harnessed. What older people thought of the Church was mixed, and while many professed satisfaction with their local church as a source of friendship, love and support, others had felt unwelcome and ignored. In investigating what older people felt they could do for the Church, Knox found a reticence on the part of many older members. He concludes by suggesting that a truly caring church would, through its pastoral support and activities, enable older members to feel valued and supported, and he draws particular attention to 'the forgotten people' in care homes, or caring for loved ones at home, who can feel particularly isolated.

Other important contributions

Founded in 2001, the Leveson Centre for the study of ageing, spirituality and social policy[3] arose from a conviction that the contribution of older people to society was often undervalued and that the Church shared in this. The Centre has hosted a number

---

3 www.leveson.org.uk.

of seminars and conferences and produced various publications, including the impressive 'Leveson Papers', which deal with such subjects as understanding the needs of older people, illness, dementia, death, the humour of old age and the policy challenges of an ageing population. Of particular interest is the publication, produced jointly with the Church Army, *A Mission-Shaped Church for Older People?* (Collyer et al., 2008). This offers a modular training course for churches to raise awareness of the potential for mission to and by older people, suggesting many practical applications.

For the past 15 years, the Outlook Trust[4] has provided a training and support network, primarily among evangelical churches, with an emphasis on outreach. Such a focus would seem to be justified by the anecdotal evidence that older people in churches can be effective 'friendship evangelists' as they get alongside other older people, offering support in stressful times and encouraging them to cross the threshold of churches which otherwise they might not feel able to surmount. This could, of course, become less likely when future generations of older people may well have had no previous contact at all with the Church or the Christian religion.

Valuing Age (Woodward, 2008), based largely on the author's experience as Director of the Leveson Centre and his earlier work as a hospital chaplain, is rich in its scope and depth. Woodward seeks to sensitize those involved in pastoral ministry to the spiritual needs of older people, which seem all too often to be ignored. He identifies the importance of help with prayer, reconciliation with others, reflection on the meaning of life, the need to be rather than to do, and coming to terms with diminishment and dying. There are specific chapters dealing with worship (including people with dementia), memory, retirement, pastoral engagement with older widows, and men and age. His firm conclusion is that 'we must never forget what an enormous resource older people are' (p. 87).

---

4 www.outlook-trust.org.uk.

In their book, *Crying in the Wilderness: Giving Voices to Older People in the Church*, Hawley and Jewell (2009) bring together their experiences of researching the spiritual needs of older people. In his preface to the book, Keith Albans, MHA's Director of Chaplaincy and Spirituality, comments on the paucity of advertisements in church newspapers relating to older people, compared with the abundance of those involving work with children, young people and families: 'The message seems to be that, in a generation, we have gone from wrongly speaking of children as "the church of tomorrow" to wrongly implying that older people are, in effect, "the church of yesteryear"' (p. 4). The book challenges the false assumptions often made about older people, encourages churches to provide safe spaces for them to reflect upon their life journey and deep questions, is illustrated with case studies, and offers relevant Bible focuses. The following ten questions for ministers and church councils to address can provide a basis for working out a pastoral strategy:

1 What is the proportion of those aged over 65 in our church?
2 Is it known how many in the church community are affected by dementia?
3 In what ways does our church show that it really values older people – or are they rather taken for granted?
4 Are our older members pastorally visited on a regular basis, and by whom?
5 In what ways are we relating to older people in the wider community?
6 Do we have a group in which older people can share and discuss their gifts, needs and doubts?
7 To what extent are death and dying addressed in our church?
8 How can we help longstanding servants of the church to 'let go' without feeling guilty?
9 How aware is our church of the need to safeguard vulnerable older people, and how can we raise that awareness?
10 How can we help our church become more 'dementia-friendly'?

What can local churches do?

In addition to the organizations detailed above, which have a country-wide remit, there are others with a more regional focus that seek to involve and enthuse local congregations. One example is Faith in Elderly People (Leeds), which has for 20 years organized conferences and produced resources concerning the spiritual care of older people, especially those with dementia. Another is Faith in Older People,[5] which is located in Edinburgh. Its vision is 'To mobilise faith communities to understand, celebrate, promote and support the importance of the diversity and social and spiritual needs of older people in their congregations and local communities'. In collaboration with Alzheimer Scotland it has produced a DVD, *Spirituality: Have You Found Any Yet?*, which uses the voices and experiences of people with dementia. A third example is PSALM (Project for Seniors and Lifelong Ministry),[6] which is based at St Pancras Church in London. This has the strap-line 'taking ageing and faith seriously' and offers a wide variety of lectures, workshops and seminars addressing matters of interest and concern to those over 60 within Greater London.

Although there are many other local initiatives, it is clear that the challenges and opportunities identified above remain largely ignored and are yet to be widely addressed. The vital task of the local church therefore has two main emphases: to urge that the fruits of ageing be valued and the gifts of older people affirmed, and to recognize and address their distinctive spiritual needs.

Valuing and affirming

Within the Old Testament and continuing Judaism, ageing and sage-ing are virtually synonymous and respect for older people is axiomatic. If there is relatively little in the New Testament about older people, this is probably because the early Christians simply took for granted their Hebrew heritage in so far as it related to respecting and caring for the aged.

---

5 www.faithinolderpeople.org.uk.
6 www.stpancraschurch.org/index.php?id=114.

However, despite the great preponderance of older people in the mainstream churches today, and the fact that many congregations rely heavily upon them, church leaders often give the impression that they are much more concerned about the children and young people who are largely absent from their congregations than about their many congregants who are old. All too often, so-called 'all-age worship' and 'fresh expressions' of church do not seem to be truly inclusive of the very old, and most mission statements that local churches produce display a marked absence of any mention of older people.

Because of their experience of life and their individual faith journeys, older people often excel in pastoral ministry and have much to share in inter-generational contexts. Regular visiting of the housebound and those in care homes is particularly needed. Lay pastoral visiting teams can effectively fill this gap, and of course many individual older church members do so quite informally. It has already been noted that older people are natural 'friendship evangelists', and can be particularly good at bringing their contemporaries into the church family. Janet Eldred (2006) has investigated the specific contribution of older women to the 'community, connection and caring' that she sees as necessary for a healthy church.

One of the predicaments faced by older lay leaders in local churches is that they may become exhausted by their church work and might dearly like to retire from their roles or change them. My long pastoral experience has shown me that for an office holder to hang on until someone else volunteers rarely brings a positive outcome. It is only when the resignation or removal actually happens that such a progression can be made. It is sad but hardly surprising that when some individuals who have faithfully served for decades, perhaps in the same office, move elsewhere in retirement, they may choose not to darken the doors of a church again for fear of once more becoming over-committed.

Canon Michael Butler has drawn the attention of readers of the book *Spiritual Perspectives on Ageing* (Butler, 1998) to the practice in two Sussex churches:

Every two years older people who have given long and faithful service to the church and community are publicly and appreciatively admitted by the bishop to the 'Companions of St Mary's', a brief account being made of each individual thus enrolled (researched by the church wardens). The thank-you letters received afterwards by the vicar signal the appreciation of such affirmation on the part of the new companions. (p. E4).

The spread of similar practices is to be commended.

Older members not wishing to continue serving on church councils or in a particular office represent a rich cumulative resource and it is a pity if they are so rarely consulted. Often they provide the prayer support and direction that every church needs. One woman in her eighties regularly wrote encouraging letters to the young people she knew in her church and was slightly taken aback to be told that this was a valued ministry; receiving a personal letter was in fact a rarity for the young people concerned.

Whether in formal or informal roles, the contribution of older people in church and community needs to be affirmed, and not taken for granted – which sadly is the impression too often given.

Meeting spiritual needs

In the previous chapter, Keith Albans has outlined the spiritual journey of ageing, and I want here to focus on how the churches might respond. We need to recognize, of course, that older people are not somehow a different species: they share with those of all age groups such basic human needs as to receive and give love, to be creative and to find hope. However, the diminishments that often accumulate in later life, and the sense that death is that much nearer, do lend a particular focus. The following headings highlight some of these needs, which local churches do well to recognize and address.

Finding meaning and purpose in life

It was the contention of Viktor Frankl (1964), drawn from his experience in wartime German concentration camps, that prisoners needed some sustaining purpose of life if they were to stand any chance of surviving. While not suggesting that older people face such an extreme threat, it does seem that people of any age need a sense of purpose in order to thrive. Retirement can mean, for some, the opportunity to do what they lacked the time to pursue fully in the midst of busy lives. Hobbies and different forms of creative expression can be very sustaining. But retirement from regular work, or the empty nest when children have left home, may also trigger a deep ennui that can be truly soul-destroying.

Betty Friedan, in her book *The Fountain of Age*, suggests seven 'tasks of ageing' (Friedan, 1993, pp. 427–8), two of which are particularly important for churches to understand. She writes of 'the need to review, reflect upon, and sum up one's life'. Erik Erikson (1982) defined this process as 'integrity', which may be best understood as the pulling of one's life together so as to make some sense of the whole (Jewell 2002). Do churches provide encouragement and safe places where this may be done? Friedan also writes about 'drawing mental boundaries beyond which it is not reasonable to expend the remainder of one's time and energy' in order to 'focus total attention and energy . . . on what is one's truest concern' through a process of selection and optimization. In activist churches there is often too little understanding of the paramount need in older people to let go and rediscover the God within.

Finding reconciliation and peace

High on the spiritual agenda of many older people is the need to die at peace: with other people, God and themselves. This is something that goes much deeper than the often rather peremptory prayers of confession and absolution offered in most church services. Much of the 'spiritual baggage' accumulated by older people has to do with the hurts – received and inflicted – that most of us experience within the skein of close relationships. Not infrequently a fracture may go back into the distant past. Many are the cases of parents and children, siblings or former friends, who have fallen out, sometimes for reasons long forgotten, and have never made peace. The knowledge that this is quite common is no remedy. The danger is that such a sense of hurt or grievance can become deeply entrenched and corroding. It is all too easy for a pastor to sidestep the issue and seek to persuade the older person that he or she should forget this falling-out and put it behind them. The pastor may give the impression that it doesn't really matter – but for someone wanting to die at peace, it most certainly does. Bringing people together before it is too late can be wonderfully liberating for those concerned.

Finding confirmation of faith

The commitment, steadfastness and long service of older members of most congregations is impressive. However, it is easy to overestimate their 'faith-ful-ness'. Some older Christians do indeed evidence a serene and unswerving faith despite the trials and tribulations of life. For others, however, holding on to their faith is a real struggle. They can find the multiple losses that come with advancing years deeply troubling. I was particularly struck by a member of a former church who wrote to me at the age of 94, wishing to find some solution to the problem of suffering – he had lost his wife to cancer some 40 years before.

The trouble is that very often older Christians are either ashamed to give voice to their doubts, or afraid that they will rock the boat for younger believers whose faith may seem fledgling. They may not wish to speak to the minister because they fear somehow losing face. In his seminal book on faith development, Fowler (1981) posits a path from rather infantile and dogmatic levels of faith towards more reflective forms that are capable of living with paradox and a multi-dimensional view of truth. Whether or not one wholly accepts Fowler's developmental theory, the challenging questions and doubts posed by life's experience, and the soul-searching that they engender, can lead towards a much more mature faith rather than the loss of faith that some may fear.

The challenge for churches should be clear. It is to ask: where in our churches are safe places to be found where it is acceptable to pose questions and express doubts? Graham Hawley believes from considerable experience that workshops for small groups of older pilgrims, suitably facilitated, can provide a focused forum in which 'the paradoxes and ambiguities of life can be more readily faced' (Hawley and Jewell, 2009, p. 38). This may not be a task that ministers feel they have the skills, time or inclination to pursue, but in most churches there will be older mature Christians, around whom such a group can be gathered.

Becoming prepared for death

In my research interviews with older Methodists the matter of death and what may lie beyond was discussed, and quite often those interviewed expressed gratitude for this rare opportunity to talk about a vital subject that seemed not to feature anywhere in the curriculum of their local church. Three-quarters of the respondents in my study (Jewell, 2010) displayed a positive approach to death, seeing it as a pathway to a fuller life beyond, some even expressing real excitement. However, although only a quarter said that the prospect of their own demise aroused anxiety, more than twice as many were perturbed about dying a painful or slow death. The study showed little evidence that helping older people approach death is currently high on the agenda of many churches.

Vulnerable older people and churches

Many churches do recognize, at least in theory, that they have a special responsibility towards the most vulnerable both within their ranks and in the community at large. In this final section we shall examine, first, vulnerable adults in general and, second, those with dementia in particular. Although the latter is examined in more detail by Margaret Goodall in Chapter 10, it is appropriate to devote some space to it here in relation to local churches.

Safeguarding vulnerable older people

For some years now, churches of all denominations have been required to adopt safeguarding procedures to protect children from possible abuse or neglect. Subsequently the Churches' Agency for Safeguarding (formerly the Churches' Forum on Safeguarding (CFS)) has added 'vulnerable adults' to its remit and recommended that participating denominations develop good practice guidelines based upon the CFS agreed policy along with the government guidelines set out in the Department of Health *No Secrets* publication (Department of Health, 2000). The generally accepted definitions are that:

- 'Vulnerable adults' comprise those who may be at risk or in need because of physical, sensory or mental impairment or who are unable to protect themselves from significant harm or exploitation (including teasing).
- 'Abuse' can take many forms including physical, sexual, emotional, psychological, domestic, financial, discriminatory and spiritual, as well as neglect, and can usually be seen as the outcome of a misuse of power, control or authority.

The category of 'vulnerable adult' is thus a wide one. Indeed, it can be argued that every older person, as they become frailer, is potentially open to abuse, sometimes from those to whom they are closest. Physical and mental abuse can happen when a family carer reaches the end of their tether. Financial abuse may take place when other people are involved in 'managing' the finances of an older person. Spiritual abuse can take the form of pressurizing the older person into some belief or practice that is contrary to their known preferences, or in some cases it may involve ritual abuse.

The churches have been somewhat slower to take up the challenge to safeguard adults than they were with children. The Baptist Union of Great Britain has produced a very user-friendly

Safe to Belong publication (Hammond and Owen, 2006). In the same year, the Church of England produced *Promoting a Safe Church* (Church of England, 2006). The National Catholic Safeguarding Commission, established in 2008, is working across the dioceses to implement the 83 recommendations of *Safeguarding with Confidence*, the 2007 report of the Cumberlege Commission (Cumberlege Commission, 2007). The United Reformed Church set out its policy and procedures in 2009, and the Methodist Church, which shares a Joint Safeguarding Liaison Board with the Church of England, issued an updated safeguarding course in 2011, *Creating Safer Space* (Methodist Church, 2011). All denominations are currently rolling out training programmes regionally and locally.

Sadly, it has to be said that implementing the protection of vulnerable adults has met with some resistance in places. Whereas it is obvious who children are, the identification of vulnerable adults is seen to be far less straightforward. It is not always clear when, or in what circumstances, an older adult becomes vulnerable. Churches take different views about which officers and leaders should be specifically vetted and trained. Some ministers seem to regard the procedures as an unwarranted intrusion on their pastoral integrity. However, it is undeniable that adult abuse, including the intentional or unintentional marginalizing of some older people, does occur in churches and few would distance themselves from the declaration in the preface to the Methodist safeguarding adults policy: 'The Church's vocation is to be a place where men and women, children and young people, those who are hurt and those who are damaged, may find healing and wholeness' – and, one might add, protected from any abuse in the first place.

Older people with dementia

Currently, an estimated three-quarters of a million people in Britain suffer from Alzheimer's disease and similar conditions such as vascular dementia. As many as a third of those passing their sixtieth birthday are likely to develop some form of dementia during the remainder of their life, and almost all church members will know someone with this condition. Since we have seen that the age profile within the churches is far higher than in society at large, the implications for the local church are obvious.

However, there is too little evidence that this challenge is being heeded. Indeed, few ministerial training courses devote much time to the pastoral care of older people in general, let alone those with dementia. The outcome is that most pastors feel uncomfortable in dealing with this group of vulnerable elders. After visiting a 99-year-old dementia sufferer whom I knew well from the distant past, I asked her daughter whether her minister visited and was told he did so every month. On enquiring further I was informed that what he did was to go into her room, enjoy a cup of coffee, pick up her daily paper to read and depart after a few minutes' sitting there. Diligent in attendance, he obviously had little idea about what to do in such circumstances. And yet the woman was surrounded by photographs of her life with her deceased husband, also a minister, and she had been one of the early female doctors in England, if only her minister had taken the trouble to find out. His successor was very different: they would chat together and share Holy Communion and prayers along with the woman's daughter.

It is worth spelling out some of the lessons ministers and pastoral visitors can learn. It is good to visit the person with dementia regularly rather than taking the view that he or she will forget almost immediately that you have called. The 'afterglow' will in fact remain for some time. Such visits cannot be rushed, nor can the conversations that take place, so it is important to be relaxed, and prepared for the other person to be rather repetitive because of short-term memory loss. Family carers may be very tired and need a break, so it is good to give them the opportunity to have time to themselves for a change.

Congregations (and preachers) are usually pretty tolerant of babies and children disturbing church services but far less so of adults with dementia, taking the view 'they should know better', when clearly they cannot. Because the concentration span of such people is limited, they may feel happier in a short service at home or one specially arranged for people with dementia. Nor should those in care homes be neglected on the false assumption that all their social and spiritual needs will be met through the staff.

Researcher David Snowdon has carried out an interesting study of Notre Dame nuns in the USA (Snowdon, 2001). He was amazed to find that when the brains of deceased members of the order were examined there were advanced levels of brain deterioration in some sisters who had displayed no signs of dementia when they were alive. Pondering whether this lack of symptoms might be because of their diet, freedom from earthly worries or other factors, he came to the conclusion that it was most likely the outcome of their corporate life and regular pattern of praying together, which simply carried them along in a secure and sustaining way. They felt they belonged and were valued. Although local churches can hardly offer such an intense experience as a convent, it may well be that the ongoing regular worship and fellowship life they do offer can to a degree act as a similar prophylactic for people with dementia – provided always that the opportunity is given to them. The closer the community, the more sustaining it may be.

Three helpful booklets are produced by MHA in conjunction with CCOA: *Spiritual Care and People with Dementia*, *Visiting People with Dementia* and *Worship with People with Dementia*. CCOA is currently working with others to produce resources to help in the development of genuinely 'dementia-friendly' churches.

Conclusion

All the evidence is that David Jenkins' challenge, with which I began – do we see the ageing Church as a geriatric burden or an elderly blessing? – will not disappear in the foreseeable future. The evidence also suggests that while the challenge has been largely ignored for the past generation, the need to rise to it now is overwhelming. As we hear the testimonies in this book of those who have reached extreme old age, it is hard to ignore the importance of the task of ensuring a different experience for those who make up the next generation of the oldest old.

References

Appleton, N., 1998, *Respecting the Gift of Years*, London: United Reformed Church.

Ball, P., 2010, *Matters of Life and Death: Reflections upon Ageing and Spirituality for Churches and Individuals*, URC Eastern Synod, www.urc-eastern.org.uk/td-locall-church/focus-booklets/matters-of-life-and-death.

Bano, B., 2009, *It's Still ME, Lord* (DVD), London: CSAN.

Brierley, P., 2000, *The Tide is Running Out*, London: Christian Research.

Burke, G., 2007, *Spirituality: Roots and Routes*, London: Age Concern.

Butler, M., 1998, 'Spirituality and growing older', in Jewell, A. (ed.), *Spiritual Perspectives on Ageing*, Derby: MHA and CCOA.

Church of England, 1990, *Ageing*, report for the General Synod Board for Social Responsibility, London: Church House Publishing.

Church of England, 2006, *Promoting a Safe Church*, www.churchofengland.org/media/37405/promotingasafechurch.pdf.

Coleman, P. G., McKiernan, F., Mills, M. and Speck, P., 2007, 'In sure and uncertain faith: belief and coping with loss of spouse in later life', *Ageing and Society* 27:6, pp. 869–90.

Collyer, M., Dalpra, C., Johnson, A. and Woodward, J., 2008, *A Mission-Shaped Church for Older People? Practical Suggestions for Local Churches*, Solihull: Leveson Centre and Church Army.

Cumberlege Commission, 2007, *Safeguarding with Confidence*, www.cumberlegecommission.org.uk.

Department of Health, 2000, *No Secrets*, www.gov.uk/government/publications/no-secrets-guidance-on-protecting-vulnerable-adults-in-care.

Eldred, J, 2006, *Like Spring without Flowers: Why Older Women and Churches Need Each Other*, Derby: MHA.

Erikson, E. H., 1982, *The Life Cycle Completed*, New York: W. W. Norton.

Fowler, J. W., 1981, *Stages of Faith*, San Francisco, CA: HarperCollins.

Frankl, V. E., 1964, *Man's Search for Meaning*, London: Hodder & Stoughton.

Friedan, B., 1993, *The Fountain of Age*, London: Random House.

Hammond, G. and Owen, S., 2006, *Safe to Belong*, Didcot: Baptist Union of Great Britain.

Hawley, G. and Jewell, A., 2009, *Crying in the Wilderness: Giving Voices to Older People in the Church*, Derby: MHA.

Howse, K., 1999, *Religion, Spirituality and Older People*, London: Centre for Policy on Ageing.

Jenkins, D., 2002, 'Geriatric burden or elderly blessing', in Jewell, A. (ed.), *Ageing, Spirituality and Well-Being*, London: Jessica Kingsley Publishers.
Jewell, A. (ed.), 2001, *Older People and the Church*, Peterborough: Methodist Publishing House.
Jewell, A., 2002, 'Nourishing the inner being', in Jewell, A. (ed.), *Ageing, Spirituality and Well-Being*, London: Jessica Kingsley Publishers.
Jewell, A., 2010, 'The importance of purpose in life in an older British Methodist sample: pastoral implications', *Journal of Religion, Spirituality and Aging* 22:3, pp. 138–61.
Knox, I. S., 2002, *Older People and the Church*, Edinburgh: T&T Clark.
Methodist Church, 2011, *Creating Safer Space*, www.methodist.org.uk/ministers-and-office-holders/safeguarding/creating-safer-space.
Snowdon, D., 2001, *Aging with Grace*, New York: Bantam Books.
Woodward, J., 2008, *Valuing Age*, London: SPCK.

4

The Narratives of Old Age

JAMES WOODWARD

Older people are marginalized because we largely fear what they represent for us. The challenge to befriend the elderly stranger within ourselves remains an essential task of learning and of spiritual growth. In this book, therefore, we are looking to open up what emerges when we read old age in the light of our own narratives. Reading old age challenges us about who we are learning from and what we are not learning, and, as I have outlined in greater depth elsewhere (Woodward, 2008), the margin is one of the places where energy and life remain persistent and possible.

Each of us is a biography, a story. Each of us is a singular narrative, which is constructed, continually, unconsciously, by, through and in us – through our perceptions, our feelings, our thoughts, our actions, and not least our discourse, our spoken narratives. Biologically and physiologically, we are not so different from each other. To be ourselves we must have ourselves – possess and, if need be, re-possess our life stories. We must 'recollect ourselves': recollect the inner drama, the narrative of ourselves. Each person needs such a narrative, as Phelan and Rabinowitz (2008), among others, have emphasized.

In Part 2 of this book, we are able to listen to the stories of 15 older people, but in this chapter I want to focus on four published narratives of old age, in order to explore how these stories have the potential to shape our own – to inform and challenge the unlearning that must take place if we are to think and feel differently about old age. These particular narratives are quite random and make no claim to be representative, but I share them with a hope that they will help to open up the area of autobiographical approaches to age.

May Sarton

May Sarton (1984) was a writer, poet, novelist and chronicler until her death in 1995. It is not surprising, therefore, that her many years of immersion in literature as a poet gave her the ability to describe and therefore connect with her world through language. What is distinctive about this narrative is its honesty and quality of articulation of the world, *At Seventy*, as Sarton experiences it?

At the beginning of the book, Sarton defines age:

> I do not feel old . . . I suppose real old age begins when one looks backward rather than forward, but I look forward with joy to the years ahead and especially to the surprises that any day may bring. (p. 10)

Although I suspect Sarton was temperamentally an optimistic person, her life was not without its incompleteness, its pain and regrets. Throughout the journal she acknowledges the inevitability of unfinished business described as 'the unsolved, the painful encounters, the mistakes, the reasons for shame or woe'.

There is a wonderful sense in this book of the advantages of being old. Sarton writes: 'I am more myself than I have ever been. There is less conflict. I am happier, more balanced, and . . . more powerful.' So the narrative proceeds to name a number of significant things as they emerge. These include the importance and complexity of time, the challenges of keeping a focus, and the necessity for older people always to consider how best they might live. The challenges of downsizing and uncluttering are constant themes.

In her consideration of the physical aspects of growing older, Sarton takes inspiration from women who for her are examples of good ageing. She discusses Golda Meir and Eleanor Roosevelt. She does not romanticize or idealize age and she tackles some of the physical aspects of growing older as she asks: 'Why do we worry about lines in our faces as we grow old? A face without lines that shows no mark of what has been lived through in a long life suggests something unlived, empty, behind it' (pp. 60–1).

Sarton was blessed with friends, but she reminds her reader that some people are uncomfortable around old age. She wonders aloud why this might be. 'Youth is a kind of genius in itself and knows it. Old age is often expected to recognize that genius and forget its own, so much subtler and gentler, so much wiser' (p. 76).

In the silence and the seeing – the sheer wonder of nature and the necessity to keep on being creative, Sarton asks what we are becoming in old age: 'We are not meant to be angels, no we are not meant to be angels but human beings' (p. 86). Her narrative challenges her reader to reflect on both the possibilities and the limitations of what it means to be human.

In all of this one should not underestimate the security that is based on a good pension and a home that is both manageable and workable. In the obvious blessings of life, as Sarton describes them, comes a constant theme – that of being thankful. She gives voice to the liberation that comes from this sense of gratitude. We need to be aware, she argues, of the things that bring us to life. People and what emerges when we really open ourselves up to others are a key part of her sense of well-being. In the opening up and giving out, time for recovery for the self is important, including plenty of sleep. This space is also important time to face the self and the pain that shapes and misshapes us. Sarton concludes by stating her belief that our chief responsibility is not to change others for the better, but to change ourselves.

David Shields

My second example introduces an entertaining and somewhat candid view of ageing. David Shields (2008) has written a biography of his own body, alongside a narrative of the body of his father, who persists into very old age. Shields is 51 while his father is 97. Towards the beginning of his book, Shields sets out his agenda: 'This book is an autobiography of my body, a biography of my father's body, an anatomy of our bodies together – especially my dad's, his body, his relentless body' (p. 8). Reflecting on his father, he comments: 'He's strong and he's weak and I love him and I hate him and I want him to live forever and I want him to die tomorrow.' The narrative is over-tidy as it subdivides into four sections: infancy and childhood; adolescence; adulthood and middle age; and finally old age and death. Shields is adept at making interconnections between these areas of his life journey, and shows his readers that there are particular challenges and opportunities associated with these stages. His argument is that failure to negotiate some of the hurdles during these stages of life inevitably shapes its development and growth.

One of the strengths of this narrative is that there is a good deal of physical detail – Shields believes that it is important to listen to the body and the wisdom that exists in the body. In reflecting on his father, he comments on a dependence on medicine to combat anxiety, depression and sleeplessness. This opens up the story of the relationship between our physical and mental health – and the importance of good mental health for creative ageing. Shields is intrigued by how we judge what is fulfilling and indeed what makes us happy. How we connect with and interpret experience remains a key part of spiritual insight.

There is a good deal of reference to body image, body weight and sex, especially in middle age and old age. The innate sense of 'laddishness' in the text resists any spiritualizing of experience – making meaning doesn't seem to concern Shields. He defines man as a pleasure-seeking missile and, while there is some acknow-ledgement that the process of living is rich, unpredictable and ultimately uncontrollable by any ideology, he urges his reader to a good life that resists giving in to the inevitability of how things might or should be. He refrains from wanting to offer advice or tell others how they should live. Living with the possibility of change keeps his narrative energized.

Free as his narrative seems from religion, it is interesting to note the candour with which Shields discusses death. He asks how much choice we have in life and especially in old age. 'Each man builds his own hill to die on,' he suggests. There is an acknow-ledgement of the inevitability of death and a close link between this and sex. He seeks no glory and detects some deep male dissat-isfaction in friends who are over-dependent on the status and role afforded by work, echoing the words often attributed to Charles De Gaulle: 'The cemeteries of the world are full of indispensable men.' Shields' realistic philosophy might be summed up as 'everyone tries, no one wins, everyone dies'.

From my perspective, as one listening to the spiritual music within this score, I hear some spiritual force in a story where life is viewed as refreshingly simple, tragic and eerily beautiful. The terror of old age is that of pointlessness and boredom. I wonder if that is so dissimilar to what some of us struggle with in middle age.

Carolyn Heilbrun

Third, I turn to a short book by an academic, Carolyn Heilbrun (1998), entitled *The Last Gift of Time: Life Beyond Sixty*. In this narrative Heilbrun informs her readers that she vowed to end her life when she turned 70, but on the advent of that fateful birthday she realized that the golden years had been full of unforeseen pleasure. This narrative celebrates those pleasures from the point of view of someone who had been spending her life rather dreading the last chapters! The text is encouraging, honest and bittersweet.

In the Preface to this book three interesting questions are posed:

1 How do we plan to live our lives?
2 What re-adjustments do we make or need to make in order to live our lives as we would wish?
3 What are the rites of passage that help us or that we need to consider?

What emerges is the reality that for Heilbrun the period beyond the age of 55 is a time of questioning and profound change. Heilbrun wrestles with a core spiritual challenge: whether we ourselves define life, or whether it defines us. Choice, intentionality of action, environment and people are a key part of understanding a life shaped by both accident and fortune. This is a struggle. The narrative allows us to hear that struggle, and to see the movement of Heilbrun's view of age, from loss to gain. She is brutally honest about the privilege and comfort of her position, which has allowed a post-retirement period to be one of serenity and purposeful and interesting activity.

This narrative urges the reader to connect with their relationship to age. For Heilbrun, age takes on importance and significance. What construction we build around it can offer the possibility of both shape and deeper meaning. Within the narrative, her challenges are:

1 Why is it good to be old?
2 Can we be ourselves in old age?
3 What freedoms does it bring?
4 Will our old age be conventional or unconventional?
5 What is our circle of friends – is old age enriched by a range of ages?

In the discussion of memory and meanings, Heilbrun considers what might be the cause of the involuntary return of usually inconsequential memories. She questions whether memory is a trustworthy ally like dreams, 'experience, once we have processed it, becomes a part of our present consciousness and can no longer . . . be called memory at all' (p. 45). This poses all kinds of questions about learning. One question is how far any of us can mend the past as we struggle with the present and, indeed, what we make of our sense of regret and even disappointment in self, others and work. What is it reasonable to expect? Why can so few of us live in the present moment? We need to relish the present and speak of it in its own terms: 'those of us in our last decades . . . every time we allow memory to occur, we forget to look at what is in front of us, at the new ideas and pleasure we might enjoy firmly in the present' (p. 124).

There is a desire to be radical, and for Heilbrun that means being liberated from fashion and listening to different perspectives, other than the dominant ones of men and younger people.

She considers mortality in this way: 'a person . . . plants a tree under whose shade he or she will never sit, but we who are near the end of our lives must also, I feel certain, have confidence in the quality of that shade' (p. 206). In this digging deeper there is a kind of darkness that emerges out of her perspective as she questions what is the point to living on and on for so long? And so the narrative returns to a common theme: delight in and seize the moment, grasping life and rendering it full of possibility and potential. It is worth considering one of Heilbrun's images here: 'dancers ought not to worry about the whole ballet, its meaning, its significance, but should – just dance the steps'.

Bernard Cooper

My final narrative is the story of a complex relationship between father and son, exploring the universal mysteriousness of having parents. Bernard Cooper (2006) writes a narrative about his father, Edward, who is clearly a hard man to know – dour and exuberant by turns, Edward's moods dictate and dominate the mood of the Cooper family and home. Balding, an octogenarian and partial to a polyester jump suit, Edward Cooper looms larger than life for his son and is a baffling and overwhelming presence.

The title of the book – *The Bill from my Father* – emerges from an invoice that Edward Cooper sent his son asking him to repay the money expended on his education, holidays, food, clothing, housing and upbringing. The narrative is a searing meditation both on the economic and emotional indebtedness of children to parents and parents to children – and deeper than that, in the context of old age, a reflection on the mysterious nature of memory and love. Anger, disappointment, frustration and sheer confusion about whether Bernard will ever understand the cold harshness of his father are the notable themes of this narrative.

Much has been made of the genetic similarities between parents and children; this narrative is about differences between children and parents and the inevitable gaps and distances that emerge as people grow apart, if indeed they ever had the opportunity to grow together in the first place. Cooper describes his father's 'sheer incuriousness' as simply infuriating. His father chooses to take on life as it is without any probing or digging or questioning or reflecting. This mode of narrating life is quite beyond his gay East Coast therapist son. What a combination!

Cooper is not unsympathetic to his father. Bernard is the only remaining son alive. Bob, one brother, died when he was 20 from cancer, Richard at 31 and the third brother from heart disease at 50. This experience of multiple losses is not something that Bernard Cooper explores in any depth, let alone how this experience might have shaped his father's emotional and spiritual world. What he does describe are the indignities of old age and especially the horrors of the slow advance of dementia.

The honesty of this narrative is compelling. In this exchange Bernard Cooper waits in a hospital with his father:

> He turned to face me, his glasses flashing. 'I don't want you to watch me grow old.' 'Believe me,' I said, 'there are plenty of things worse than growing old . . . Such as not growing old.' For a moment we were allied in silence, remembering Bob and Gary and Ron [dead sons and brothers]. Their deaths were done, but their dying survived them. 'Look at it this way,' I said. 'We're growing old together.' 'It's happening faster to me.' 'No, Dad . . . You and I are aging at the same rate.' 'Time goes faster when you're older.' 'It only seems to go faster. It can't go faster for you than it does for me.' (p. 91)

This narrative asks us to consider who shapes our story. How can our parents be both so like and so completely foreign to us? How do we deal, as we learn, with individuals and views so different, alien or even offensive to us? And in our own narrative how much honesty are we to exercise about our flaws, anger, sarcasm and eccentricities? While there is in this story a soothing undercurrent of the importance of love and the endurance of family bonds, Cooper reminds us that there is no untangled life and that few of us can escape (or even name) our own self-destructive impulses.

The ordinariness of the dignity and courage and honesty expressed by Edward Cooper reminds us that, in learning, perseverance and hope are key virtues to be nurtured in self and others.

Conclusion

The narratives explored here offer a range of starting points for a deeper understanding of age and the varied shape that it can take in our lives. Attending closely to the experience of older people in this way offers us a radical way of putting the older person at the centre of our discussions about policy, provision of care, and social and theological theory.

Knowledge of the person's story is vital if we are to put the person at the centre, but most older people have neither the desire nor ability to see their own story in print as in the accounts examined in this chapter. When, at the end of life, older people are no longer able to tell their story, who will remember for them? Although the facts may not necessarily be accurate, our lives are essentially stories that contain 'truth', as memories of all the things that have happened to us are edited and transformed as a way of making sense of our lives. The story may have been repeated many times internally, but unless this is shared with someone, or there is someone at hand to try to interpret, then the person's identity becomes shadow-like. Reflecting on the end of life of his grandmother, one writer expresses it like this:

> She was all bones, curled up into herself. She muttered and murmured to herself. I could not make out what she was saying. I wanted to know what she was thinking, what she was feeling. She had never cultivated a language of intimacy . . . Now she was physically incapable of communicating her experience. And I did not have the resources to imagine her experience. (Woodward, 1991, pp. 24–5)

The stories that are shared in Part 2 of this book are examples from those who have committed themselves to listening to the spoken, or unspoken, story of a person in order to affirm the self of that individual. And as we will see in Chapter 10, even in dementia, where skilled listening is required to understand the meaning behind the communications offered, some very profound insights into the essence of the person can be gained through providing space and opportunity for getting alongside those whose stories have been extended and varied through the passage of time. For as the body ages, the self is not destroyed but requires a relationship in which, through the telling of story, the self can be held, find meaning and flourish.

References

Cooper, B., 2006, *The Bill from My Father: A Memoir*, New York: Simon & Schuster.

Heilbrun, C. G., 1998, *The Last Gift of Time: Life Beyond Sixty*, New York: The Dial Press.

Phelan, J. and Rabinowitz, P., 2008, *A Companion to Narrative Theory*, Oxford: Wiley-Blackwell.

Sarton, M., 1984, *At Seventy*, New York: W. W. Norton.

Shields, D., 2008, *The Thing About Life Is That One Day You'll Be Dead*, New York: A. A. Knopf.

Woodward, J., 2008, *Valuing Age: Pastoral Ministry with Older People*, London: SPCK.

Woodward, K., 1991, *Aging and its Discontents: Freud and Other Fictions*, Bloomington and Indianapolis, IN: Indiana University Press, quoted in Hepworth, M., *Stories of Ageing*, 2000, Buckingham: Open University Press.

PART 2

The Testimonies of Age

5

Listening and Accompanying:
The Essence of Later-Life Chaplaincy

ANDREW NORRIS

The role of chaplain

At the heart of this book are the stories of 15 residents who are living or who have lived in Methodist Homes care settings. They are recounted by people who have been appointed chaplains to those settings. The major role of the chaplain is to be alongside residents and ensure each one's life story has an opportunity to be heard and can continue to gain expression in their life and the life of the home in which they live. What has been written is not a verbatim account of what the chaplains have been told or learnt, but provides suggestions of conversation reflected within the context of lives that have been lived. We are not concerned here (nor is it a priority in the role of our chaplains in their work) with historical fact or accuracy. Indeed, the way in which each of us recalls our own life story will not only be different in manner and style but also reflect personal perspective, our own editing, interpretation and distillation of that story. It is important to discover the story's meaning not only behind the shape and path of a person's life journey but also through the way it is told.

In Chapter 12 of this book, we shall look at how the practice of active listening fits into the broader context of the history, evolution and purpose of chaplaincy in general and within the context of social care and later life in particular. For now, we shall take the opportunity to explore in more detail some of the skills that are needed to ensure an older person's story can be told, heard and interpreted, shared and be given expression in an appropriate manner. As the title of this chapter implies, the heart of the chaplaincy task is to listen and accompany.

In each of our MHA homes and independent living with care schemes, dedicated chaplaincy time is provided, reflecting the importance attached to this work in the care we provide. This is not to say that everyone who works in our care settings cannot or does not provide a listening ear and spend time alongside residents. Sometimes this happens as part of the many other duties that have to be performed. However, time in care settings is generally under pressure, which is why it is all the more important to ensure that there is someone whose main purpose and priority is to 'be alongside residents' and offer space for them to express and celebrate their story and share their joys, gifts and concerns.

We emphasize to our chaplains that they are not there to be counsellors or therapists, merely to give the opportunity for a story to be told. As facilitative listeners, the role is one of offering unconditional acceptance, welcoming, affirming and being guided by the willingness and co-operation of the storyteller to share what they will. The invitation is with the raconteur – the role of the chaplain or any other active listener is as an interested, empathic (where necessary compassionate) accompanist and companion.

Some of what is shared will be influenced by the context of the interaction and by any preconceived assumptions as to the listener's role. So, for example, there may be an initial assumption that our chaplains are only concerned to engage in stories and issues about a person's religious life or end-of-life needs. This is not inappropriate but it may be limiting. Indeed, many of our chaplains say they spend half of their time trying to convince people that spirituality is more than just about religion and the other half helping people to explore how religion, worship, ritual and prayer can be relevant and enriching to their lives at whatever age or stage they might happen to be. Most preconceptions are quickly dispelled as trust and relationship develop.

Characteristics of active listening

While the act of listening is something in which we can all engage, active listening requires particular skills, not only to hear what is being said but also to understand its meaning. Such skills include encouragement, facilitation, empathy and patience. Also, as the 15 stories that follow illustrate, these skills may be shared in a variety of ways and be expressed through complex and interwoven themes. The stories will also have been subject to many different influences that need to be grasped and understood. Further skills may be needed in order to understand and interpret the stories of those living with dementia, and these will be explored further in Chapter 10.

Discovering the course, content and dynamic of a person's life is primarily, but not exclusively, reliant on verbal exchange of information.[1] However, their story is one that we have no inherent right to know, nor may the person wish to share it. The important point is that we must be ready to hear it – to make space for it to be shared – and to be responsive when the invitation and opportunity are given to us. Making space may literally mean finding a quiet time or private location in which conversation can take place. It may also mean ensuring that we ourselves are in a psychological (and spiritual) state of readiness to receive and respect that story.

Listening to older people

If you ask any one of our chaplains what they feel about the work in which they are involved they will almost inevitably respond, 'It is a privilege'. This is because they find themselves coming alongside those who have experience and wisdom accumulated over many years, invited into someone else's world to share its joys and its challenges; often learning so much, not only about the person they are with, but about life and about themselves.

---

1 For an exploration of the importance of non-verbal and interpretative communication, see Chapter 12.

However, this does not necessarily happen automatically or very easily. Insights into someone's life can come spontaneously and in the most unexpected of contexts, but it is more likely that the themes that characterize each person's life reveal themselves in the context of ongoing and developing relationships, where familiarity, trust, knowledge of the individual and their idiosyncrasies, and understanding of them as a person can develop.

In the context of the social care environment for older people, where there is a greater opportunity to develop and nurture relationships over a period of time, chaplaincy is a particular privilege, although it will be interesting to see what impact the trend towards increasing frailty of admissions to care facilities may have on the ability to develop extended relationships. It also means (and this is reflected in the stories gathered for this book) that a person's life journey will have time to unfold and be shared – not just on one occasion or in one go, but over a period of time as re-membered experiences are brought back to mind, new insights gained and the end of life is anticipated. An important aspect of chaplaincy, as will be described in Chapter 12, is that chaplains need to be generally available as part of the everyday life of residents if they are to be trusted at special times.

The benefits of storytelling

For those who are (more than) willing to share their story, time may be of the essence – having some but also having enough! This leads us to examine the importance and purpose of telling and listening to *story*, as discussed in Chapter 4. As previously suggested, in engaging with someone's story, we are not looking for historical accuracy. The benefits of sharing stories are evident to both listener and storyteller. Thus we have probably all experienced the sense of satisfaction and fulfilment that comes from having someone else show an interest in us; but the satisfaction that spending time with and listening to older people brings to them is also very easy to observe. This derives from a sense of well-being and of being valued and respected as an individual, which someone giving time and attention to their story may convey. It may also relate to the fact that, particularly as we get older, the opportunities for nurturing that sense of well-being can become diminished and therefore, when they do occur, are valued even more.

Robert Butler (1963) suggests that reminiscing can aid the process of life review, which enables a person to look back over their life in an attempt to make sense of it and address any unresolved conflicts from the past. However, McMahon and Rhudick (1964) identified that not everyone enjoys the opportunity to tell their story. Some may use what they have to say as a smokescreen behind which to hide their true selves; with others, their stories about themselves may be characterized by unwarranted exaggeration, regret and/or guilt. Each one of these styles of interaction will reflect a need. However, the permission to respond to that need lies with the storyteller.

The stories

We have endeavoured to provide a little shape to the stories that follow without betraying their content or style. This shape echoes what we expect of our chaplains in the work that they do in getting alongside our residents and enabling them to share and celebrate their stories. First, there is introduction – getting to know someone and defining the context in which their story can be told. Next, there is the process of accompanying the individual as they map out the biographical story of their life. In the context of this book, we have taken a particular interest in those elements of each person's story that relate to what might be termed the 'spiritual' aspects of their journey – what gives it meaning and purpose and influences their current sense of well-being – as well as their hopes and dreams. We have also included some reflective material, comparable to the process of taking a step back and endeavouring to understand the meaning behind the story in which it is important for our chaplains to engage during the course of their work. Whether this reflection process is explicitly shared with the storyteller has to be a matter of judgement and consent but should never be abandoned, given that continued (spiritual) growth and development are always possible. Inevitably, the way a story is told and lives are lived means that what happens to us doesn't fit into neat categories, but this kind of framework may be helpful in understanding the importance and value of the listening and accompanying process.

References

Butler, R., 1963, 'The life review: an interpretation of reminiscences in the aged', *Psychiatry* 26, pp. 65–76.
McMahon, A. and Rhudick, P., 1964, 'Reminiscing: adaptational significance in the ages', *Archives of General Psychiatry* 10, pp. 292–8.

6

The Testimonies of Age

Story 1

Mary's story – A generous friend

Mary came to live in the care home as she was approaching her ninety-eighth birthday, and although mentally alert and lively, her mobility had reached a stage where she could no longer manage on her own. Both her feet were turned over sideways and walking, even with a frame, looked excruciatingly painful, but she was never once heard to complain.

Mary grew up in the inner city, as many in her generation did. Her father had been badly wounded in the First World War. She had worked all her life in the Post Office and spoke warmly of the friendship of those among whom she worked. Mary never married, but remained close to nephews and nieces and their children, who were very fond of her and always invited her for Christmas. She was an honorary aunt to many other children too.

What stood out about Mary was her exceptional gift of generous friendship. There were many examples of this and how it called forth reciprocal responses from those she befriended. Latterly, Mary and some other women had shared the same taxi each week to go to church; she quickly became friendly with the taxi driver, who in consequence would help her into church and make sure that she was all right. When she moved to the care home, a young man had helped her with the move. One of the things she missed from her old home was the garden. The young man realized this, took a photo of the garden, had it framed and presented it to her, and it stood in a place of honour on her window ledge.

Fortunately, the care home had a very good garden too, and she enjoyed spending time in it.

Mary's capacity for befriending people continued when she moved into the home. She showed a sense of empathy with other new residents, particularly those who felt lost and unhappy, and would befriend and support them. Frequently, when I went into the lounge, I would find Mary in the middle of a small group of residents, leading the conversation, sharing in laughter (she had a great sense of humour), and building up group friendships between the residents, so that newcomers became integrated into the community of the home. She accepted her own limitations and pains cheerfully, and was thoughtful to others.

Perhaps Mary's most remarkable friendship was with Elsie, the oldest resident at the home, aged 104. Elsie had been a professional pianist, playing for silent movies, until she was made redundant in 1928, when the talkies came in. She had clearly been a strong and interesting person, but by this stage had lost her capacity for conversation or involvement with others. Mary took to sitting with Elsie at services and community hymn-singing, first holding her hand and then beating out the time of the hymn. Gradually Elsie herself started singing again and joining more in the life of the home. When Elsie died, her granddaughter brought Mary a large bouquet of flowers, and said that she felt that Mary was now her grandmother – perhaps the last of Mary's honorary relationships until she died shortly before her hundredth birthday.

Mary was closely involved with her local parish church, and her vicar continued to visit and bring her Holy Communion once a month, as he had done in the time before her entry to the home when she was no longer able to attend church regularly. Mary had missed her links with other members of the congregation, and was surprised and grateful when the vicar explained that in this way she could remain part of the church family. Receiving communion, she said, made her 'feel better'; it certainly had that effect on those who shared it with her. No doubt, too, those regular services were also a time when she could catch up with news of her church friends.

Church was clearly part of Mary's life. She had, as far as we know, always attended church from childhood, as would have been much more common for people of her generation. There had never been a moment of sudden conversion: rather, her story seems to fit the pattern of the story George MacLeod told of the Scottish minister who would pray at baptisms: 'May this child be so well baptised that she need never be converted' (MacLeod, 1956, p. 109). Churchgoing remained a natural part of her life, and one of the points where, as for so many people, she was linked into membership of a community, which was particularly important to someone like Mary who did not have an immediate family of her own, but who valued and responded to social contacts.

This is not at all to say that Mary attended church simply for the company. Her religion had an important meaning to her as an individual person. She valued opportunities for worship, at church and in the care home, and she accepted changes in patterns of worship as she got older. She was happy to join in new hymns (and to sing familiar hymns to different tunes when she entered an MHA home!) and was fully accepting of less formal all-age worship. She loved children and was not in the least one of those older members of the congregation who tut-tut when children are boisterous in church. She took her faith seriously and was prepared to think and question things, such as discussing with the vicar why a close friend and neighbour had died of cancer. I never discussed her personal prayer life with her, but there was a Bible at her bedside. Her faith was an important point of support in her life.

Mary's life reflected very closely the fruit given by the Spirit that Paul lists in Galatians 5.22, including that most elusive gift of joy; they were evident both in her own love and patience, and in kindness and generosity to others. This leads to the question of how far these gifts were specifically derived from her faith, and how far they would have been a natural part of her character, whether or not she had been a Christian with strong church links. There is no easy answer to this. Mary was, almost certainly, the kind of person who would naturally have been outgoing, warm and friendly.

We can only guess that this was something which she learnt within her family, and perhaps, as a single woman without an immediate family to express this love to, it spilled over into her relationships with neighbours and members of any community of which she was a part. In Mary's particular context, love was expressed to and through the church – to her friends in the church, and through that back to the wider community. Whatever personal gifts Mary had inherited and developed, her kindness, generosity and concern for the well-being of others were able to flourish in a setting where those gifts have been valued and built up. We may, I think, conclude that Mary's faith enabled her gifts to grow, and that they were supported through her church life.

Furthermore, these gifts were passed on from Mary to others in the home. The kindness, support and cheerfulness that she gave to others helped to sustain and build up the community that makes a care home a home and not an institution. People in the care home, including myself, felt better for having contact with her. Her vicar commented that he would put Mary last on a list of people to be visited during the day, partly because he knew that it could be a long visit, but also because he would himself be cheered and encouraged by spending time with her, and I felt the same visiting her in the home. Looking back, I see Mary as one of a series of unrecognized but important 'auxiliary chaplains' who have contributed a great deal to the work of chaplaincy in the care home – sometimes through hinting that this or that resident needed special support, but more often because they were there all the time, giving support and building up positive relationships within the home community. Mary's own example of patience and cheerfulness, and her generous kindness to others, had an immeasurable effect on the life of the home and are surely an illustration of why the gifts of the Spirit are indeed gifts.

Story 2

The story of what Pearl experienced with her husband at the end of his life came to be told by accident. It arose when the chaplain was enquiring about another resident, whom Pearl knows well, but it quickly became evident that the story of Pearl and her husband Walter was the one needing to be told. It took the chaplain by surprise, and she left Pearl's flat 90 minutes later feeling she had just experienced a spiritual and rather special time.

Pearl and Walter's story – God's hand at work in people's lives and in death

Pearl was an only child, brought up in a strict Christian home and, as a result, her upbringing had been very restricted. For example, she had always wanted one of those lovely straw hats decorated with beautiful flowers, but in her parents' eyes that was vanity, so no straw hat! There were no playing cards, drink or cinema visits, and throughout her childhood Pearl had felt some pressure from these restrictions. But Pearl recalls vividly her baptism at a Brethren meeting at the age of 17, and it was just after this that she moved away to college to train to be a teacher. Her first teaching position, at the age of 21, was at a public school for boys, and they had their own chapel and padre. For the first time Pearl experienced a sense of freedom; the pressure she had felt had been lifted. However, because of her parents' ill health, four years later Pearl moved back home and started teaching at a local secondary modern school, where her main subject was English and Pearl became deputy head.

Taking a deep breath, Pearl recalled meeting Walter at the age of 29 and how she fell in love with him. Circumstances were not easy for them, and Pearl had a break from teaching for two years, but the devotion they had for each other was strong, and in time they decided to get married. They joined the local Anglican church and were members there for 60 years, for 14 of which Walter served as churchwarden. Pearl remained in education throughout her working career, including a period as a headteacher, and she retired at the age of 59.

Pearl and Walter lived out a happy retirement in Devon, eventually moving to their last home on the edge of Dartmoor. It was here that life became difficult, as Pearl began to lose her sight because of macular degeneration, and the layout and stairs of this apartment were not suited to the physical needs of Walter, who was now in his nineties. Pearl explained how things gradually became more difficult and demanding for her, speaking of her struggle to meet Walter's care needs, both physically and emotionally. She said, 'I was at my wits' end, I really did not know what to do. It was a difficult time, and I wondered how we were going to continue to manage this situation.' Pearl laughed when she recalled Walter's delusions of grandeur in the various properties they had lived in over the years. This had troubled Pearl at the time, because she knew a move to somewhere 'more suitable' would be made harder for a man with a character like Walter's.

Pearl said, 'I prayed very much asking God to show me what to do, and others were praying for us too.' She then told of how a house became available which they felt would be suitable, but the sale fell through. At the time they were disappointed, but looking back Pearl felt that God was directing their lives and answering prayer, and that this was not the right property for them. Pearl described how her daughter-in-law and son encouraged them to visit Acorn Lodge, and to put their names on the waiting list. Walter at 98 years of age was of course very much against this as it was a place for old people and he certainly had not reached that stage. He told Pearl that he really felt that he was not ready yet for Acorn Lodge and was quite horrified by it all.

However, Walter was becoming frail and the stairs to the first floor were very difficult, so when a telephone call came from Acorn Lodge offering them an apartment, Pearl said, 'I felt this was God telling us where we should be' and that, through her faith and prayer, God had answered and it was perfect timing. They went together for a visit and they both loved it, although Walter did comment that the restaurant was full of old people!

Acorn Lodge was an amazing answer to prayer for Pearl. She had prayed and had had faith, and here they were in a lovely apartment and the comfort of others around them. Pearl felt God had been faithful and she said that the staff at Acorn Lodge were there to meet their needs and were absolutely fantastic.

In telling the next bit of her story, Pearl had to pause and there was a silence as she regained her composure. She described how five weeks before Walter's hundredth birthday he had had a fall from which he never really fully recovered. However, the previous week he had been able to attend church in his wheelchair, which was positioned on the front pew where he always sat, and after the service they visited 'The Green Man' with friends for a carvery Sunday lunch. This memory brought a contented smile to Pearl's face, although she recalled that this was just seven weeks before Walter died.

Walter had his hundredth birthday and really enjoyed his celebrations, and Pearl emphasized just how lovely it was that he had felt special and important about it all. But she became emotional as she described how Walter was frail and bedridden for the last week of his life, and he faded gradually for the ten days after his birthday, desperately wanting God to take him home. But Pearl added that she felt pleasure and a sense of blessing that Walter's mental faculties lasted until the day he died, and his family were around him. She said, 'On the Friday I knew Walter was nearing the end, and I was so grateful for the care staff and their expertise and knowledge, all the necessary things were done, and in such a dignified and good way.' Pearl was glad that her vicar happened to be at Acorn Lodge when Walter died, visiting another member of their congregation, and that he had with him his prayer books and oil and so he had anointed Walter and prayed with her.

Pearl spoke of some special moments during Walter's final days, such as when their granddaughter had been able to read the newspaper to Walter when he was so poorly, and one of their grandsons had wanted to be near to his granddad at this difficult time. She was also sure that although she was saddened by Walter's death, she did not wish him back, because after a long, active life full of sport and activities within the church he was a shadow of his former self, and he knew it was time to go, and he was ready.

In telling her story, Pearl clearly felt that her prayers for their personal needs were answered, and she recognized how God goes before us. He is an intimate God, a God who knows and cares about the details of our lives and the importance of them to us. It is the small things that matter, and he reaches down and touches our lives at just the right time, and in such a personal way.

Pearl spoke of how she prepared the funeral service so that it was a thanksgiving service for Walter's life, and all they had enjoyed together. Pearl said, 'I will never be sad thinking of Walter's funeral, it was a joyful celebration, of a long and full life.'

Pearl described how she feels now and her feelings about the future. She acknowledged that her prayers had been answered in so many ways and spoke of feeling blessed to have had the privilege of living with Walter at Acorn Lodge. She added, 'I feel that I am in the right place, and if I can help people by listening or in any other way or even by making them laugh, this is my life and I feel very blessed in it.'

Pearl has been able to reflect on her end-of-life experience and final days with Walter, with the belief that God's hand was on their lives and cared for them in all the small details in those final days. Pearl is comforted in this knowledge, and at peace, strengthened in her faith to be able to bless others now, through God's grace.

Pearl's interactions with the other residents make it clear that she has the ability to sympathize and empathize. They find her easy to talk to and will share with her, and she can create laughter whichever group she is spending time with. The loss of Walter seems not to have taken something from Pearl, but instead Walter's life and relationship, and all that they did together and experienced, have given something to Pearl. So she continues with a richness of life, and is an inspiration to many who can see in her an example of how in your nineties you can still support others, and give out through your Christian faith to make a difference every day to them. Although Pearl struggled and found her Christian upbringing strict, that seed of faith sown in her childhood has continued to sustain and support her right through her life to the present time. Pearl still attends her church every Sunday, and sometimes she still goes to 'The Green Man' for Sunday lunch with friends.

Story 3

In this story the chaplain shares the consequences of what has been a journey of discovery for herself as well as Nancy, with whom she develops an important relationship.

Nancy's story – Finding faith at the end of life

In 2008, I took up the position of chaplain at a care home for older people offering nursing and dementia care. According to the job description, the chaplain's role is 'to be a focus for the spiritual life of the home and scheme, ensuring that the spiritual needs of service users and staff are addressed' (MHA *Chaplaincy Manual*, 2011 Section 2, p. 5). I knew that first I would need to build relationships in order to gain people's trust before I could nurture and support them in their spiritual journey. I encouraged joint acts of worship in the form of church services; however, it was the care of the individual and their spirituality that I struggled with. I read care plans and gleaned the background information that I needed, but the question was, how could I accomplish that without using the tools that years of nursing had taught me, as my role no longer allowed me to give physical care?

Some residents of the care home were fully able to communicate, so conversation leading to relationship was usually straightforward. These relationships have often led to privileged trust when learning of an individual's inmost beliefs, thoughts and faith journeys. Other residents were less able to communicate and they, like me, must have become tired of my feeble attempts at talking about the weather or the news.

I was three years into my role when I met Nancy. By this time I felt I had improved my own communication skills to some extent. However, even up to the point of meeting Nancy, there was always the compulsion to want to do something practical for the person I was visiting. I wanted to converse, read or sing to them, or perhaps it was more 'at' them. In Nancy's case I could do none of those things, because she asked only for my presence. I admit that in those initial few moments I felt awkward and ill at ease.

The care staff did everything to make her comfortable, the nurses did what they could to manage the pain, but Nancy was clearly uncomfortable. As I sat on the chair near Nancy's bed, I felt useless doing nothing as we occasionally exchanged glances when Nancy opened her eyes. After a few moments, I began to relax and mostly filled the time switching between my own thoughts and prayer. My prayers were mainly asking God for his presence in the room and discernment in knowing what to do next. What comforting words could I say on leaving Nancy's room when I knew that she had no fixed belief? When I realized that even having a companion in the room was exhausting for Nancy, I knew it was time to leave her. By this time I had relaxed in her company and the pressure to 'do something' had gone. I offered the best I thought I could give her, which was just 'to be' with her: companionship. I was delighted when she agreed for me to visit her again as it affirmed my actions, or indeed lack of them.

Nancy was a woman in her eighties who had been admitted to the care home's nursing unit following some time in hospital. She had lived alone in her own home for seven years following the death of her husband. Nancy had no children, but she had a brother to whom she was very close and a niece. Both relatives lived nearby and visited Nancy frequently. Nancy came to the unit with a history of falls and multiple health conditions, one of which required frequent treatments at the local hospice. Nancy had full mental capacity. She suffered from anxiety and needed lots of reassurance and support. Nancy's religion was recorded in her care plan as 'Church of England, not practising'. In the spirituality section of the notes it is recorded that Nancy had 'no fixed belief' and 'religion is Church of England – chooses not to attend church services'. On entering the home, Nancy had expressed her anxiety for her future: 'I would like to feel more capable. I feel inadequate. I am frightened of the future. I am left here alone to cope, everything is such an effort.' Nancy's wishes for each day were that she be helped to get up and sit in her chair in her room. She enjoyed watching television as she felt she had control over what she could watch. She did not want to socialize with other residents, preferring her own company.

Over the months she lived at the care home I visited Nancy, and she would tell me stories of her life: her hobbies, family and employment. She was a good communicator and seemed to enjoy the opportunity to be prompted to talk about times gone by. Nancy never spoke about faith or church, nor did she talk about what gave her life meaning and purpose. She was frightened because of her deteriorating health and I would sit with her and try to reassure her. One day, I was asked by the nurse to visit Nancy. She was dying. Nancy invited me into her room on condition that we would not converse. She was lying on her side in bed. She said, 'Please don't talk to me. I have no interest in talking about anything. I don't know anything any more.' I understood Nancy's request and asked if I could just keep her company. She agreed. We stayed in each other's company for quite a time in silence. Nancy lay on her bed, and I sat on a chair nearby. I could see that Nancy was getting tired and I thought it would be best for me to leave. She thanked me for visiting, and I asked whether I could come and visit her again and just be with her. Nancy agreed. As I was leaving, Nancy called me back into her room and said, 'There is nothing that I am interested in and there is nothing that I know other than the fact that I trust Jesus.' I came back into the room and offered to pray with her. Nancy said that she was wary of prayer, because the church prayers that she had once heard were so long and complicated that she could not understand them. I offered to pray a short prayer in simple language. I prayed that Jesus would make his presence known to her and that he would be her comfort and friend. I did not have the opportunity to visit Nancy again. She died a couple of days later.

The unexpected had happened. Nancy had called me back into her room and shared her faith. I was stunned and I found myself desperately praying that I would not mess the next bit up. I had only read about end-of-life conversions to Christianity. This was the sort of thing that happened to high-profile Christians who then went on to speak to thousands of people in stadiums. I felt humbled that God would allow me to witness and be a part of this moment in the life of one of his children. I had done nothing to enable this person to make such a decision and I knew this was exactly the right thing to do – nothing. It was God who worked in Nancy's life and had allowed me to watch this life-changing experience.

My professional background is in nursing. And in my previous role, community nursing, the care of an individual was mostly centred on physical care and procedures. Emotional, mental and spiritual care were often given alongside physical care; for example, in banter and conversation over intimate acts of care such as washing, dressing and changing a wound dressing. Due to time constraints and a mainly task-orientated job, emotional and spiritual care was often superficial, although understood to be as important as physical and mental care. My faith was a big part of my life then, as it is now, and spiritual care, particularly of those who were terminally ill, was something I wanted to explore more.

In my own faith journey, I have worshipped at churches where service to God has been expressed through doing. The Sundays at one particular church I experienced as a child were hectic. We had six separate meetings to attend. As a church, we were so busy that there was little time to just 'be' in the presence of God and allow him to work his grace and power in our lives.

Since meeting Nancy I am becoming more at ease in being with people whose communication is limited or who are very ill. Sitting in quietness together is a form of service and care to an individual; it is a ministry important in its own right. It is companionship, being a comfort in being present, and an expression of Christian service. It is fellowship and encouragement in silence when important truths are being revealed and decided upon. It is giving space for God to be able to minister in the quietness and stillness.

Story 4

This story highlights the role the chaplain can have in being alongside people of no declared faith and demonstrates that we can never know when a person may be ready to move on in their spiritual journey.

Sidney's story – Faith discovered late

Starting work at The Brambles, I took my time to meet and listen to all our residents. Initially, the conversations were brief and polite, as it can take a while for people to open up and trust.

In MHA there is good provision for Christians, especially Non-conformist Christians, with regular church services and links to the local churches. I did become increasingly concerned about how to meet the needs of those of other faiths and especially those of no faith. I do not want to convert people but I believe that we all have a spiritual dimension to our lives, which some recognize in organized religion, some through art, painting or poetry. Some do not recognize it as a need, but it is part of being human.

Meeting with a Hindu, and having done meditation with Buddhists, led me to start a meditation group. This varied from week to week; sometimes guided meditation, sometimes complete silence. It proved to be a very powerful and moving time.

Sidney introduced himself as an atheist. I responded by saying that I am there for everyone regardless of belief, and not there just to talk about my faith. I did not invite him to the services but visited him in his room. He was warm and welcoming, talking about his long and very interesting life. He was a highly intelligent man who had been a committed communist with very strong socialist beliefs. In his life he had contributed much towards positive change in this country, and indeed in other countries. All the staff loved him, his humour, gentleness and great intellect. I did not meet the energetic, vivacious Sidney, but could tell from the twinkle in his eyes, the photographs in his room, family members and the staff's love towards him that he had been a strong character – a real gentleman.

Towards the end of his life, while under palliative care, he expressed an interest in Methodism, so I lent him a book introducing John and Charles Wesley. I believe Sidney was impressed with the Wesleys' social activity, and he started to talk about them and Methodism in a positive way. What interested Sidney was how Jesus' words have been put into action – reflected not only in the social actions of the founders of the Methodist Church, but, indeed, in the formation of MHA itself.

Shortly after that, Sidney asked if he could come to the services that we hold on Thursday mornings. I double-checked, to be certain that he was sure and not feeling under pressure to please me or the (Christian) staff. He was adamant that he wanted to attend, so I took him in his wheelchair. He did not join in the hymn-singing or appear to be very engaged with the service, and by now he was failing in his health. However, he came along to the service each week for six weeks.

After one of the services, it seemed right to invite Sidney to the meditation group. On this particular week I guided the group into ten minutes of complete silence. At the end, particularly sensitive to Sidney's atheistic beliefs and lack of experience of this kind of guided silence, I asked if it was okay and if there was anything the group wanted to share. Sidney said, 'It was a great privilege,' then paused and said, 'I saw God.' I paused (as the atmosphere was one of quiet) and felt it was okay to ask, 'What did he say?' Sidney replied, 'He said, "Welcome" – and called my name.' There was not a lot to say after that! It made the power of group silence very real.

When asked by the palliative care doctor to give his 'faith' for the forms, he said 'Christian', to which his daughter said, 'You are not, Sidney, you are an atheist.' 'No,' said Sidney adamantly, 'Christian'. I heard this from the manager and feel humbled how God works in ways above our understanding or expectation. I certainly hope I put no pressure on anyone to become a Christian, but am happy to support them if that is the journey they choose to take.

Two weeks after that event in our meditation group, Sidney died peacefully, holding the hand of his daughter, with his grand-daughter and great-granddaughter in the room; the last thing he would have heard was the laughter of his great-granddaughter. It was an enormous privilege to be there at the end of his very eventful life and to sense the depth of peace this encounter brought to him. I was with Sidney in the last hours of his life and said to him, 'Sidney, what a lovely picture of the circle of life, you, your daughter, granddaughter and great-granddaughter all in the room together.' His daughter (not able to reconcile his new faith) was moved and said, 'I hadn't thought of it that way.'

Sidney and his family had been committed atheists, serving his country as a socialist with strong communist ideals. He was very intelligent and had made a mark for the better on our country and in some of the least developed countries in the world. It seemed to me that he had been more 'Christian' in his life than most 'Christians', living in a self-sacrificial way and working for the good of humankind. I felt that he was indeed the expert on life, having lived a far longer, more thoughtful and helpful life than myself. I regarded him as my teacher, sharing his socialist concerns and ideals with me. Perhaps this attitude of learning from people brings out an openness towards me, especially from our atheist friends, as since this incident there have now been three atheists who seem to have warmed to me, enquiring a lot about God and occasionally asking me to pray for them.

As I reflect on my time with Sidney, I feel he had a lot to teach me and I had little to teach him, but was honoured to think that he wanted to learn more about the Methodist Church and come to the services and meditation.

I have learned that God speaks in silence. I often feel lost for words when dealing with people with such great intellect and life experience, so I do not try to argue any point, but simply accept them as they are, listening with interest. Perhaps it is the Christ way, as I am sure the non-believers, poor and outcasts all felt comfortable to be with Jesus. The time of silence was, and continues to be, powerful. Shared silence is something we do not do often, but Sidney's comments are a clear example of God speaking in the silence.

Another Christian teaching is not to judge, but Christians seem to be good at judging others. I have found the discipline of practising non-judgemental acceptance a long and difficult one to learn. I have pretended to myself I am not judging but simply trying to understand where they are so that I can 'help' them (hidden agenda 'be better people'). Sadly, after messing up my own faith journey and mixing with non-believers with no belief system whatsoever but who lived generous loving lives, I learnt I am not in a position to judge anyone. Who am I to know whether people are right with themselves and God? Am I in a position to help them? I hope that I am open to God's spirit working through me, an empty vessel, to bring people to a peace with themselves and God.

I am always surprised and honoured to have been with Sidney at this very powerful time. Working at a care home I am in a very privileged position of seeing people at the end of their lives and feel drawn to be with people in their last days. I am not sure why, but I do feel I have a gift of comfort to those who are dying, and by staying quietly beside them, perhaps holding their hands, perhaps praying but always listening, I sense God speaks to them all in surprising and unusual ways. Certainly Sidney's story is not one I would have ever predicted, hoped or expected.

I feel a little sad that Sidney's family remain atheist. This is not because their being atheist troubles me, but that they would be horrified to hear this story. It would not have given them any comfort, so I made sure not to tell them. However, many families, of faith or no faith, have been comforted to hear that their loved one came to a place of peace, and had experiences like Sidney, which I feel privileged to be part of.

I feel my qualification for chaplaincy is not the training or work in the church that I have done, but rather my own personal struggle with my Christian faith. Having been through difficult times, I now feel comfortable with people of all faiths and no faith, and feel it is important to be there for everyone in a non-judgemental place.

Story 5

Robert's story – Faith made stronger through adversity

Robert was the youngest of seven children born into a Christian family in Bridlington. He was brought up in a guest house and recalls how all the family worked to help cook and clean and care for the guests. For the first few years of his life, on parental command, he had to attend the Congregational church three times on

Sundays but he was not really aware of a personal faith. He says his first 'sin' was at the age of seven, when he and his brothers would spend half of their penny collection money on sweets!

His second 'sin' was to sit up in the balcony of the church throwing sweet papers down on to unsuspecting ladies below for which his punishment was to pump the organ. A later punishment, at ten years old, was to teach the babies in Sunday school, but he maintains that he probably shouldn't have taught them some of the things he did! At the age of 11, he won a scholarship and went to a grammar school that also housed 300 boarders, so his boyhood pranks were somewhat curtailed.

Just before the Second World War, he made friends with a group of Catholics and was nearly persuaded to convert. But the war put paid to any ideas of faith or religion and doubts started to creep in when Robert was 16. His family were forced to move from Bridlington as his mother was ill, and they moved into, in his words, 'little more than a doss-house', which was not a pleasant experience. After leaving school, he worked in an insurance company, helping older employees to collect the money, and it was at this time that he became aware of the plight of young girls suffering from TB in the slums of Leeds. Robert has always been very socially conscious and believes in fairness, justice and freedom. He was so incensed with this awful poverty that he began to go round the youth clubs with his friends preaching communism, believing this to be the way to a fairer society. This continued until he was old enough to join the RAF, where he had set his sights on ideally being a Spitfire pilot. Sadly for Robert this wasn't to be, but he joined as a member of the aircrew, being both a wireless operator and a rear gunner. Having had many traumatic experiences during his time fighting for his country, he certainly had no thoughts of Christian beliefs and maintains that all his RAF friends were atheists. He and his fellow airmen could not believe in a God who allowed such suffering. But his crew survived the war and it was probably the thought of being protected from danger and saved from becoming a casualty of war that caused Robert to re-evaluate his position of faith.

After the war, he married a Congregationalist, and eventually they moved to Birmingham, where he joined the Birmingham City Police. It was at this time that he came across the horror of back-street abortionists and the terrible suffering of some young women, a real problem in post-war British cities. He remembers vividly the films they were shown of such evil, barbaric deeds and how that image of pain and suffering has always stayed with him. But this time, instead of doubting the existence of God in this suffering, he began to feel that faith and compassion were very much needed in this dire situation. He was attending church with his wife but had made no real commitment. He did, however, attend various churches, including Seventh Day Adventist, with his mother-in-law, a born-again Christian, and having experienced many different styles of worship, he found he was beginning to seek a deeper faith, and actually loved all forms of worship. In fact he still does appreciate all styles of worship from lively, charismatic services to quiet, prayerful meditation.

Having worked in the Inland Revenue Robert trained to be a customs officer and moved to Ipswich where he started regularly attending the Congregational church. Over the years Robert was to find that he was more and more aware of a gradual increase in faith but had no 'Damascus road' experience.

In the 1960s, Robert became a member of Ebenezer Methodist Church, the nearest church to where the family was then living, and the church he continues to serve to this day. He had by this time a very strong faith and the whole family was involved in the life of the church. After retirement, he occasionally worked as a volunteer at the local Shaftesbury home for disabled adults, living out his faith. He helped wash and dress the residents, feed them, help with personal care, play games or take them out, always willing to do whatever it took to make their lives bearable. He found this an extremely worthwhile and fulfilling experience.

However, it was to be his wife's illness that really increased his dependence on faith. In 2004, Hazel, who was already ill with emphysema, was also diagnosed with dementia. Robert became her carer and looked after her faithfully until her death in 2008, an exhausting and traumatic period in his life. But he really believes that God was his strength and support during those difficult days. After Hazel's death, he became increasingly aware of the support he found from his faith and within the fellowship of the church and is still a very active member of that church.

Robert came into Charlotte House in October 2011, having had his name down for the new 'housing with care' flats. He decided that rather than wait another year for them to be finished he might as well come straight into residential care, but that certainly hasn't curtailed his activities. At nearly 90 years old, he is a church steward, reads the lesson, attends weekly prayer meetings and still drives his car, transporting people to and from church and other functions. He plays bridge twice a week, goes out every week to lunch with friends and takes them shopping, helps run a senior citizens' club in the town and organizes outings for them.

He recently had to have another assessment to receive his blue badge for disabled drivers, as he struggles with walking. His reaction was: 'It doesn't matter if I don't get it as long as I can still drive.'

On occasions he has organized services at Charlotte House on a Tuesday or Sunday and is always willing to participate in all activities. He has now taken over running bingo on a Friday morning and thoroughly enjoys himself. At Christmas, he sang a solo and did a reading. He really enjoys coming down to the dementia care floor to help with services, and says he gets a great sense of satisfaction and finds it very moving seeing the residents joining in the singing and enjoying the worship. He regularly attends Bible study and will often choose a topic to study, coming prepared with passages to look at and always willing to share his insights and his story of faith. He recognizes that he was far from perfect as a young man and has some regrets, but he really knows God's forgiveness and accepts that it is not by our works we are saved but by faith. Having said that, his actions illustrate his faith and he helps others whenever he can, always willing to be the spokesperson for the residents if things are unsatisfactory, always concerned about people's rights.

Robert's son-in-law has been stricken with Parkinson's disease at the age of 60. It pains Robert to think of a relatively young person suffering, and it is a real worry for him, but being always the compassionate and caring father he has given his daughter and her husband his blessing, as they prepare to move away to be nearer their family. He says that now he is settled in Charlotte House it is important for them to be where they can get help.

He is certain that his faith will continue to support him for the rest of his life.

In the book *Crying in the Wilderness*, Graham Hawley and Albert Jewell have this to say about the ministry of older people:

> We usually think of older people as those who need being cared for and visited. But . . . sometimes just the knowledge that they are doing something of value, rather than being done to, can be the encouragement needed, and acts as an antidote to becoming absorbed by one's own needs and concerns . . . Paul in his concern for the emerging churches demonstrates a strong level of care . . . emphasised in 1 Corinthians 13. (2009, pp. 60–1)

Appropriately one of Robert's favourite readings is 1 Corinthians 13.

Story 6

This story traces the evolution of the personal theology of a lifelong Christian and shows how her faith has changed and developed over the years, sometimes in contrast to the teachings and doctrine of the church to which the person belongs.

Joyce's story – A faith evolved

Having been a teacher during her working life, Joyce is now 93 and has lived in an MHA home for the past year. She describes herself as a lifelong Methodist. 'In the early years I was brought up in a strong Primitive Methodist tradition with a Christian Socialist outlook', she says. Her father was a Primitive Methodist local preacher, who lived and worked among the coal mining community during the 1930s depression. He had a robust and straightforward faith, devoid of ritual, which was about giving practical help to those worse off than they were.

Joyce trained as a teacher at a Methodist teacher training college, and her brother trained to become a Methodist minister. While a student she resigned from the League of Nations Union and joined the Peace Pledge Union, which was non-political and promoted non-violent solutions to conflict. When she got married, Joyce attended the local Methodist church with her husband. There they became class leaders and were both very involved with collecting for Christian Aid.

Growing up, Joyce became rather uneasy with evangelical forms of Christianity and the insistence that some people have on asking if you have been 'saved'. Instead she became interested in more liberal expressions of Christian faith and her own continuing search for the truth.

Joyce talked about a time when she and her husband were in their seventies. At more or less the same time they came to a point in their faith life when they felt that they did not fully accept some of the conventionally held beliefs of the Church, as contained in the creeds and especially in the words and sentiments of many of the hymns.

It is mainly the Church's continuing focus on 'blood and sacrifice' that Joyce is not happy about; she thinks that although this aspect had real meaning for people in Paul's time when the New Testament was written it has lost its significance to today's world. We discussed this aspect of faith and the fact that many people find comfort from the narrative of Christ's suffering, because it is through this we know that God understands when we suffer, and we know that he is with us in our suffering. Joyce says that she understands this may be helpful to some people, but it is not helpful to her. She certainly rejects the idea that the God of perfect love would send Jesus to suffer for our sake, as set out in atonement theology and emphasized by many Christian preachers.

One image of the cross that rings true with Joyce is seeing the horizontal beam crossing out the 'I' of the upright beam. In other words, she says Jesus' death crosses out our selfish, egotistical self-centredness. Joyce knows that Jesus suffered and died but she

doesn't like to think about it too much because it was such a terrible death. She says that in talking about the death of Jesus it is
important we remember that it lasted a relatively short time. In
comparison, she knows people who have suffered terribly from
pain and illness for many, many years.

This led on to the question of, 'Does God have control of the
bad things that can happen to us?' Joyce thinks that God does
not cause bad things to happen but he is with us when they do.
Very often, she says, the bad things are man-made, as in the case
of disasters and illness caused by the way we choose to live. There
are also factors like our genetic make-up, which depends on our
parentage over which we have had no control. If God controlled
and destined everything that happened to us – good and bad – she
says, we would have no free will.

In later life, and particularly since moving into a care home,
Joyce says, 'The aspect of faith which has become most important to me is carrying out, or at least attempting to carry out, the
message of love, and understanding how this can be practically
lived out.' This desire to live out her faith practically goes back,
I believe, to the very good example she had within her own family from an early age. She has continued to pursue her interest in
liberal theology, and says that she identifies with some of the ideas
promoted by progressive Christianity movements and continues
to read about this and discuss it with friends.

Joyce now has a more inclusive, wider faith, she says, and has
moved away from the idea that she once had of Jesus as a friend,
an idea that she thinks came from her parents. She feels that to
closely identify with the humanity of Jesus is helpful for some
people in order to feel close to God, but now, in this stage of
her life, she feels a direct closeness to God. That does not mean
that Jesus is any less important because she says we can only
understand God's will for us through the teachings of Jesus, especially the Sermon on the Mount. However, the direct closeness
to God that she feels now means that the Trinity has become less
important to her.

When thinking about mortality and her own death, Joyce says
her views have changed over the years. Several years ago, her

thoughts on death followed her childhood teaching on God's judgement: the good would go to heaven and the bad would be banished. Now, however, she is not so sure and it is something she is working through in her mind. Joyce is also not sure, but thinks she will be with her husband again – something that gives her comfort. She has often felt his presence with her, and has talked to him and asked him about things in her mind over the years.

Joyce says that although she has had a lifetime of going to church and saying prayers she does not pray now as such. We discussed how her faith had been much more about action and practice, but that now she is in the care home perhaps her thoughts are in some way like prayer – communication with God.

James Fowler (1981) describes a moving on for some from our faith stance of late childhood. He writes about a framework of how faith can develop over a person's lifetime, and goes on to describe a final stage of faith which he thought of as being rare, which is a selfless faith and involves the relinquishing and transcending of the self: 'Stage VI: Universalizing faith'. Henri Nouwen saw this progression as being less systematic. He observed that the movements of the Spirit:

> tend to come in cycles throughout our lives, with only a broad and hardly predictable progressive order. Instead of stepping up to higher and higher stages, as if achieving one stage leads to the next level then the next, we tend to vacillate back and forth between the poles that we seek to resolve. (Henri Nouwen et al., 2010, p. 134)

We 'become more aware of the different poles between which our lives vacillate and are held in tension'. In the process, Nouwen says, 'we gain greater awareness, personal freedom, and spiritual connection to God and others'.

Joyce's faith in the final years of her life seems to me to have moved very much towards a spiritual connection to God. Her faith has been pared down to what is its essential element – to what can be described as the 'primacy of love'.

Joyce does not like to talk to her friends or to other residents about how her faith has changed. When asked why, she says that they may have retained a more traditional faith from their childhood and she does not want to introduce questions that may cause them to lose their faith. I can understand her concern because from my own experience I know several older people who have decided that a fixed set of beliefs taught by the Church or formed over the years suits them. To question themselves too closely would be disturbing, so they avoid it.

Joyce, in her search for meaning, says she has confidence in what is described in the Epistle to the Hebrews – 'being sure of what we hope for and certain of what we do not see' (Heb. 11.1). The one thing that is most important to her is God's love – which she feels is an 'otherness', the complete opposite of the materialistic world we live in now. The words of a verse from a hymn by Frederick William Faber particularly resonate with Joyce's faith.

There's a wideness in God's mercy,
Like the wideness of the sea;
There's a kindness in his justice,
Which is more than liberty.

Story 7

This story illustrates how spirituality, manifested not just in churchgoing, worship and devotion, but also in the service and exercise of everyday lives, lies at the heart of what can give purpose and meaning to life.

Arthur and Alice's story – Faith sustained by finding God in the commonplace

'You will come to our seventy-first party, won't you?', Alice said, as we finished speaking. 'Of course,' I replied, 'I'd be delighted. When is it?' 'Next Thursday,' she said; and we left it at that.

Arthur and Alice had been married for 71 years – quite a time!
I wondered how they had become so serene.

I'd sat for some time with Arthur and Alice that day. He'd settled into his chair by the window and I'd sat next to him, and we
talked about the bowl of bright blue scillas I'd brought him (we
share a passion for flowers). I had gently massaged his large work-
man's hands and shared a favourite psalm, 'The Lord is my light
and my salvation, whom shall I fear?' (Ps. 27). His eyes closed,
but Alice was alert. 'Come on then', I said, 'tell me your story.'
So she began.

They were country folk, both born between the wars. She an
Anglican by birth and he a Methodist, they spent some of their
courting comparing hymns. She grew to love Wesleyan poetry:
deep truth simply, memorably and sing-ably expressed. They
married, had their first child who was to be one of seven (six girls
and at last a longed-for boy), and she became a Methodist. He
went away to war: a hard war, a time of great stress and sadness,
friends killed and maimed. He spoke little about it.

At home, their lives were full. There were many family responsibilities and work. Arthur turned his hand to anything: building,
plumbing, repairing cars, growing things. 'The rhythm of sea-
sonal life keeps you steady.' He was a nurseryman, specializing
in fuchsias, regal pelargoniums and cut flowers for market. Alice
would bunch and pack them, and sometimes one of the children
would help. It was backbreaking work. Up early and in the cold
they filled the boxes and sent them off. And it was risky. Who
could predict the arrival of mould spores that wiped out the whole
cyclamen crop: two years' work gone at a stroke; or the transport
difficulties that meant the cut flowers arrived unsaleable?

So Arthur went into partnership with his brother and built a
thriving garage business. Happy days, these were, but long and
demanding too.

How hard Alice worked alongside! Babies and small children
and their friends filled the house. So much to do when they were
small, and those years stretched out. She looked after her own
mother at home, arthritic and chair bound, right up until two
days before her death. They took vanloads of kids to hear Billy

Graham at his rallies. There was village life to be part of, as well as the nursery and later the garage: Alice worked the pumps, too.

Retirement was a great joy, a return to horticulture without the pressure of the bottom line. Their garden was a delight, no matter what the season: perennials and bulbs, vibrant shrubs and trees. And not only their own. A local stately home had an unloved garden, and they joined a team of restorers to nurture it into sparkling health once more. In the winter months, Arthur would copy and post out cassettes of Christian conference speakers. It seemed there weren't enough hours in the day; they would gladly fill them all.

Arthur had always been a patient man, 'Wonderfully patient; he never grumbled. And gracious.' One day he collapsed, 'completely tuckered', a victim of physical and mental exhaustion. It took him years to recover a quiet mind. The great grief of losing his older brother affected him deeply. Family were not only close, they were and are essential.

Later, he was involved in a serious accident when a car came screaming round a blind corner and his leg was broken in seven places. He would not have the driver prosecuted, but rather endured who knew what pain as he waited two long years for it to heal. He had prostate cancer, and the radiotherapy treatment left him doubly incontinent. This was the only incident in the whole story about which Alice expressed any regret: 'I wish we'd never agreed to it.' Thinking about it later, I remembered that Arthur had had to come into residential care because of his incontinence rather than his dementia. Alice had not relinquished her caring role easily, but it was obvious that they now enjoyed their time together, rather than Alice being overwhelmed by being on duty 24/7.

Arthur and Alice were both involved in the church, serving in any way they could: preaching, stewarding, flower arranging, befriending and visiting. They opened up their home. Alice was a skilled lacemaker, a craftswoman; her leisure was filled with creativity. There were often exhibitions to prepare for.

She and Arthur spent time together each day in prayer and reading the Bible; there is always something to learn. Alice still reads new books, wrestles with new ideas, but it is hard to share these now with Arthur who can only concentrate for short periods and only cope with what is familiar.

Truth earthed in real life is precious. It was a lay preacher whose explanation of difficult Scriptures in 1951, *along with his lived goodness*, had led to a new depth of understanding and commitment which sealed all that had gone before and helped them to face whatever lay ahead of good or ill; perhaps even to see the patterns develop.

Alice struggled with the carer's many-sided burden: her children, her mother, her husband all needed her, one after the other, but she 'got on with it' with very little in the way of complaint. Her joints grew painful as she entered older age, her shoulder especially. No matter. 'Lord, heal my daughter's cancer,' she prayed in the Abbey. She felt a light touch, someone behind her, a curious fullness of heart, and then no pain: 'So, God is here, and I never knew it.'

Alice walked a steady road then, and does now. Though 90, she retains a 'reasonable independence' and still offers hospitality whenever she can. The children, now with their own grandchildren, come and go; so many can share in Arthur and Alice's care, but the eldest girl remains the most frequent visitor, the closest companion.

Arthur's dementia came on slowly, but the diagnosis was 'no surprise'. It meant relocating to be nearer to the oldest daughter. It was hard to leave the village where they had lived, worked and then been retired for so very long. They were involved in the same local Methodist church for over 80 years. And leaving the garden was a wrench, a bereavement. But the timing was right, somehow. It felt like God's.

Alice has taught her children her craft skills, and they have passed them on to their children; the great-grandchildren are still at the baby and toddler stage. She feels the circle is completed; a sense of contentment, 'with God in the middle'.

Alice's only comment on the lives of the young today, whose situation she in no way envies, is that there are 'just too many distractions'.

Arthur and Alice have always been focused, and not only because need drove them. They loved to work purposively, each exercising their gifts and talents which made them and others feel whole. Their life has always been *life in connection*: connection to the earth, to family and families, to ancient skills handed on, to the rhythm of the seasons.

In some ways, however, their experience of life is particular to them and to their time. Arthur's skill with his hands is still seen in many young people: brickies, sparkies and chippies; but it is harder and harder for them to find an opening. Small businesses can rarely access much-needed capital, and, even if they can, many do not survive more than about two years, the competition is so fierce.

Rural life today presents different challenges, as farmers, nurserymen and women, market gardeners and garages have been largely replaced by mega-businesses that completely dwarf them and price them out of the market, leading to high unemployment. The housing bubble has left most rural folk unable to afford to buy homes in villages. And all these factors have perhaps hastened the decline of village life, including the village church that was such an important expression of Arthur and Alice's faith life.

In other ways, though, it is their internal life, their daily devotions together, that broaden their story to embrace all the faithful, because their walk with God has utterly transformed their characters. And it is who they are rather than what they have done that is important. Still essentially themselves, aged 90 and 96, they are also like Jesus in faith, hope and love.

Their lives are the complete opposite of the image Jesus offers of the cup sparklingly clean on the outside, but inside coated with all sorts of horrible stuff. No, whatever material their cup is made of, it is beautifully transparent.

Story 8

It is a reflection of attentive ministry that relationships between care home chaplains and residents deepen as minds meet, connections are made, reciprocity is shown and God works visibly in and through us. The relationship with Edith exemplifies all these things and for this reason, Edith's life story offers such a rich tapestry of a life lived in and for Christ, which continues to be so as she enters the closing stage of her life's journey. Edith shares here the journey of her life – which is a story of faith – and the encounters in life that served only to deepen and strengthen her.

Edith's story – God, an ever-sustaining presence

Born in Oldham, an industrial northern town that was home to many working-class families like hers, Edith grew up attending the local parish church with her family, where she was baptized and later confirmed. Edith told me that she became a Sunday school teacher because 'telling children from an early age about the love of Jesus was (and still remains) important to me'. As she reached her early twenties she became a youth leader in the church, working with groups of teenagers and with other local churches.

Edith had always been open to the spirit of ecumenism (including worshipping in a local ecumenical partnership) and true to that spirit married a man from a staunch Methodist family, even though she made the decision to continue worshipping at her parish church. This was until she was rudely forced by the curate at the church to make her 'choice' between being an Anglican or a Methodist. Edith told me that not surprisingly she chose Methodism! This was a turning point in life and the Methodist tradition became important to her faith and helped sustain her spiritual life.

In the Methodist church, Edith told me that she first became involved in organizing social events, groups and trips, but felt that something was lacking, when 'one evening in worship I felt that I was being called to be more than a church member'. Having found someone with whom to share this sense of calling, and after a period of exploration, Edith offered for training as a Methodist local preacher and was duly accepted and trained. This was 41 years ago, and she told me, 'I felt that God was with me all this time, giving me strength and ability – not only to preach, but also to teach.'

Around the time she started local preaching, Edith told me that she was diagnosed with motor neurone disease (MND). Although it was difficult to deal with, and she had to live with the unpredictability of the disease, Edith told me that she felt upheld in her faith throughout, feeling God's presence all around her, guiding her future and supporting her husband and family. Despite the diagnosis Edith never stopped local preaching, as she maintained full cognitive function. It was a blessing to her that as her condition deteriorated it was limited to affecting the movement and use of her shoulders, arms and hands and latterly the strength in her legs. Edith did not need prompting to respond to the question of 'Why me, God?' Instead of being resentful about her condition, Edith responded, 'Well why not me? Jesus suffered much more than I have.'

The strength and resolve of Edith's faith does not come from a place of pious self-sacrifice with its emphasis on death and crucifixion, but is a positive forward-looking perspective incorporating the message of resurrection and hope in every aspect of her life.

Edith's story embraces more than 40 years of fruitful local preaching, many more years of happy marriage and motherhood, a professional teaching career spanning 16 years; she was an ardent traveller and forger of friendships along the way. Edith is now 84 years old, having been a widow for 15 years, and is no longer in what she describes as 'the best of health'. A heart problem gives her great discomfort, but she told me she tries hard to place herself in the hands of God, as she has done throughout her life, and trust that he will help her in her discomfort. Edith's approach to age is liberating; she told me that her age really does not matter, because God is always with her. She said, 'I don't dwell on getting old, because I know that God will take me home when the time comes.' At this point she quotes a passage close to her heart, John 14.2–3: 'In my Father's house there are many dwelling places . . .' She says that it is not for her to know the time or place when God will call her home – but she knows that she is entirely in his hands and says: 'He will bring me to that heavenly house. I have no fear of dying, except that I do want the reassurance of his presence and my family at the time of death and that my dying wishes are fulfilled.' Even in her final lap of life Edith hopes that others will find strength in her faith and Christian witness – a thread that runs through the tapestry of Edith's life. Edith speaks of that hope even in old age; the words of Psalm 71.18 come to mind as the psalmist prays, 'from my youth . . . generations to come'.

Prayer has always been central in Edith's life. Even as a small child, prayer helped her to deal with conflict in the family as she learned to speak to God every night, taking her concerns to him. Edith believes that prayer connects her to God and gives her a sense of God's omnipresence, sustaining and guiding her. Edith said that all major decisions in her life were made seeking God's wisdom through prayer; as she took the step to move from the Anglican Church to the Methodist Church and become a Local Preacher, and from independent to dependent living. Even now when she sees fellow residents in need she prays for God's love and care for them.

Being loved by God (and her family) encourages Edith to deal with all that weighs heavily. Edith has lived out the gospel throughout her life, even in the midst of frustration from the loss of much of her independence. She has remained faithful to Christ and can truly understand what is at the heart of the gospel: that in giving we receive and in dying we live.

Edith explained that she relocated to live nearer to her daughter and family after her husband died. She continued to be a local preacher and developed her links as a volunteer in the care home where she now lives. Three years ago, having experienced further problems with her health, Edith realized that she needed 24-hour care and she felt that it was important for her to live in a nursing home with which she was already familiar. Being rooted in faith and the communities in which she has lived have been prevailing themes throughout her life. Although it's hard at times to be in the care home, Edith shared that she appreciates she couldn't have remained living at home alone. And yet despite those frustrations, she still tries to be of service to others and to God. She told me that she doesn't 'resent being old, my faith has helped me feel God's hand caring for me as it has always done'.

Throughout her life and now in the care home, Edith told me that she 'feels sustained by God and notices the kindness of others'. Of her continuing links with local Christians, she says, 'the care of and being connected with the people from the local Methodist church is important for me'. Edith's attendance at monthly Bible study is important and she feels valued and included as she assists the chaplain in planning and running some weekly Wednesday morning services. It is here that she has been able to continue to fulfil her lifetime call to ministry, albeit in a small way. The last three years in the care home, like much of her life's journey, have been a time for spiritual growth.

Being cared for in a Christian home, Edith told me that it has been important for her to be part of a community of people who share a Christian faith irrespective of denomination. This spirit of ecumenism has remained with Edith throughout her life and has helped her make sense of what it means to be part of the one Church of God. Edith has always passionately read and studied the Bible and still derives much satisfaction today reading and conveying the message to others. An integral part of her faith has been to evangelize and she says she's 'not stopping now'.

Throughout her life Edith has recognized the need to respond to the needs of others and now describes the care home as a place of need; and so it continues to be her mission to be a witness for God until the day she dies. During Edith's life the desire to preach the Word, to live out the gospel, to pray, to be part of a Christian community and to be rooted in Christ have helped her not only to maintain a hold on her religious faith, but to grow in strength as she has deepened her relationship with God.

Story 9

Joan's story – Making sense of the life lived

Joan was the youngest of several children and, having been born a few years later than the others, enjoyed a childhood where she was spoilt by her siblings and allowed to join in all their games, and yet where she also spent a lot of time with her parents. She enjoyed their company, and they had more time to do things with her than they had with the older children. She inherited a love of literature and a reflective approach to faith from her father and many practical caring skills from her mother.

The family lived in a rural location and Joan loved the time they spent exploring the countryside and enjoying the environment in which they lived. She did not marry and cared for both her parents in their old age.

Joan was trained secretarially and worked mainly for charitable organizations. She had been brought up to go to church and devoted a lot of time to supporting church activities. When her parents died she moved into smaller accommodation and became very involved in the South London community into which she moved. Joan had many opportunities to travel but spent most of her later life in the London suburbs. She had been very well provided for financially so that she was able to live comfortably.

In her early nineties, and suffering from a terminal illness, Joan arranged to move into an MHA care home. She was familiar with the home, having previously visited friends who lived there. She was a very quiet, undemanding person who appeared quite shy, but I think she was just the sort of person who needed time to think about what she wanted to say and never desired to push herself forward. She always listened to others and rarely said anything about herself unless asked direct questions. Yet she said to me on many occasions that she wished the staff would have more conversations with her when they were offering personal care. I think the staff, and other residents, found it difficult to engage her in conversation and quickly gave up, and so Joan spent a lot of time on her own. However, with people she knew well or felt comfortable with, Joan was a wonderful conversationalist and could talk on a great many subjects.

Joan had a very strong faith and when she was no longer able to get to church services she spent much of her time reading Christian literature. She read her daily Bible notes every day and appreciated the opportunity to discuss the passages she had read. She had a keen interest in the work of missionary societies around the world. Even when writing became more difficult she still managed to correspond or keep in touch with friends by telephone, and members of the church she attended and other friends visited frequently.

Joan appreciated opportunities to share in prayer. She was aware that she was terminally ill, and was accepting of the situation and always thanked God in her prayers, although her main desire in prayer was for the concerns of the world.

One day the manager asked me to go and talk to Joan as she had become very agitated and was being difficult with the care staff, not wanting them to assist her, which was quite unlike her, and they didn't know what to do. When I chatted with her, she told me that there was much about her life that she had never shared with the wider family, and she knew her time was now limited. She wanted the younger generations in her family to know her story, and for various reasons it had not been possible for her to share this with them directly. I sought the permission of the manager to sit with her for a couple of longer sessions and write down her story. I sat with my laptop and, as Joan talked, I typed everything just as she was saying it. Joan freely talked with me and poured out her whole life journey and included feelings and emotions and reasons why she had made certain decisions in her life. (There was nothing in this story that would have been hurtful or difficult for others to read.) When this was done, I printed it out in large type, and she read it through and put it in an envelope for the family. The following day she was admitted to hospital, and I went to visit her; she thanked me for what I had done and said, 'I can let go now.' She died that evening.

As the chaplain, this was quite a watershed moment for me. I had often shared in discussions or training sessions where we had looked at the importance of ensuring that a person has the opportunities to 'put their life in order' before being able to die. I was also very well aware of the importance of receiving forgiveness and why as Christians we put such an emphasis on being able to hand over to God all concerns and worries and to know that we are forgiven. Here I saw at first hand the immediate sense of release in someone being able to share something that had been weighing on their mind. Having the opportunity to do this simple task for Joan was a moment of true awareness for me, because I witnessed the sense of release and peace for her in being able to speak out all she was feeling and to know that she had been able to leave behind a complete life story, with all the emotional impact as well as the factual details.

There are many families today in which, for a variety of reasons, people are not always able to have the contact they would like. My experience of working with Joan to write her story demonstrated to me how important it is to be able to find a way of helping someone achieve what is on their mind; sometimes this is not difficult. Finding release from something that is bothering us can come through simply being able to tell someone else. It is not always necessary to do more.

One of the things Joan said to me was that, if circumstances had been different, she would have liked to have shared with the younger generation some of the wisdom she felt she had learned in her life in order to help them in the decisions and choices they would face. Clearly this had become a burden on Joan's mind, and no one could have known how often she went over things mentally, wondering how she was going to communicate this information. Joan told me that she had always planned to write this down herself, but had never quite got round to it, and then it was too late as she was physically unable to do it.

As the chaplain, the sorrow and sadness for me was that we had not been able to do this sooner and so have given Joan the spiritual freedom she craved for a longer period of time. Jesus says in Matthew 11.28, 'Come to me all who labour and are heavy laden, and I will give you rest.' It is not always easy to know if people have things on their mind, but this has made me much more aware of the need to ask people if there are things they want to do or say before they die, or at any time, to give them the opportunity to share and to help them to see that sometimes there are very simple ways I can help.

Putting things off for another day is something that many of us do, as is keeping issues that are worrying us tucked away inside and maybe not even admitting to ourselves how much of a burden they are. Joan believed in the power of prayer, was used to praying with others and welcomed prayer for herself. She had never previously given a hint of anything that was worrying her, and I like to believe that this issue had been a part of her private prayers and that God enabled her prayer to be answered.

Joan's faith sustained her to the end of her life, and having got to know her over her last few years I had a fairly clear idea of how important her faith was to her. But it was seeing so clearly the way in which unfinished business, once attended to, can allow someone to let go and find peace that was so remarkable for me.

Story 10

This story illustrates the effect that a conversation with a resident who has reached an advanced stage of memory loss can have on the chaplain. She had known Ada for almost three years, and Ada started talking about her memories of the day she had attended the chaplain's ordination as a deacon in the Church of England the previous year.

Ada had been absolutely delighted to be invited and able to come to the service. It had been a great day out for her, and even now as she is reminded of her presence on that day, and the delight her being there gave to the chaplain, she responds with a great smile and the memory – somehow – remains. This was a big event for Ada. Her son, when he found out that she had made the trip and spent the day at such an important celebration, was bowled over. He could barely believe she had done it. But we have the photographs to prove it, and Ada loves her photographs!

As the chaplain and Ada sat together in her room and spoke about her memory of the day, the details are now fading fast, but the emotional memory of happiness and being part of something so special remains. And yet having spent a lifetime in the Baptist Church, acknowledging the leadership of women in the Church may not have been something she would have known a great deal about. So they spoke about what she could remember of her life and being part of a church.

Ada's story – Am I justified by faith?

Born in the southern Home Counties, Ada was approaching 93 years old. Her husband, to whom she was married for 59 years, had been a Baptist minister. Ada had supported him in his ministry for many years and, in keeping with the church tradition, had always been there for him and those he ministered to.

Ada was mother to two children, a daughter who sadly died in her teenage years and a son, born in the mid-1950s around the time of the death of the first sibling. The death of their daughter caused considerable sadness for Ada and it was for this reason that the conversation did not trespass on to this sensitive territory.

Ada is an interesting person who is very warm and loving. She loves art and we sense that she must have learned art at school or at college later in life (or perhaps she was self-taught). She has a unique style of painting, preferring the use of pastel colours mixed with water to give subtle tones in her pictures. She can't remember having learned to paint, but she certainly has a great gift for it. And while her paintings are far superior to those produced by many of her fellow residents, Ada can never see how beautiful and precise her paintings are. She always feels that they are not good enough. When we do a jigsaw puzzle together she does not recognize her innate ability to fit together the pieces, drawing on shapes and colours, and when we do flower arranging she rarely feels her arrangement is up to the mark.

Ada can recall how important church worship and prayer had been, helping her to deepen her faith over the years. She says that 'throughout my life, my faith has been such a blessing and I give thanks to God for all that he has done for me'. Yet when in the course of the conversation Ada shares that she has always been burdened with the feeling that she is 'far from perfect', the observations I have made suddenly make sense. For some reason, although she tells me that her faith has been a blessing, she goes on to say that it has also been a challenge because her faith has made her consider her imperfections and shortcomings. I discover a real paradox in the way Ada's faith is expressed both as a blessing and a challenge. For it is through what she knows of God and how she falls far short of him that she has considered and recognized her imperfections. Immediately my thoughts turn to the nature of this God that Ada loves but also fears and needs to be 'put right' with before she dies.

As this point is gently pressed further, Ada tells me that she has 'always had this sense of being imperfect before God; it is not just a feeling that has developed with age. It is a reflection of what I have been taught over the years.' The thought that she has been made to feel imperfect before God is a deeply troubling one, and it is, then, hardly surprising that she feels so burdened with the image of God as judge, one whom we will always fall far short of and one who punishes. And yet the striking thing is her dogged persistence as she tells me 'all my life I wanted to follow Jesus – and I did'.

As we spoke about her sense of not being good enough we explored the importance of God's grace for us, and the idea that we can never earn or deserve God's grace. It is quite simply a gift from God and it is unmerited.

God's great mercy for us reveals that he is slow to anger, for he is a compassionate God and very patient. The greatest act of God's grace is the gift of salvation, which is available for all through faith, not by works that are judged by God with a score chart for goodness (Eph. 2.8–9). Our conversation led us into a time of prayer together calling to mind Paul's letter to the Corinthians: 'My grace is sufficient for you, for my strength is made perfect in weakness' (2 Cor. 12.9). We spoke about the real extent of God's love for us being greater than we will ever understand.

At the very heart of this conversation, Ada expressed her need to be put right with God before she dies and in so doing raised a number of issues for those caring for the spiritual needs of elderly residents in the final lap of their lives. In particular the conversation reveals the importance of creating a foundation for building loving and caring relationships with elderly people as soon as they enter the care home, and giving time to listen to their experiences so that it is not too late to gently offer new possibilities and ideas. While it is not possible to 'undo' damage, we are able, by using sensitive prayer, to allow God's healing to come into their situations and to ask for God's peace, to take them beyond the hurt they may be experiencing.

The importance of confession and absolution may be vitally important for some people struggling with past guilt and shame, so creating the right climate in which they may be released of this burden is crucial.

Ada told me, 'I don't feel that I have dealt well with my loss of independence and my old age.' Ada struggles with feeling very low on some days, on occasions enough to prevent her coming to our weekly 'church' service in the home. But usually with love and encouragement she will come along and will always feel better for having done so. It is when we are in a good relationship with our residents that these things are known and can be handled with love and care.

Throughout our conversation Ada kept looking at a photograph that shows a picture of the face of Jesus Christ, which was hanging on the wall of her living room at the house in which she lived some years ago. She knows that it was a special picture, and with a little bit of investigation I find out that it was bought in a local shop at the seaside resort on the south coast where she lived many years before. The picture was special and had been with her throughout her married life, although sadly now not in her room at the care home. She also kept staring at the oval green plaid hassock that sits under her dressing table in the room. She knows that this also has been very special to her in the past, but she can't remember its place of origin or where it had been used. It could have been her husband's. She cannot recall the detail; it's simply the happy memory she attaches to them both. It is reassuring that Ada is also able to attach happy memories to her walk with Jesus.

Story 11

This story is recounted in a slightly different way from the others in that it is told verbatim by Sally. It emphasizes the importance of faith needing to be exercised in the context of a community of believers. This section concludes with a reflection on the story by the chaplain.

Sally's story – *The importance of faith exercised in community*

When I was in a church it was quite different! Being part of a church community meant that I always had a close Christian friend to talk about the sermon to, or to study the Bible with. I also felt that I had some sort of role, a purpose to fulfil. When I reached the age of 93, however, I came into a care home and stopped being able to go to church. In many ways, this has been the most difficult aspect of growing old – being away from the church continues to affect me greatly.

Initially, the only Christian visitors to the home were trainee vicars on a one-week placement and, knowing how important my faith was to me, the staff always used to point them in my direction. I enjoyed speaking to them, but then I had to say goodbye, and it reminded me again just how much I missed being with other Christians. That said, those visits did keep my faith alive until, after a couple of years, the local vicar was appointed as the honorary chaplain. David would come in to take monthly communion services, and occasionally we would have a chat. That helped a great deal too, but now we've got a paid chaplain (who is a Baptist like me), whose arrival has been like the icing on the cake.

I went to the local parish church as a child – and as a young girl I walked four miles on my own to get there (my parents weren't churchgoers). When the evenings were light enough, I used to go to the evening services as well as in the morning. I was keen to know more about the Bible, and always came top in Scripture at school. It wasn't until I was about 40, while attending a Baptist church, that I had what I call a 'conversion experience'. I have always tried to help people, however, and maybe having a daughter who was born with severe disabilities has helped me to understand other people's problems. Even the pastor of my church confided in me once when he was going through a particularly difficult time. Maybe it's because I used to go with him as encouragement when he preached elsewhere? I still try to help people, but it's not always easy now.

When I came to the care home it was because I had a fall. I prayed to God about my fears, questioning him about the situation – and somehow I knew that I could trust the Lord, believing that he would have a purpose for me being here. Indeed, I had been in for a fortnight of respite previously, and God had used me to help care for another resident, a lady called Winnie. She had had a failed spinal operation and used to scream and shout continuously. The care staff only had so much time they could spend with her, and so I began to sit and talk with her, and it gradually calmed her down. I would often sit by her bed all day, and at night until she went to sleep. It really wore me out, and I realized what I was able to do to help others would be limited, but it gave me a sense that God could still use me, even though I am as old as I am.

There was a really good Christian friend from my church who would come and visit me, and yet soon after I moved into the care home she died very unexpectedly. I really missed the fellowship we had together and really questioned God as to why he had to take her away. One of my daughters, Gladys, comes to visit me regularly, and although Joyce, my daughter with disabilities, can't get to see me so frequently, we often speak on the phone, and as a Christian she encourages me to keep going in my faith. It isn't always easy, but growing old is just another of life's challenges, and God will help me through it.

Indeed, it feels that my life has had more than its fair share of trials. My first husband died at the age of 24 from tuberculosis, leaving me a widow with three children. On his deathbed he converted to Catholicism and, for some reason or another, as a non-Catholic I wasn't even able to attend his funeral. I also had my own life-threatening illness, and because this happened while I was pregnant with Joyce, I think that is probably why she was born disabled. Thankfully, God blessed me with my second husband, who took me and my children as his own, and made me very happy for more than 50 years. In later life, however, he too took ill with a problem in one of the veins in his neck. It meant that he could die suddenly at any moment, and for a period of three or four years I would always worry when I was at home on my own and he was out for a walk or something. My prayer was that he would not die alone – and I praise God that I was with him when, at the age of 84, he did pass away peacefully in his sleep. Nonetheless, his death still hit me hard and I needed a number of years of help from Cruse (bereavement care) to come to terms with my grief.

Everybody in the home knows that I am a Christian; my faith isn't something I hide. When I arrived, I thought I was going to be a great evangelist and get everybody else to believe too. That hasn't been the case – in fact, although lots of people went to Sunday school as children, it's been a hard job to find anybody else who was a regular churchgoer before they came into the care home. The trouble is, when I do have opportunities to talk about my faith, I can't remember all of the things I've heard in sermons and used to know about God. I still read some Bible study notes each day, but I don't always understand or remember what I have learned. I'm now starting to forget people's names too.

There's a bit of me that thinks as a Christian old age shouldn't happen to me – but it does, just the same as everybody else. At my age I suppose dying is going to be something that happens quite soon, but I don't really think about it like that. Two of my great-grandchildren always talk to me about me reaching 100 years of age, and although I will miss seeing them, and the rest of my family, I've come to the conclusion that my time to go will be at the Lord's choosing, not mine. At first I said I wanted to be resuscitated, but now I've said no. It's hard to think about dying. I can't really imagine it happening at all, although I know that it will. I'm not afraid of dying, but bewildered about what happens afterwards. Where will I be? What will I be doing for all eternity? Who am I going to see – just other Christians? What about those I love, but I don't think believed, like my mother, my husband and my eldest daughter? If I'm honest I'm also a little bit fearful, even though I am a believer. I think that's normal. I wonder whether it's really going to be like I was taught; I guess that's where faith comes in.

As we get old we lose all sorts of things: physical abilities, places and people we love, even our memories. Faith is something I've always had, so why should my old age make any difference? Even if I lose everything else, I know I'm not going to lose that!

Reflection

Sally is a remarkable woman who has offered her own power-ful insights into the role of faith in later life. Sally's particular care home has only been part of the MHA family for a decade or so, and does not, therefore, have the same faith heritage as other homes that have a much stronger link with the local Christian community. Sally's story shows how, for people who have always been involved in the life of a church, the loss of fellowship with other believers can be a significant cause of grief when moving into the care home environment. For this reason the provision of a chaplain, who can facilitate regular services, along with oppor-tunities to study the Bible and share fellowship, is of vital import-ance. In any context it is hard to maintain a living faith when isolated from other believers, and as 1 Corinthians 12 implies, this is not God's intention for his Church. When congregations seem to ignore the needs of their members who have moved into a care home this inevitably creates avoidable pain and grief for the individual involved. Moreover, the church also misses out on the wisdom that people like Sally can bring, and the encouragement that comes from hearing how they have overcome such great obstacles in order to keep going on their journey of faith.

Story 12

This story illustrates how a person's faith can shine, even through confusion.

Daphne's story – A deep, emotional and hard-wired faith

Daphne is 106 years old. She started playing the organ in church during her teenage years and continued well into her 80s. Evidently faithful from a very young age, she continued to demonstrate her dedication to the service of God when she qualified as a local preacher, and preached for 50 years. Indeed her name still appears on the Circuit Plan with the annotation 'not preaching this quarter'! Many members of staff (myself included) believe that if the occasion required it, Daphne could deliver a sermon that would make other preachers sit up and listen.

Now Daphne is often confused and doesn't always know what's going on. She asks if her mother is well, and when she can see her. Daphne calls out to say hello to people and is very friendly, though occasionally other residents feel frustrated and perhaps disturbed by Daphne's calls. Often when I talk to her, Daphne tells me that she is very frightened, and looks of fear and terror may dart across her face as she grips my hand and pulls me close.

When Daphne calls for her mother, and the look of fear crosses her face, it is easy to feel helpless. Who could blame someone for not knowing what to do when this person wants the comfort of a mother who is of course long departed? There is a desire to help but a worry about not knowing how to do just that. Some may evade the question by asking another: 'How old would your mother have been, Daphne?' 'What was your mother like, Daphne? Would you tell me about her?' Not unreasonable responses, and certainly better than turning away and finding someone else to visit. Talking about her mother may well help Daphne, and certainly in her reality her mother is only a train ride away. But the fear remains; even if we can talk about her mother together, Daphne remains concerned that her mother needs her, and is upset when she realizes I am not going to take her to the train station to go to meet her.

Daphne isn't always able to participate in conversations or acts of worship, but despite this there are glimpses of the faith that has always sustained this remarkable woman.

One such moment came when a chaplain who had been visiting the home for several months had come to his last day, and was invited to lead grace at lunch-time. When the chaplain picked up the microphone, before he had the chance to start, Daphne spoke up clearly and audibly and beautifully recited the words:

The grace of our Lord Jesus Christ,
the love of God,
and the fellowship of the Holy Spirit be with us all,
evermore. Amen.

It was a touching moment for staff and residents. Those who recognized the words were overjoyed to hear them being spoken,
and those who didn't were in some cases overcome by the clarity
with which a much loved resident spoke out words that evidently
meant a lot to her.

At other times, Daphne will recite lines or verses from hymns,
sometimes as they are being sung during worship, or sometimes in
a few moments of quietness. She'll often utter a prayer out loud,
and even when things seem most confusing, prayer still reaches
Daphne, and her faith is still evident:

I lift up my eyes to the hills –
where does my help come from?
My help comes from the LORD,
the Maker of heaven and earth.
(Ps. 121.1–2)

In one particular moment when Daphne looked at me with fear
on her face, pulling me close and gripping my hand, it occurred
to me that the answer was already there. I'm not the one who
can comfort Daphne, not really. But I can look to the hills, and
see that not only my help for dealing with this situation, but also
Daphne's help in her fear, comes from the Lord. I can help to
bring her the comfort of the God in whom she has always had so
much faith. Kneeling in front of her, meeting her gaze, I asked her,
'Daphne, shall we say the Lord's Prayer together?' 'Yes please,'
she responded. As I started the prayer, keeping my eyes focused
on hers, Daphne joined in, and slowly, right there in front of the
fish tank, with other people bustling around, we said together the
words that Jesus gave us. After the prayer, I couldn't move away.
It felt wonderful to share comforting words with Daphne, but I

knew I wasn't done. The tension in Daphne's face had lessened, but it was still there.

'Daphne, you are safe here, everyone here is looking after you. There's no need to be afraid.'
'I'm frightened.'
'We believe that Jesus keeps us safe, don't we, Daphne?'
'Yes, Jesus loves me. Jesus makes me safe.'

For Daphne, it seems the world can be a scary place. Perhaps that's a result of confusion, perhaps a result of lucidity and terrifying awareness that she is very old and no longer as able as she has been. Whichever it is, the world around her is not one in which Daphne feels safe, at least some of the time. As I learn more about how to be a chaplain to Daphne, I realize that the groundwork was already laid way back before even my grandparents were born. Her lifelong faith, so deeply ingrained, has sustained her so far and will continue to do so. My job is to remind her of the loving and comforting God she believes in when she finds it hard to remember for herself. The faith she has never seems to disappear, but, as with all of us, sometimes it's hidden beneath the cares of the world. For me, those cares might be about getting the house straight, saving money or spending time with family and friends. For Daphne, the scary world itself must be put to one side in order for her to remember how she is held by God.

When I hear Daphne saying aloud the words of a familiar prayer or hymn, with others or alone, I wonder what other people see. I see a woman who needs to feel the closeness of God, and whose faith tells her that this is always available when she calls.

The Lord will keep you from all harm –
he will watch over your life;
the LORD will watch over your coming and going
both now and for evermore.
(Ps. 121.7–8)

As she is no longer able to participate fully in conversations, Daphne may seem like someone who is 'winding down'; still present but not as fully as in previous years. That is a great challenge to me and many others. When we're unable to participate in the world as much as we have done, can we really participate in faith? Will there come a point where I can't even remember my faith? Perhaps. That's a worrying prospect, or it would be. But here's the wonderful thing. What Daphne shows me is that God never ever forgets us, and still breaks through into our lives, however unlikely that may seem. God comforts us when the world can offer us no comfort. God is present with us when reality may seem different from what we thought it was. God is with us in our past, our present and our future. God was there in the relationship between Daphne and her mother, and can still offer to Daphne the safety that she once found in being mothered. God is with Daphne in the moments when she is scared or confused and when she recites familiar words; and God will have his glory seen in those moments! God will be with Daphne both for the rest of her earthly life, and for ever after. And Daphne knows it. Somewhere deeply hidden, Daphne's faith resides, decades upon decades old: a faith so hard-wired into her person that it will stand the test of time. God gives us the gift of himself. All we need to do is believe, and he will hide within us a faith that can sustain and comfort us, even when the world around us is not a safe and happy place to be. For me, as a chaplain, I need to remember that it is not me who brings comfort to those who need it, it is God. My purpose is to bring God close when the world, and indeed perhaps their own mind, creates distance.

When I started as a chaplain in the home in which Daphne resides, I wondered whether life could have purpose when one is very old. It's not a question I asked for very long. At 106, Daphne's life has purpose. To me, and to others, her life reflects the beauty of a very present God, and the desire of the soul to cling to God, to worship God and to share God with others. Her faithfulness helps me to be faithful. And I am grateful to her.

Story 13

Elizabeth is somewhat younger than most of the other people featured in these stories, and although her story is not unique it does reflect some of the issues and 'spiritual baggage' that some older people carry into later life.

Elizabeth's story – Faith that survives despair, anger and fear

From a very young age, Elizabeth was brought up in the Baptist tradition and, together with her parents (who were also caretakers of the chapel), was a dedicated churchgoer. Elizabeth remembers very definitely making the choice to be part of the fellowship at the Baptist church and recalls with great joy watching the full-immersion baptisms that often took place at her church. She particularly remembers the baptisms of the American servicemen from the nearby airbase during and following the Second World War.

Elizabeth married David in a church service, and seven years later, in February 1964, their son Neil was born. During the first 24 hours of his life, Neil experienced severe breathing problems and was seriously ill. He suffered from oxygen deprivation to the brain, which left him disabled with learning difficulties, epilepsy and a dependency on full-time care which, until very recently, Elizabeth and David provided entirely themselves. Without Elizabeth or David's knowledge, the hospital staff arranged for the newborn Neil to be baptized, and he was taken from his crib to the end of the ward for this to take place. The first Elizabeth knew of the baptism was when 'some vicar' appeared at her bedside with a baptismal certificate – he was told in no uncertain terms to go away!

Elizabeth says that her life has been difficult and, as much as she loved David and wouldn't change him, their married life was a struggle.

Elizabeth, David and Neil were the first people to purchase a property at the housing scheme, where the family moved so that there would be stability for Neil should anything happen to his parents. They planned that they would leave their home of many years and purchase an apartment, which would then become Neil's home for the rest of his life.

Elizabeth's relationship with God is probably best described as rocky and honest. She often speaks to God, although sometimes this is primarily to shout at him and to vent her anger. She is still very angry that Neil's baptism took place without her knowledge or consent, and very much against the beliefs of her chosen denomination. She feels very let down by God and more especially 'the Church'.

After many years of not attending and feeling disconnected from 'the Church' (although she would often visit cathedrals and churches across Europe and the UK while on holiday), she has become a regular attender at all the services at the scheme. She contributes to our weekly informal Café Church service in a questioning and enquiring way, which shows her keenness to explore and understand her faith better.

After David was diagnosed with terminal cancer, Elizabeth asked me about re-baptizing Neil, and a service was arranged to reaffirm his original baptism. The joyful service, which I led, was held in the scheme with Neil surrounded by his fellow residents, friends and many of the staff members; coincidentally, it was held on the anniversary of his original baptism.

Following David's untimely death, Elizabeth was determined that he would receive a 'proper' full Christian funeral and a memorial service in celebration of his life. In David's final days, he promised me and Elizabeth that he would come back and let us know what heaven is like – we are still waiting for him to make the great journey back to us.

Elizabeth feels very restricted by her life, especially as now, without David, she is Neil's primary carer. Neil lives a life that is structured by routine and fixed points in his day, and Elizabeth works around this, although she finds it highly frustrating, leaving no room for spontaneity or changes without pre-planning. At times, she is quite angry and resentful with God, frustrated and annoyed by the life she has been given.

Despite this, Elizabeth continues to speak to God, keeping the channel of communication open in a continuing dialogue with him. Her faith has been very volatile at times; there have been times of closeness and coherence in her relationship with God, but there have been more times of distance and resentment.

Elizabeth is at a stage where she is moving towards a tolerance and sceptical closeness with her God. She doubts some of the core elements of Christian teaching and actively seeks to discover more knowledge and understanding, but the basic closeness and acquaintance with the Lord is real and tangible.

Elizabeth is a very strong woman; she has dealt with the difficulty of life with a real determination and realism. I know that Elizabeth would not want anyone to pity her, or feel sorry for her. She is a woman of amazing resourcefulness and possesses an inner strength of which many of us could be envious. What she would want us to reflect on is that sometimes a relationship with God can be difficult, troubled and, in her words, 'rocky'. I might almost say that she is at times cynical and disbelieving of people who enthuse about their closeness to God.

I think that now she has become part of this community, and has developed an understanding that, although she hasn't always realized it, God has always been a presence in her life.

I have become very used to coming into work and being greeted by Elizabeth with 'You need to have words with your boss (God)!', which tells me that something has gone wrong or that there is an issue that I need to look at with her. This way of referring to God is done in a completely respectful way. I am always impressed with the fact that Elizabeth continues to have a knowledge of God's sovereignty.

One question that Elizabeth's story raises is why the hospital staff didn't seek permission from Elizabeth or David before performing the sacramental act of baptism on Neil. Many of us would feel violated by a church that did this. It was perceived as an enforced baptism, which went against the beliefs that Elizabeth then held, although I believe that the hospital staff and the church felt they were acting in the best interests of both Neil and his parents as there were genuine concerns that Neil might not survive.

Elizabeth is resilient and brave. Her life has been difficult and she has faced many disappointments. But throughout it all she has lived a life of 'practical Christianity' with genuine concern for neighbours, family, friends and colleagues. I doubt that she perceives this as a Christian way of living and would simply state that she is doing her best.

Being on the fringe of the Church has allowed Elizabeth to retain a very pure understanding of her faith without it becoming too 'churched'. This practical manner of understanding faith and her relationship with God is without many of the additional 'hang-ups' and conditions that the 'churched' can sometimes accumulate and this gives her a very practical and open faith that many of us might wish for.

I have never had a doubt about the strength of Elizabeth's faith – it is what it is.

She knows and respects God, she vents her anger at him, but also shares her frustrations and joys – the Church may have let her down, but God didn't. He may not have 'given her an easy ride', but she has coped with and dealt with all that life has thrown at her. There have been times recently when she has expressed embarrassment for the way she has spoken to God in the past and for the anger that she has shown to him. Together we have agreed that God has very broad shoulders and is probably just happy that she keeps on talking to him.

As her chaplain, it has been a privilege to be part of Elizabeth's journey. She questions the traditions of faith and actively seeks to understand why things are done, and what things are for. This is wonderfully refreshing and helps to challenge my own knowledge.

Perhaps the Church needs more 'Elizabeths' to make sure we challenge the faith that we are taught. I also believe that Elizabeth's example could show the 'modern world' that adversity is something that can be worked through and lived through and doesn't stop a good life from being lived – in fact it can make us stronger and much better people.

Story 14

This is a story of a faith and devotion to God that has spanned over 100 years.

Winnie's story – A story of enduring faith and devotion

Winnie Charlotte Brown, affectionately known as 'Lottie', was born in Norfolk in 1911, the only child of a second marriage. Lottie was very intelligent, attending the local grammar school, which for a girl of her generation was quite an achievement. This did, however, affect her relationship with her friends from primary school who, being jealous of her progress, wanted very little to do with her, so she was quite a loner but not alone.

In the early 1930s, she went on holiday to the east coast and fell in love with the area, remarking on what a lovely place it was, with, in her words, 'lovely shops and lovely beaches with no vendors to worry you'.

Winnie married the love of her life, Harold, in 1937, but sadly they were never to be blessed with children – one of her regrets. But again this was an obstacle that was overcome by faith, and she continued to make the best of life. At the beginning of the Second World War, she joined the Fire Service working as a telephonist, and she talked about the bombing raids and how the shrapnel used to rain down on her tin hat on the way to work. But as she remarked, 'you just took it all in your stride'.

When Harold joined the Army and went away, Winnie decided to offer herself for the Navy, and so her life in the WRNS began. She was accepted gladly, because she was an excellent mathematician and needed no training. So she started working immediately in the clothing store on Parkeston Quay, eventually rising to the rank of Chief Petty Officer. She remembered the war clearly, especially D-Day, being responsible for driving landing craft over the water to fetch 'vittles' – as she called them – from the American ships. She used to tell how, while sitting on the quay, she witnessed the first magnetic mines being dropped over Harwich, not realizing what they were until much later. She was also there when *HMS Gypsy* hit a mine and exploded. She said, 'I felt so helpless because there was nothing I could do to help the sailors calling out in distress.' She was a very compassionate person, and this experience affected her deeply. But always being very philosophical, her outlook was, 'It was no good being frightened, you just had to get on with it. I knew God was with me.'

Winnie had several hobbies, but most of all she loved her sport. She once came across some old hockey sticks and asked her commanding officer if she could start a WRNS hockey team. Perhaps it was through her sheer determination or just her strong character that she usually got her own way, but the team was formed, and they competed all over the county. After the war, she continued playing, representing her county and also refereeing for the England team. She was also a very good runner and talked about once winning the 100 yards sprint. She played badminton until she was 82 and attributed all her gifts and abilities to God.

After the war she worked as an accountant and recalled how she used to collect the rates and cycle back with a lot of money with no fear at all. Winnie was determined to succeed in whatever she tried and would not let fear get the better of her.

Winnie loved her church and was very involved, running the youth club and becoming honorary aunty to many young people. She also enjoyed performing in variety shows, plays and pantomimes. Sadly the church closed after being damaged during the gale of 1987. This caused her some distress and she missed the old building, but, having become a member of a joint Methodist/ URC church, she remained very active and was much loved and respected. She was also a pastoral visitor and spent many hours helping and chatting to housebound elderly people. She used to say to me, 'It seems funny that I used to do what you're doing now.'

When her husband was ill, she nursed him tirelessly, an extremely exhausting and emotional time for her, but again she took it all in her stride, her faith helping her to cope. After Harold died, she continued with her commitments to church and really lived life to the full. Winnie enjoyed going out to lunch with friends and loved the water, thoroughly enjoying boating with friends on the Norfolk Broads; she was rather good at being at the helm steering. I think that was pretty typical of Winnie, wanting to be in charge of her destiny!

It wasn't until 2008 that Winnie became unable to care for herself at home and moved into Victoria House at the age of 96, again showing her determination to remain independent for as long as possible. At first, she was reasonably mobile, and always joined in anything at the home.

Latterly, Winnie had most meals in her room but did go up for a special tea to celebrate her hundredth birthday, a day she really enjoyed; she was surrounded by cards, flowers and friends, exhausted but happy. About six weeks before she died, she was persuaded to go up to the dining room for lunch, which she also enjoyed and afterwards sat in the lounge overlooking the sea and chatted once more about her life. Even at her great age, Winnie was always ready to learn something new. She once borrowed John Wesley's Journal, so she could learn more about him and was interested in what she read, although she did say, 'He wasn't a very nice man really, was he!' She had a remarkable brain for a centenarian. She was very popular with both staff and other residents and was a wonderful character, 'a very special person'.

As she grew older her eyesight failed, and after a couple of falls she lost her confidence and was very reluctant to leave her room.

Winnie attended church with her grandmother from the age of three and used to talk about the box pew with the family name on it, which was so high she couldn't see over. The experience of church life affected her deeply and church was to become the mainstay of her life for the next 97 years. She became a Sunday school teacher of the 'tiny tots' as she called them and was always involved in the life of the church, particularly the choir. She had a wonderful alto singing voice and used to tell of her first solo in church at the age of nine, a very proud moment for her. She always used to harmonize during the hymns at our services at Victoria House, and she even sang to me just a few days before she died, in a very clear voice and remembering all the words, her favourite hymn, 'Summer Suns are Glowing'.

In an article on memories, Margaret Cundiff (2003) wrote:

God gave us memories that we might have roses in December –
but roses often have thorns and we can hurt ourselves if we
don't handle them with care . . . What matters is the way we
see and deal with unhappy memories. True wisdom, I believe,
comes from being thankful for all good things . . . and being
able to place into God's hands those things which cause us hurt
or regret, knowing he understands, and heals.

Winnie really believed this.

Winnie regularly attended quiet time in the mornings and Bible
study, always ready to contribute some pearls of wisdom and
share her faith. She enjoyed Tuesday Fellowship and Sunday services and loved anything musical. She used to love being taken
out to the park where she would sit enjoying the sun and chatting
for ages about her past and the importance of her faith. It was a
great disappointment to her that she began to lose her sight and
couldn't read the words of hymns.

Towards the end of her life Winnie was tired and used to pray
every night that God would take her, almost to the point of being
disappointed when she awoke in the morning! I used to tease
her and say God wasn't ready for her yet, to which she always
laughed. She never lost her sense of humour and appreciated
someone with whom she could share her faith. Her strength of
character and great faith always shone through, and on several
occasions she said, 'I don't know where I would have been without God. I started when I was three and he has given me strength
to get through life.' But even so, she still wished she had more
faith and she longed for others to share that faith.

When asked, 'Shall we have a prayer?', she would answer, 'Oh
please, I would be very disappointed if you hadn't asked', and she
would join in and pray for others. I gave her a picture of the image
of the Laughing Jesus, which she liked to look at when she said
her prayers, feeling he was there with her. Winnie lived life to the
full, a life of love, faith and devotion to God. She was a remarkable character.

Story 15

This story illustrates the important role other people can play in helping individuals continue their faith journey into extreme old age.

Barbara's story – Faith in the face of confusion

Barbara was a single woman who was politically active and devoted her life to work for peace and reconciliation in this country and abroad. She had written a booklet of poems and reflections on becoming an octogenarian, and had also written down many thoughts and feelings about memories from the past and ideas for the future. Her writing had a light, humorous tone to it.

Barbara was brought up in a Christian home. Her parents were fairly well off. After schooling she had a secretarial training, which she put to good use in the services during the Second World War. Civilian life led her to secretarial work in London before spending a number of years travelling and working abroad, mainly in Asia, where she embraced the culture and way of life and made many lifelong friends. During her retirement years she lived in South London and was a regular churchgoer.

She came into the MHA home when she could no longer manage physically. She hated losing her independence but recognized that she could no longer cope with living on her own. She had a very strong faith and joined in life in the home very well. She made it her business to talk with other residents and to get to know people, and showed a great concern for the needs of others. She read very well and so participated in the life of the home by giving some poetry recitals and sharing details of her life story with groups of residents. Initially she was able to continue attending church and fellowship groups at her church, to go out with friends and have many visitors.

As she developed dementia things changed, and changed very quickly. She was a very intelligent and articulate woman, and she could see and understand what was happening to her and was very despondent about this. She was angry and frustrated that she could not do anything to halt the progress of this illness. I think the fact that she had been such a contained and independent person for so many years made it very hard for her to see things happening in her life over which she had no control, and this was not just with the illness; it affected things like what she would wear or when she would be able to have her hair done. She found it difficult to keep asking members of staff to arrange things for her. The care staff tried very hard to enable her to remain as independent as possible with her personal care, but even so it was quite a trial for Barbara that it took so long to achieve so little.

Barbara described her faith as a journey of learning and growing, at times quite a hard journey. And she often spoke of the reward in later life when she had more time to 'be still' and listen to God and reflect. As the dementia became more apparent, the saddest thing was the way it caused her to question her faith and even the existence of God. She felt that God had abandoned her and could not understand how God could allow this situation to arise.

Unfortunately, this sense of abandonment came also from friends who found visiting or telephoning difficult, as they felt Barbara did not understand what they were saying. Visitors from the church also stopped coming regularly, as they found it difficult to be with her. I tried to explain to both these groups of people that Barbara did understand what they were saying, but needed a considerable amount of time to process the information before she could respond. I had discovered that if I waited several minutes after saying something, Barbara would respond.

Barbara loved receiving postcards, and although these had to be read to her, she clearly knew who the people were and gained a lot of pleasure looking at them. Towards the end of her life it did become quite difficult to understand what she was saying, but with careful listening it was possible to glean enough to know what she wanted. A couple of strokes made life much harder physically, and she became very despondent. However, every time I asked her if she would like me to pray with her she smiled and seemed comforted by it, which makes me think that deep within she still held on to her faith and hope in God.

Many times in ministry I have experienced situations where people who have worked devotedly for the Church all their lives have a crisis of faith and start questioning the existence of God when old age becomes difficult. It feels as though all the while we have a level of independence and can be actively involved in expressing our faith, we feel as though we are journeying with God, even through some very difficult times. When old age or dementia cause us to cease being independent, this can be a very low point in faith for some Christians. There is a lot in our Christian teaching about letting go of self and trusting in God, but that is easier to subscribe to while we still have a degree of ability to take care of ourselves, and a positive mental attitude to life, than when we are totally dependent on others and confused in our thinking.

From her late teens Barbara had always taken time in each day to be quiet and still with God, to listen for God's promptings, so it is not as though she had always lived out her faith solely in action, although this was a very large part of her faith journey. She was used to 'waiting on God'. For her, the illness had taken away the ability to have stillness of mind and the peace that comes with that, which I imagine is why she felt that God was no longer with her, but she clearly held on to a degree of hope because it was evident that she found prayer helpful. Even at the very end of her life when it was extremely difficult to understand what she was saying, she managed to tell me that prayer was comforting. Barbara's story shows us that when we are forced to let go of a sense of control or independence in our lives we need others to be the words for our continuing faith journey.

People seem to feel very uncomfortable in the presence of those who are suffering with memory loss or dementia. Part of the problem appears to be an inability to cope with the fact that they no longer seem to be the person they were, and the other part is an assumption that they won't want the same sort of conversation so that communication often becomes very difficult, or seems to be totally one-sided. Visitors feel very inadequate and often give up, feeling their visit has no purpose. Greater understanding of the need to maintain visits and to find new ways of communicating are clearly very important, as is a greater understanding of this stage in life. This presents a challenge to individual Christians as well as to the Church in supporting and enabling everyone to be able to remain active in their faith despite physical or mental disability. Paul in 1 Corinthians 12 speaks about how the different parts of the body are all interdependent and Barbara's story is an example of how, within the body of Christ, we need to be supportive of one another in new ways.

References

Cundiff, M., 2003, 'Wisdom and memories', in Albans, K. R. (ed.), *Old in Years and Young in Soul*, Derby: MHA, pp. 4–5.

Fowler, J. W., 1981, *Stages of Faith: The Psychology of Human Development and the Quest for Meaning*, San Francisco: Harper; cited by Elizabeth MacKinlay, 2006, *Spiritual Growth and Care in the Fourth Age of Life*, London: Jessica Kingsley Publishers, p. 70.

Hawley, G. and Jewell, A., 2009, *Crying in the Wilderness: Giving voices to Older People in the Church*. Derby: MHA.

MacLeod, G., 1956, *Only One Way Left*, Glasgow: Iona Community.

Methodist Homes (MHA), 2011, *Chaplaincy Manual*, Derby: MHA.

Nouwen, H., Christensen, M. J. and Laird, R. J., 2010, *Spiritual Formation: Following the Movements of the Spirit*, New York: Harper Collins.

7

Distilling Meaning through the Stories

MARGARET GOODALL

These 15 short stories are examples of the hundreds of stories listeners hear from those who are among the oldest in our society, now living in our care homes and housing schemes. Through these stories we have seen how the chaplains are able to listen, within the context of an ongoing relationship with the person and while giving focused attention, to those who want to share some of their life with them and then reflect on the meaning of the stories they have shared.

Themes

It would be easy to suppose that, in matters of faith, the oldest old will have arrived at one of two points. Either they will have worked their way through any questions they might have had and are now just biding their time, safe in the knowledge that they are at peace and 'at one' with God. Equally possible is that they have decided that there is nothing beyond this life and are content in that knowledge.

However, what our stories show us is that there is much more fluidity of belief, and that reaching the end of a very long life does not make it any less likely that there will be questions or doubts. The stories also describe, in very real ways, how reflecting on the life lived offers opportunities for a person to make sense of that life in relation to their faith journey.

Instinctively, it might readily be assumed that those who reflect on a life of faith will do so either in the context of their own involvement in church or, particularly with the oldest old, that ideas will have been fixed and all the questions will have either been asked, forgotten or are no longer of any interest. However, the examples we have here show that it is perhaps only when engaged in conversation that ideas begin to take shape, and that listening to their story can sometimes result in action to help a person address a need, hope or fear. At other times, when there is no answer, it is perhaps enough that the thought is shared, and while the idea of 'doing nothing' is not easy, the opportunity for expression might itself offer some form of release or healing.

The themes that come from our stories, and the reflections on them, fall under four main headings: sharing faith together, living the faith, spiritual growth, and, finally, change and decay as the end of life becomes a reality. The stories are all individual accounts and while that makes them unique, there are commonalities of approach that might enable the reader to understand the process and the response of the listener. These responses are sometimes practical in that they offer to try to address a problem, but often they are simply a raised awareness of the depth that is the person the listener meets. Being aware of the past hurts and sorrows of those to whom they listen is not easy, but these chaplains have developed a lightness of spirit that enables them to empathize with the person while maintaining perspective that enables them to reflect.

We shall now look at how each of our identified themes is expressed and illustrated in the stories that have been shared.

Sharing faith together

In reflecting on the stories, the chaplains noted that many of the conversations were situated around belonging, especially the importance of belonging to a faith community. In Sally's story (Story 11), she places much importance on visits made to her by local clergy, as they kept her 'faith alive', when she had come to live in the home. The visits of a Christian friend enabled the fellowship for which she longed, but after a time her friend died.

One of the challenges Sally sees in living to a great age is outliving friends who have been supportive. In this case, the chaplain understands that Sally finds it 'hard to maintain a living faith when isolated from other believers', and so facilitates services, along with opportunities for Bible study and sharing in fellowship. Here the chaplain offers ways to connect to a new Christian fellowship and so encourages Sally to share her faith with others.

Involvement in a community of faith is not always positive, however. In Elizabeth's story (Story 13), we meet a person who has been damaged because long-held beliefs and practices have, in effect, been trampled on by the system. Here the chaplain reflects on the actions that have caused the hurt, and although he is able to offer Elizabeth some way through, he is not able to undo the harm done. However, it does offer the opportunity to learn from what has been shared, and he reflects that 'adversity . . . doesn't stop a good life from being lived'.

Living the faith

Even in very old age many still seek to be good disciples and live out their faith in practical ways. In Mary's story (Story 1), the chaplain reflecting on her life both in the community and now in the care home sees Mary as 'one of a series of . . . "auxiliary chaplains" who have contributed a great deal' to his work in the home. Looking at her character now, he reflects back with her on her life to glimpse the factors that contributed to her gifts, especially those of kindness, generosity and concern that he sees her exhibit even at 98 years old.

Others also reveal faith that is sensitive to different beliefs, and is not threatened by them. In Joyce's story (Story 6), the chaplain reflects that 'Her faith has been pared down to what is its essential element – to what can be described as the "primacy of love".' Joyce had developed an understanding of faith that had changed but was not challenged by the more traditional faith of others; neither does she try to disturb the faith of others by posing questions. The chaplain describes how by sharing her journey he is able to honour that faith which is vitally important to her. It is a sharing of the secrets of the heart with someone who can both listen and affirm the life lived. This is the case in Arthur and Alice's story (Story 7) of their rooted and grounded faith, of which the chaplain reflects that 'Still essentially themselves, aged 90 and 96, they are also like Jesus in faith, hope and love.'

Sharing stories of lives in which faith has stood the test of time is a characteristic of many of the stories, and this is especially true in the examples where the person has signs of confusion. In Daphne's story (Story 12), the chaplain writes how opportunities to rehearse words that have embodied faith over the years still have the capacity to calm and comfort and bless. Those who are watchful note the power of familiar words and music that seems to break through any confusion, especially when the words are part of a 'deep, emotional and hard-wired faith'. Providing opportunities for these words to be repeated is important, and while it may seem to some to be simply repetition, to those who see the effect it is the doorway to accessing faith.

Spiritual growth in the last stage of life

For some of the oldest that we meet, faith is something to hold on to that sustains in times of trouble and change, or something that is itself continually changing and growing. And yet for those who have never found faith, late life can be a time of searching.

In Nancy's story (Story 3), the chaplain reflected on how she could meet the needs of Nancy who, with no fixed belief, was near the end of life. She was too tired for talking, and the usual aids of reading or singing used by the chaplain when visiting – actions, she noted, that help us to feel useful – were not wanted, nor were her prayers. What was needed was someone not 'to do' anything, but just to be a companion. This offering of vulnerability, just 'being present' in the moment, gave the space for Nancy to share her trust in God.

Likewise Sidney was a person who, given the space, found a faith that he had not known before. In his story (Story 4), the chaplain suggests that meeting him in a non-judgemental way opened up an opportunity. She reflects that previously she had been 'trying to understand where they are so that I can "help" them', with a hidden agenda of helping them to be 'better people'.

With all the pressure to do and to achieve, the chaplains here recognize that it was not in 'doing', but in offering companionship and non-judgemental accompanying that they gave the opportunity for these people to recognize the faith that was inside them. In the stories of Nancy and Sidney, the chaplains look at their own practice and the twists and turns of their faith journey, as they reflect on the faith of the person they have met.

In Ada's story (Story 10), the chaplain offers an example of a life story that is the launch pad for an exploration of spiritual development, in which Ada's faith is expressed as a blessing, but also as a challenge. The feeling of never being good enough had stayed with her all her life, and was now firmly embedded. Having recognized what was on her mind the chaplain was then able to talk with her about God's grace and loving kindness, and offered opportunities for her to have fellowship with others, giving continual reassurance.

Reflecting on the end of life: change and decay

In Edith's story (Story 8), the chaplain reflects on a life rooted in faith and love where the changes of old age are faced. Although Edith now needs help, she 'doesn't resent being old, my faith has helped me feel God's hand caring for me as it has always done', 'I know that God will take me home when the time comes.' But not all the stories show this acceptance of a life completed well. The chaplain in Winnie's story (Story 14) reflects on the hurt that unhappy memories and unresolved issues can cause, and that 'True wisdom . . . comes from being thankful for all good things . . . and being able to place into God's hands those things which cause us hurt or regret' (Cundiff, 2003). In Pearl and Walter's story (Story 2), the chaplain observes this same wisdom in Pearl who, despite struggles and difficulties throughout life, now 'continues with a richness of life . . . an inspiration to many'.

Where an older person has been able to come to terms with their life the listener's role is to feel the emotions of the story and to mirror back the sense of completeness that can be evident when facing the end of life. However, when the story told is one of a sense of abandonment, by friends or family or the Church as well as by God, then there is other work to do. In Barbara's story (Story 15), the chaplain reflects that as Barbara was unable to pray in the way she once knew, she now needed 'others to be the words of (her) continuing faith journey'. The need for companionship and the continuing support of others spurs the chaplain to look at the idea of the many parts of the body of Christ being 'interdependent' and how we 'need to be supportive of one another in new ways'. These insights influence how the listeners respond to the person, but also how they work to encourage others to maintain the contact and relational links that are so important to emotional and spiritual health.

The importance of the story to enable listening

While some are able to rationalize and accept the lack of independence that older age brings, along with other changes that are neither welcomed nor looked for, others rail against those changes and the dying of the light. This is especially so when the person is not able to express their thoughts because of cognition difficulties.

An example from my own experience offers an illustration of this and how important it is to know the person and their story. When I was sharing some time with Anna, a woman with moderate dementia, she asked a question for which I had no answer. She asked why God had allowed this love. Her story was that she had married but had then left to live with another man. The pain was evident, and she seemed haunted by the confusion she now experienced. All I could do was to say that I didn't know. She was reassured by my continued visits that God loves her and I did not judge her.

There are times, however, when being familiar with the person's story can give an insight that no one expects. Hilda had dementia and repeated the phrase 'God help me!' over and over again. It was thought that this was a symptom of her dementia; however, reading her story we discovered that she had been a churchgoer until her marriage but had then stopped because her husband didn't want her to go. We invited her to the service in the care home, where she joined in the hymns and prayers. The calling out stopped. She had found peace.

One important thing comes from these stories and that is that everyone is different. There may be some common themes, which I have drawn attention to, but the way the stories are reflected on and acted on – or just listened to – will depend on the individual person and the attention of the listener.

To listen carefully in this way, with an open heart and an imagination that offers insight beyond the words, is both a gift and a skill that can be honed. Through these stories we meet real people who have been listened to. The chaplains have recognized the importance of trying to understand and distil meaning in conversations, which goes beyond the normal acts of kindness or just listening. They have used the skills identified in Chapter 5 and have been willing to share themselves with the people they meet.

Reference

Cundiff, M., 2003, 'Wisdom and memories', in Albans, K. R. (ed.), *Old in Years and Young in Soul*, Derby: MHA, pp. 4–5.

PART 3

Making Sense of the Stories

8

Long-Life Discipleship:
The Fruits of the Journey

JOANNA WALKER

The purpose of this chapter is to explore that which sustains faith and spirituality in later life and how older people and their supporters can recognize what will help them grow on the journey. In particular, it will aim to cover:

- What we know about adult development and ageing into late life and how this relates to lifelong spirituality.
- What faith communities can do to support and enhance long-life discipleship.

Discipleship implies a journey following a master and growing to maturity in a chosen way of life and faith. Both the individual and the community dimensions of this journey will be considered.

What do we know about later life that will help spiritual development?

Ageing, at any age, is a difficult process to understand, mostly because it is unconsciously experienced and because it has contrasting internal and external characteristics. That is, most people will say that not only do they *not feel old*, but also that they do *not feel any different* from their youthful selves. Accounting for and describing what manifestly does happen to people over a lifetime is therefore a challenge. There is also a challenge for the ageing individual, who perhaps feels misunderstood because of the increasing mismatch between how they feel and how others perceive them. Coming to terms with change and pursuing the gifts of later life are therefore keys to spiritual growth. Examples of the fruit of lives well lived with God are to be found in the stories section of this book (Chapter 6).

Life courses and journeying

A recent approach has been to think about ageing over the whole life course, including both the transitions and the continuities that are significant features in life's changing landscape. This is a readily acceptable notion for Christians, familiar with the concept of a faith journey and life as a pilgrimage. It can help reduce the feeling of 'us' and 'them' with regard to older people, and allow recognition of greater experience and wisdom in those who are further on down the road. Older people may, by the same token, be out of touch with where younger people are, and the geography may be different by the time the younger ones get there, but at least we can all perceive a common journey and a sense of mature people's progress.

John Hull, a Christian educationalist, reminds us 'we know God biographically and not just doctrinally' (Hull, 1985). He goes on to say that God speaks in and through the structure of our life course and our ways of thinking, which change over time, just as much as through the propositions, traditions and symbols of our faith. If true, this is great encouragement to understand ourselves better so as to hear that voice and also to relate to our fellow travellers. Hull speaks of 'an evolving faith for an evolving self' and applies this into late adulthood.

Joyce's story (Story 6) illustrates this evolving spiritual self very well. Her account records faith development from early to late in life, where she still continues to grow. The chaplain's commentary links the 'inner' and 'outer' elements of her faith experience to the thinking of Henri Nouwen, who also understood the spiritual life as a journey – both into the heart and out into community and life's mission (Nouwen et al., 2010). The inward journey is towards understanding oneself and knowing God, which is formational for the outward movement of reaching out to relate to others and for our action in the world. However, this 'formation' is not a once-for-all process; the two aspects of the journey feed each other and we progress not by stages but by what Nouwen calls dynamic movements back and forth, more like musical movements where themes recur. He observes that some societies value and look for linear progress in all things, including spiritual development, but that cumulative stages and 'measurement' should largely be left behind 'when we speak about the life of the Spirit' (Nouwen et al., 2010, p. 130.)

A time for every season

However, the appeal of identifying processes and stages for development is prevalent in many periods of thought, from medieval to modern. A popular approach is to think of a person's lifelong development as being composed of stages or 'seasons' that they pass through, often with times of transition between them. This, again, offers an easily grasped concept of life's progress – this time as a maturing organism, growing to maturity and leaving the seeds of new life for others. What environments can we create and sustain for growth and the fulfilment of potential? There are models of human growth from lifelong developmental psychology that are particularly relevant.

As we saw in Part 1, a key figure is Erik Erikson, who was one of the first to offer a psychological account of life that included continuing development beyond adulthood into later life. His eight proposed stages of growth (from birth to death) also recognize interpersonal relationships and social forces acting on the individual; progression is not just biologically or internally driven (Erikson, 1963; Erikson et al., 1986).

Development in mature adulthood is Erikson's seventh stage (said to occur between 45 and 60 years of age) and is tasked with 'generativity' – a growth of concern beyond oneself. This is usually achieved by the mature person finding ways (through love and work, creativity and care) to contribute to the flourishing of others, including younger generations. The risk of not doing so is to move towards 'stagnation', whereby attention remains focused on meeting or being overwhelmed by one's own needs. When generativity outweighs stagnation, the virtue of care can be observed in the adult's life. Many of the chaplains' accounts of residents' stories illustrate this virtue as a late-life fruit of commitment to others, in various forms of ministry and service.

The eighth stage (60+ years) wrestles with the emotional and developmental requirements of achieving integrity versus despair. Integrity results from finding enough bases for self-acceptance and for viewing one's life as worthwhile. This implies a capacity for reflection and self-review – but one that does not require perfection or absence of regrets. Experience of both joys and sorrows, successes and failures, can be gathered and held as wisdom, which is the virtue to emerge from this last stage. The importance of both the opportunity and the encouragement to engage in reflection emerges from the residents' stories and is helpfully explored in Chapters 5 and 7.

After Erikson's death (in his nineties) the possibility of a ninth stage of 'transcendence' was proposed by Joan Erikson to address the growing experience of the greater numbers of people living to more advanced ages (90+). An extended edition of Erik Erikson's *The Life Cycle Completed* was published with this new material (Erikson and Erikson, 1997). In her new Preface, Joan Erikson speaks of how they had been influenced by the writings of Tornstam, who proposed a theory of gerotranscendence, which he described as a shift in perspective potentially available to all who live into old age. This shift is from a materialistic and rational vision to a more cosmic and transcendent one, and is normally accompanied by an increase in life satisfaction (Tornstam, 1994).

The theory predicts that a gerotranscendent person will experience feelings of communion with 'the spirit of the universe' (however defined); a redefinition of time, space, life and death; a redefinition of the self; and a greater need for solitary reflection and meditation. It has been difficult to gather evidence of such proposed effects, although Tornstam provides interview data (Tornstam, 1999). Joyce's story (Story 6), however, provides a striking description of transcendence. Neither Erikson's theory nor Tornstam's is a model of spiritual growth per se, but both could accommodate a spiritual application and indeed have influenced those who have devised more explicit accounts of lifelong spiritual and faith development.

Life as a game of two halves

A further conceptual approach to the life course is the idea of life as composed of two halves, which have differing characteristics, needs and resources. This contains two significant and related ideas about the latter half: first, that people become 'more themselves' as they age (a process known as individuation) and, second, that there comes a point, usually around midlife, when the personal values and rules that one has devised and lived by so far are no longer applicable and need revision.

Carl Jung is the best known proponent of 'second half' living and first articulated the notion that this period needs to be qualitatively different (Jung, republished in translation 1970):

> Thoroughly unprepared we take the step into the afternoon of life . . . with the false assumption that our truths and our ideals will serve us hitherto. But we cannot live the afternoon of life according to the programme of life's morning . . . For the ageing person it is a duty and a necessity to devote serious attention to himself. (p. 399)

Furthermore, Jung regards the possibilities of later life as not only superior but *constituting its true purpose and meaning*. These include, he suggests, guardianship of laws and mysteries, transmission of culture and heritage, and the development of wisdom and vision. It is therefore the privilege of later life to reflect on and make sense of experience, not only for one's own benefit, but to pass it on to others: a process known as 'generativity'. Because this is a strong drive for older people (powerfully illustrated in Edith's and Joan's stories (Stories 8 and 9)), support and encouragement for the most appropriate and acceptable ways of expressing it are important. Otherwise there is a danger of rejection, ridicule or exclusion by others who have not reached that stage themselves. Additionally, later in life where there may be fewer opportunities for such reflective conversations, people may suffer what Malcolm Johnson has described in Chapter 1 as the 'biographical pain' of unresolved issues.

Another aspect of the 'second half' worth noting is the notion that a 'shadow self' can come into play if encouraged. That is, other aspects of our personalities and of our gendered identities can be brought out in later life, once we have become confident in our primary identity and traits. Research on the Myers-Briggs personality inventory shows that, over time, the *non-preferred* modes of behaviour and thinking show up increasingly in responses. So, for instance, someone who is naturally introvert, or prefers to think and plan rather than discuss and sense, can develop some of their opposite under-used capacities. Again, the residents' stories recount the emergence of abilities and strengths at later stages of life, often expressed as grace and blessing from God who is alongside them in their everyday experience, helping them to grow.

So in all these ways, as a counter to a popular belief in decline and loss of capacity and relevance, older people contain within themselves the potential of greater personal resources. This can be strongly witnessed when life deals out difficulty or disadvantage and people describe a process of 'digging deep' to cope and then finding growth in difficult times. (See, for example, Robert's story of faith through adversity (Story 5) or Edith's sense of God's sustaining presence (Story 8).) An ongoing question about such growth is whether it is possible without the trigger of challenging events and conditions or whether learning always requires a disjunction with our experience to date.

Jungian psychologist James Hollis believes that the 'soul' or self *will* bring second-half issues into consciousness in a variety of ways, according to our situations or experiences. For him, the second half of life:

> presents a rich possibility for spiritual enlargement, for we are never going to have greater powers of choice . . . more lessons from which to learn . . . or possess more emotional resilience . . . more insight into what works for us . . . or a deeper conviction of the importance of getting our life back. (Hollis, 2005, p. 10)

This sense of needing to remake or discover our lives cannot happen earlier than mid-life, Hollis believes, because we need to have developed enough of a sense of ourselves to be able to step back and self-examine; to be willing to deal with what we perceive, including disappointment and failure; and to be strong enough to ask questions of ourselves in a committed way for the sake of our future life. For many, perhaps the leisure to do this kind of deep reflection only becomes possible in late life. Age and experience also permit the identification of our patterns of behaviour, many of which may be unhelpful, and the chance to take responsibility for change.

Richard Rohr, Franciscan priest and teacher, extends this argument to claim that it is dealing with failure and 'fallings' of various kinds that can help us discover the second-half path of life and the necessary inner journey towards greater wholeness and integrity. He offers a metaphor of life's two major tasks: the first is to build a strong container or identity; the second is to find the contents that the container is meant to hold. However, we often take the first task for the main purpose of life and our culture reinforces this with its emphasis on survival and success. But beyond 'the building of a proper platform for our early life', what is next? The move towards spiritual maturity, he says, is rarely chosen, but comes as a result of the achievements of the first half falling away or showing themselves wanting. Thus Rohr's proposal is that 'the way up is the way down' (Rohr, 2011, p. xviii).

Ageing and spirituality in later life

Religion and spirituality have recently become more significant topics in the study of ageing (gerontology), with a growing recognition of the relevance of belief and meaning-making systems to well-being in later life. Coleman and O'Hanlon (2004, p. 133) observe that religion is one of the great providers of meaning in life: 'an ultimate perspective on life's final goals and purposes, against which present failures and disappointments can be set'.

Faith and spirituality also allow older people to experience their lives as meaningful despite challenges to their quality of life: reinterpreted and new meanings can replace those that experience has found wanting. Where other forms of (physical or economic) control may diminish, the power remains to reflect and make sense of things using the resources of faith, as many of the residents' stories testify. The service that can thus be rendered to older people is to facilitate 'meaning-making'; ways of doing so are amply illustrated by the older residents ministering to each other, and are demonstrated in the role of the chaplains.

Gerontological research has increasingly linked religious faith and spirituality in older people with higher levels of life satisfaction, better adjustment and coping with stressful life events, as well as recovery from illness and bereavement. However, the greater involvement of researchers from many fields of theory and practice has highlighted definitional issues of what we mean by 'religion' and 'spirituality' when we attempt to link them to particular outcomes. These terms are clearly closely related but debate continues about whether one includes the other and whether faith in a transcendent being or power is a necessary part of the research effects being discussed.

Coleman concludes that although spirituality *is* concerned with higher levels of meaning, value and purpose in life, it is usually also associated with belief in a force beyond the material world. Other kinds of belief systems (e.g. philosophical, political) may also generate meaning and purpose but do not rely on a transcendent element, so these can be excluded from ideas about religion or spirituality. A better overall term for beliefs, values and goals that sustain meaning in life, whether derived from spiritual or humanistic sources, is 'existential meaning' (Coleman and O'Hanlon, 2004, p. 136). Some of the stories that include strong community and political affiliations illustrate the power of non-religious meaning systems that sustain people through life.

Another trap for researchers in this field is to regard religion as more of an 'external' matter, in terms of group membership and behaviours, which loses sight of its operation, meaning and effects in the lives of members. Religious ritual and practice has become an almost negative concept, with implications of meaningless activity or even of harmful effects (as recounted by some residents). However, this is beginning to change with a fresh appreciation of the value of shared activities (which are capable of change and adaptation) and of 'sign and symbol' in communal life. These can be particularly important in terms of continuity and participation for older people and can survive loss of cognitive capacity. The life of the residential home, or indeed the parish or district in the community, can offer such continuity in practices that are meaningful.

Similarly, spirituality can be narrowly conceived – for instance, as an individualistic pursuit, divorced from the social and lifelong context within which it arises. Both the inner and outer dimensions of religion and spirituality need to be appreciated, as well as the vertical and the horizontal. For research this implies a variety of characteristics to investigate: belief, behaviour, experience and understanding – personal meaning and values as well as practices and doctrines. A problem remains, however, in encouraging people to describe and account for highly private thoughts and feelings that are difficult to articulate, even to oneself. The power of narrative, and the nature of the particular stories in this book, testifies to the value of hearing the voices of older people. Those of very old people can be particularly difficult to hear and so are correspondingly precious.

The practical challenges of research, however, should not preclude the continued formulation of questions based on ideas, models and theories. These continue to arise, perhaps fuelled by a common-sense and culturally based understanding that the meaning of life becomes more salient as people age and that accumulated experience and reflection have something to say on these matters. Psychologists, sociologists and educationalists have suggested models and frameworks that seek to explain the processes involved in developing greater spirituality or religious capacity *as we age.*

Stages of life and faith

Following lifespan psychologists such as Jung and Erikson, discussed briefly earlier, more recent theorists have attempted more explicit linkages between life and faith stages. As with the life-stage models, the faith-stage models involve successive changes, sometimes including transitions, turbulence and struggle, but usually leading to re-direction and harmony.

In *Stages of Faith*, Fowler (1981) was the first to apply life-stage theory to faith development over the lifespan. His first two stages describe how the child develops ideas and beliefs about God and faith. Stage Three is characteristically the faith of adolescents, but is also a common stage found in adults in modern western societies. Hull (1985) finds that some adults will stick here because they find moving on uncomfortable and unnecessary. The chaplain recounting Joyce's story (Story 6) makes specific reference to Fowler's stages, as commentary on the further journeying that Joyce felt drawn to make.

The characteristics of Stage Three are that faith can be strongly believed and experienced but is perceived only within the belief system, not examined or compared with other symbols or meaning systems. Values and truths are not examined individually but are seen as part of a whole, and differences in religious outlooks are accounted for by differences between people rather than any part played by culture or history.

The passage into Stage Four can be difficult, as the great sense of personal relatedness and wholeness of the belief system in Stage Three makes any form of development involving questioning seem like doubt or betrayal. Seeking to move on can even provoke crisis or abandonment of faith. The prize for perseverance, however, is a more explicit and personal responsibility and commitment to one's beliefs, as these have now been translated into propositions that have been accepted through analytical processes. Now the adult is an 'apologist', having a critical appreciation of their own faith in relation to other faith systems.

The 'reasonableness' of faith as conceived and lived out in this fourth stage will later, however, lead to a longing for greater complexity, even mystery, pitching the mature adult into Stage Five. Here, the hallmarks are an ability to entertain paradox and to hold polarities in tension and then to live self-consciously and creatively with ambiguity. Multiple perspectives on reality are embraced and uncertainties tolerated, recognizing that understanding is always going to be provisional, especially in the face of mystery. Analysing and choosing one's interpretations give way to allowing symbols to speak and being open to the Spirit.

There may be parallels between the movement to this stage and the recognition that the rules and understandings of the first half of life will not suffice for the second.

The residents' stories illustrate their struggles with these issues, perhaps moving between Stages Three and Four, or from Stage Four to Stage Five. They may feel that they are departing from the 'truth' of their earlier faith and are reluctant to talk about their 'loss', especially to a minister. Fowler's model suggests that they are developing spiritually on the basis of learning and experience; people could be reassured that such changes are not unusual or due to a lack of faith.

Effects of spirituality on ageing?

How else can the relationship between spirituality and ageing be conceptualized? As well as the models discussed above, gerontologists have attempted to track 'outcomes' of a spiritual dimension on the quality of later life. 'Spiritual well-being' is a popular idea that can be correlated with other factors in older people's lives, such as health and resilience. The dimensions of spiritual well-being have been proposed to be: self-determined wisdom; the discovery of meaning in ageing; acceptance of the totality of life; revival of spirituality; preparation for death (Moody, 1998). Such indicators can be sought not only in a faith community, where one might expect good spiritual care to facilitate them, but also in secular care settings where professionals are increasingly recognizing the part they can play in helping achieve such outcomes for older patients and clients. In late life and towards the end of life, it is important that other outcomes (i.e. spiritual ones) can be recognized as part of holistic care.

Linkages have been made between the lifelong spiritual journey and the idea of 'successful ageing'. For instance, Mowat (2004) defines the spiritual journey (in which all humans participate, she says) as involving the search for meaning and location of the self within the world, and as vital to our well-being and onward movement as we age. The making of meaning is also a key idea in defining spirituality for Elizabeth MacKinlay: 'that which lies at the core of each person's being, an essential dimension, which brings meaning to life' (MacKinlay, 2001, p. 52). Spirituality is constituted not by religious practice alone (religion is one vehicle we may use on our spiritual journey) but is understood more broadly as a relationship with God and with other people. Again, the link with meaning makes spirituality a useable concept within many professions and practices, not just within faith contexts, and opens the way for interdisciplinary discussion with people of faith.

In the same work, MacKinlay offers a helpful model of how spirituality interacts with ageing. In a similar way to Erikson, she proposes that there are developmental tasks demanded by older age and the process of ageing, and that learning how to achieve these tasks will resolve a number of conflicts that characterize later life. Our success or otherwise will determine the quality of our later lives and so there is a strong case for supporting older people as they struggle with these issues. The issues and conflicts she suggests we must resolve are: self-sufficiency versus vulnerability; wisdom versus provisional understanding; relationship versus isolation; hope versus fear. The associated tasks are therefore: to transcend difficulty, disability, loss, and so on; to search for final meanings; to find intimacy with God and others; to have hope. MacKinlay's model of spiritual development has been developed and tested further, including in other cultures (MacKinlay, 2006; MacKinlay, 2010) and has much to offer all kinds of professionals involved with older people. In this book we see it demonstrated by the chaplains in their pastoral practice.

Spiritual growth and maturity – a role for the Church?

Most Christians would take the view that continued spiritual growth, especially in their understanding of God and maturity in Christ, is a lifelong task. We need to avoid the assumption that older people have reached a plateau in their spiritual development and are unlikely to progress much further. Indeed, the case has been made that there is a special and different spiritual agenda that older people face. Jewell (2001) comments on older people's continuing spiritual growth needs. He finds three areas in which they can be significantly helped or hindered by the Church.

First, in the area of *encounter with God*, older people tend to report God being experienced more as a presence than a person, and prayer becoming more a matter of contemplation than petition. An emphasis on words and 'doing' may become replaced by reflection and 'being'. These reported trends link well with the life and faith stages discussed earlier, and may explain why this tendency towards 'transcendence' (the feeling of rising above and beyond your earlier concerns towards a greater connectedness) is wrongly perceived by younger adults as disengagement or lack of interest and energy for current or pressing matters. The need for greater space for reflection before response, and for silence, is featured in several of the residents' stories. Indeed, their patterns of prayer differ with each individual, but several demonstrate the lifelong value of establishing practices that can survive physical and mental losses.

Another aspect of spiritual encounter in which older people can feel misunderstood (by spiritual leaders) is the tendency to develop a more questioning type of faith, reported by about a third of older respondents in Jewell's research. This could be as a result of faith-stage development or in response to life events or circumstances. When they failed to present the stereotype of a serene untroubled faith in older age, some older Christians felt that their spiritual needs were unwelcome. The need to accompany people throughout their faith journey, including doubt and change, is all the more important if we understand these experiences to be the gateway to spiritual growth.

A second area of potential development that the Church can help or hinder is where older people are *coming to terms with later life losses and difficulties*. Helping people to believe and see a way to grow spiritually through such experiences is a theological and pastoral challenge, especially when finding meaning in old age looks overwhelmingly difficult to the (younger) observer. There is a temptation for both parties to deny the need to make sense of difficulties, or to try to find positive counterbalances, which may not be convincing where losses are great. Thinking theologically about loss and dependency may be more helpful. For example, how are our states of greater or lesser self-reliance *throughout life* played out within our relationship with God?

Third, and most closely associated with an *awareness of the end of life*, there are needs to seek healing and forgiveness where it is wanting; for reconciliation and closure; to 'tell the story' of one's life – but often not to a family member. Joan's story (Story 9) offers a striking example of this. Sometimes the timing will be urgent and the needs deep – the last hurried chapter in an autobiography that has been working towards a conclusion to make sense of the story and pull the many strands together. Jewell calls this 're-membering' as opposed to the dismembering or fragmentation that is a feature of much of our postmodern life experience.

There is something to be learned on behalf of older members of faith communities from the lessons of the 'Fresh Expressions' of Church movement, which aims to get churches to respond more closely to people's cultural contexts and how they express their faith and its values. Collyer and colleagues discuss this well in their

report *A Mission-Shaped Church for Older People?* (Collyer et al.,
2008). However, the radical rethink that seems to accompany the
later life journey of spirituality would probably have more to gain
from the 'emerging church' movement, emanating from the USA
in the last decade or two. Writers such as McLaren (2010, 2011),
Foster (2004) and Willard (1998) offer new ways to think about
the nature of spirituality that can not only accompany but also
shape a lifetime, giving meaning and purpose at every stage. It
may be no coincidence that these writers are members of the baby
boom cohort, writing from a 'second half' perspective on their
spiritual growth so far.

Discipleship is a lifelong enterprise and, as we have seen, there
is much fruit to be gathered along the way, not least in the latter
stages of life. Although often undervalued, the agenda of older people's faith and spiritual development is surely worthy of attention.
If it is true that with age we become more ourselves, more rounded
and more connected to our faith, more concerned with others and
with a drive to transcend and integrate our life's experience, then
there is huge potential, which we neglect at our peril.

References

Coleman, P. G. and O'Hanlon, A., 2004, *Ageing and Development*, Lon-
don: Arnold/Hodder.
Collyer, M., Dalpra, C., Johnson, A. and Woodward, J., 2008, *A Mis-
sion-Shaped Church for Older People? Practical Suggestions for Local
Churches*, Solihull: Leveson Centre and Church Army.
Erikson, E., 1963, *Childhood and Society*, rev. edn, New York: W. W.
Norton.
Erikson, E. H., Erikson, J. M. and Kivnick, H. Q., 1986, *Vital Involvement
in Old Age: The Experience of Old Age in Our Time*, New York:
W. W. Norton.
Erikson, E. H. and Erikson, J. M., 1997, *The Life Cycle Completed*, New
York: W. W. Norton.
Foster, R., 2004, *Streams of Living Water*, Bath: Eagle Publishing/Harper-
Collins Religious.
Fowler, J., 1981, *Stages of Faith: The Psychology of Human Development
and the Quest for Meaning*, London: Harper & Row.

Hollis, J., 2005, *Finding Meaning in the Second Half of Life*, New York: Gotham Books.

Hull, J. M., 1985, *What Prevents Christian Adults from Learning?* London: SCM Press.

Jewell, A. (ed.), 2001, *Older People and the Church*, Peterborough: Methodist Publishing House.

Jung, C., 1970, 'The stages of life', in *The Structure and Dynamics of the Psyche: Volume 8, The Collected Works of C. G. Jung*, 2nd edn, Princeton, NJ: Princeton University Press, pp. 387–403.

MacKinlay, E., 2001, *The Spiritual Dimension of Ageing*, London: Jessica Kingsley Publishers.

MacKinlay, E., 2006, *Spiritual Growth and Care in the Fourth Age*, London: Jessica Kingsley Publishers.

MacKinlay, E. (ed.), 2010, *Ageing and Spirituality across Faiths and Cultures*, London: Jessica Kingsley Publishers.

McLaren, B. D., 2010, *A New Kind of Christianity*, London: Hodder & Stoughton.

McLaren, B. D., 2011, *Naked Spirituality*, London: Hodder & Stoughton.

Moody, H., 1998, 'Does old age have meaning?', in *Aging: Concepts and Controversies*, Thousand Oaks, CA: Sage Publications, pp. 27–38.

Mowat, H., 2004, 'Successful ageing and the spiritual journey', in Jewell, A. (ed.) *Ageing, Spirituality and Well-Being*, London: Jessica Kingsley Publishers, pp. 42–57.

Nouwen, H., Christensen, M. J. and Laird, R. J., 2010, *Spiritual Formation: Following the Movements of the Spirit*, London: SPCK.

Rohr, R., 2011, *Falling Upwards: A Spirituality for the Two Halves of Life*, San Francisco, CA: Jossey-Bass.

Tornstam, L., 1994, 'Gerotranscendence – a theoretical and empirical exploration', in Thomas, L. E. and Eisenhandler, S. A. (eds), *Aging and the Religious Dimension*, Westport, CT: Auburn, pp. 203–26.

Tornstam, L., 1999, 'Late-life transcendence: a new developmental perspective on aging', in Thomas, L. E. and Eisenhandler, S. A. (eds), *Religion, Belief and Spirituality in Late Life*, New York: Springer Publishing Company Inc., pp. 178–202.

Willard, D., 1998, *The Divine Conspiracy: Rediscovering our Hidden Life in God*, London: Fount Paperbacks.

9

The Challenge of Unbelief in Old Age

ANN MORISY

My first job was as the lowly research assistant for the Religious Experience Research Unit set up by Sir Alister Hardy. Sir Alister was one of the last great scientific researchers in the field of evolutionary and marine biology. Decades on, it still feels as if this modest research role was the best job in the world. The aim of the research was to uncover the extent to which people were able to report 'an awareness of a presence or power that was different from your everyday self', regardless of whether the person called that presence God or not. For the curious, that work in the 1970s indicated that over 60 per cent of people in a large city (Nottingham) were likely to be able to describe such an experience, and given the theme of this book it is worth noting that the percentage rises well above 60 per cent for older respondents.

Age matters in relation to faith. Countless commentators suggest that our religious ear becomes more attuned to the religious realm the older we get. However, while this might be the case for some, it is not always the case. I well remember walking to the bus stop with the pianist who had played lustily at the women's fellowship we had both attended. She cheerily commented, 'I don't believe any of this stuff, I just play the piano.' More significantly, I also remember an interview I conducted with a frail old man way back in those days when I worked as a researcher for Sir Alister Hardy.

The man, whose name I no longer remember, was drawing to the end of his life. He had his bed moved downstairs, and his breathing wasn't good, but he graciously agreed to participate in the random sample of interviewees. In the ensuing interview, he spoke of an experience of a 'presence or power' when he was a wartime soldier. He told of this experience: the platoon he was part of came under attack. They dived for shelter, all his comrades ran to the new dugout, but he told me how, to use his words, 'Something most decidedly told me to go to the old dugout, not the new one.' The new dugout received a direct hit and killed all his buddies. I asked him, as I did everyone I interviewed, how he made sense of the experience, and he replied, 'My family were praying for me and I link that with it – *but it's still a question for me.*'

For 50 years, this man had had to live with this question mark in his life. Yes, it could have been God – but it was still a question for him. For 50 years, he had resisted the conclusion that he mattered to God in a way that others didn't. He refused to assent to a God who seemed to have favourites, or a God who could be cajoled into acting on behalf of some people – and not others.

I was chastened by this encounter. It reshaped my faith. As I left his house, I started to ponder what sort of God I believed in. Did I believe in a God who had so little compassion that there could be no room for a man who had for 40 or 50 years been forced to ponder an unanswerable question? Did I believe in a God who only accepted certainty and had no room for pondering 'How can this be?', to echo Mary's words at the Annunciation.

As a result of that interview, I reflected on the nature of God's love. Did the God in whom I had confidence have room for those who live faithfully and courageously with a question in their lives? For some Christians, such hesitation has real consequences. To fail to embrace warmly the God who makes himself real in Jesus Christ is to close the door on a heavenly future. In focusing on the challenge of unbelief in old age, the challenge to the committed Christian, or the Christian evangelist, is to resolve our own anxieties, as much as it is to devise methods to sway those who are hesitant or even dismissive about the salvation that comes from belief in Jesus.

Insights from anthropology

Ethically it is not the carer's business to upend an older person's 'settled' attitude in relation to the reality or otherwise of God, and this is the case for the passionate Christian, the Jehovah's Witness or the Imam. It is not just faithful believers who have to struggle with getting an ethical perspective that allows others to be understood and respected. This same challenge is faced by the anthropologist tasked with understanding those who come from, or hold to, a different world-view from their own. It is in relation to this that the distinction between 'etic' and 'emic' approaches to 'seeing' and understanding is helpful.

The *emic* approach is concerned with how the person sees things and the meaning that they give to an event or situation. For example, in the research I was involved in, it was important to find out how people made sense of their experience. However, that did not mean that those leading the research had no thoughts of their own. David Hay and Sir Alister Hardy, who led the work, had read widely and deeply about the phenomenon of religious experience, as well as scrutinizing their own experience. This conscious gathering of insight also has value and is called the *etic* perspective because it enables a specific experience to be located within a wider framework informed by rigorous reflection and wide reading. It could be said that the chaplain's skill and knowledge also equate to an etic perspective.

The skill and grace of chaplaincy is to allow the emic and etic perspectives to flow and inform each other. This is expressed both beautifully and fully in Story 4 in the chaplain's recollection of their encounter with Sidney, and the importance of respecting his atheism. The respectfulness shown to Sidney was not about distancing because of his attachment to a different camp; rather it involved engaged appreciation. The mutuality of the encounter no doubt changed both of them, each knowing more and seeing more as a result. In the context of Sidney's unbelief, the chaplain was not to abandon the insights into faith that they had consciously gathered (their etic perspective) but to allow such insights to be subordinate to the commitment to embrace the distinctive emic perspective that Sidney had developed throughout his life. The outcome of the deep respectfulness enfolded within the sensitive etic knowledge of the chaplain was that Sidney was able to exercise his personal agency until the very end of his life.

The world wants proof!

For chaplains and people of faith the pervasive etic framework will be drawn from explicit Christian teaching, including the presumption of salvation. However, there are other overarching frameworks to draw on, which, unlike the espoused faith of Christians, pass what John Rawls (1993) calls the *test of public reason*. The test of public reason equates to the old adage that 'self-praise is no recommendation'. In a secular and pluralistic world, with many rival ways of making sense of the world, the virtues of the Christian faith, when promoted by Christians, cut little ice. Justification of Christian concern for the growth in faith by those who are very old has to be rooted in what is perceived as a more objective source. It is no longer sufficient for faith to be valued in its own right; in the public domain faith is only ascribed validity for what it can do, and such efficacy cannot just be asserted by chaplains and religious organizations. The helpfulness of faith, if it is to pass Rawls' test of public reason, has to be pronounced by those outside the camp, and ideally demonstrated by academically validated research.

The research conducted in the USA by Blazer and Palmore (1976) marks the beginning of work that indicates the link between faith and resilience, especially in later life. They conducted a 15-year longitudinal survey of 272 people who at the outset were 65 years of age. They found significant and 'substantial' (their word) positive correlations between religiosity and psychological well-being, the ability to adjust to the limitations that come with later life and the retention of a sense of usefulness. Blazer and Palmore were the first among many to examine the relationship between well-being in later life and religious behaviour and religious faith. A more recent research exercise (again in the USA) by Levin and Chatters

(1998) sought to examine Blazer and Palmore's findings, but this time using a large data set rather than a longitudinal survey. Using data from three large national surveys, they too identified a direct and positive relationship between religiosity and well-being. Furthermore, this positive relationship was evidenced in all three data sets. By drawing on such large sets of data, Levin and Chatters were able to control for other things that might have a bearing on well-being: for example, age, gender, race, marital status, education and geographic location.

Research such as this has been repeated regularly with similar findings. Even in my youthful research assistant days we were finding that those who reported a religious experience were more likely to score higher on a measure of psychological well-being compared with those who had never had such experiences (e.g. Hay and Morisy, 1985). This etic-type knowledge, which reveals the benefits of a confident faith in later life, justifies the concern of chaplains and others to support the intimations of faith experienced by those who are very old. The stories in this volume confirm the ways in which faith can impart resilience in the face of the relinquishment that so often is part of being very old. For example, Pearl's ability (Story 2) to enfold her own steady diminishment, and her husband's, with confidence in a God who is close, concerned and faithful to the very end provides an exceptional illustration of how faith is associated with resilience, psychological health and robustness.

Mystery banished as unreal

The secular world's need for objective or 'researched' knowledge is the focus of Ernest Becker's book *The Denial of Death* (Becker, 1973). Becker suggests that we have been set adrift by our analytical strengths, to the extent that our thinking veers towards 'cause and effect' and the logical always trumps the mysterious. Our modern minds, convinced that everything has a scientific explanation, have been able to banish mystery as unreal and dismiss religious faith as naivety. Becker argues that this fixation on what is measurable and material means that we are unable to make the lonely leap into faith, that is, achieving personal trust in some kind of transcendental support for our life.

Becker also suggests that there is no longer any all-embracing world-view that a secularized person can depend on to provide 'some kind of affirmative collective ideology in which the person can perform the living drama of his acceptance as a creature' (1973, p. 198). Here he is referring to the inevitability of death. In the absence of anything worthy enough to give hope, or robust or big enough to be trustworthy, he says that we become, 'A miserable animal, whose body decays, who will die, who will pass into dust and oblivion, disappear for ever not only in this world but in all the possible dimensions of the universe, whose life serves no conceivable purpose' (1973, p. 201).

Becker draws on the work of Otto Rank[1] to locate a 'cure' for this unhappy neurosis that grows in the face of death. The 'cure' that both Rank and Becker identify is religion and Christianity in particular. Becker notes that religion today (unlike earlier periods in human history) is a freely chosen dependency that provides shelter from unhealthy neurosis, by enabling preoccupation with personal power to be superseded by God in the cosmos and to embrace ideals that lead us on and beyond ourselves.

Finally, Becker suggests that religion solves the problem of death by enabling the 'hero' to surrender to the reality of nature taking its toll and by enabling the sense of an expanded self – closer to God – to continue (1973, pp. 203–4). In allowing the person to face up to the reality of death, a door is opened into the possibility of hope. Becker writes:

---

1 Otto Rank, a psychotherapist working at the beginning of the twentieth century, never founded a school of psychotherapy as such, but influenced the work of Fromm, Horney and Adler as well as Becker. In particular, Becker draws on Rank's consideration of the artist and artistic creativity. 'On the one hand,' Rank says, 'the artist has a particularly strong tendency towards glorification of his own will. Unlike the rest of us, he feels compelled to remake reality in his own image. And yet a true artist also needs immortality, which he can only achieve by identifying himself with the collective will of his culture and religion. Good art could be understood as a joining of the material and the spiritual, the specific and the universal, or the individual and humanity.' From http://webspace.ship.edu/cgboer/rank.html.

Religion alone keeps hope, because it holds open the dimension of the unknown and the unknowable, the fantastic mystery of creation that the human mind cannot even begin to approach, the possibility of a multidimensionality of existence, of heavens and possible embodiments that make a mockery of earthly logic – and in doing so, it relieves the absurdity of earthly life, all the impossible limitations and frustrations of living matter.

Edith's lifelong journey of faith (Story 8) illustrates the capacity of faith to provide a positive forward-looking perspective that embraces death, and in particular her ability to incorporate the message of resurrection and hope in every aspect of her life. Edith speaks of how she doesn't 'dwell on getting old, because I know that God will take me home when the time comes', and puts her confidence in John 14.2–3: 'In my Father's house there are many dwelling places . . .' Edith is able to reflect that it is not for her to know the time, or place when God will call her home, but she knows that she is in God's hands: 'He will bring me to that heavenly house. I have no fear of dying, except that I do want the reassurance of his presence and my family at the time of death and that my dying wishes are fulfilled.' Edith exemplifies Becker's case that deep psychological health is rooted in our capacity to surrender ourselves to the reality of becoming more and more frail combined with the sense of an expanded self that is closer to God.

Beyond formal logic

Those who have trained as teachers are likely to be familiar with the work of Jean Piaget, a developmental psychologist who died in 1980.[2] Piaget proposed and tested the theory that as we move

---

2 Piaget recognized that as the child matures, he or she moves through four stages of cognitive development. Piaget suggested that these stages are universal: every child goes through the stages in the same order, and no stage can be missed out – although he acknowledged that some individuals may never attain the later stages. The four stages of development Piaget termed sensorimotor, preoperational, concrete operation, and, the fourth and final stage he identified, formal operational.

from birth into childhood and then into adulthood, we go through distinctive stages of cognition. The final stage of this cognitive development Piaget referred to as *formal operational*, where we have the ability to analyse all the factors that have an impact on a situation – and arrive at a right answer. This ability to home in on right answers is, according to Piaget, the epitome of adult thinking, and sure enough, our society places huge value on right answers, because right answers – and *precise* right answers – are essential to the life-enhancing technology that surrounds us. This shaping and prioritizing of the rational has served to make embracing a religious faith more and more difficult, because it requires us to expand ourselves trustingly into the non-logical, into the terrain that is truly beyond belief.

Perhaps Piaget should have studied 'adult thinking' for longer and not have been fooled into thinking that adulthood is achieved at the same time as physical maturity, because Riegel (1976), following up on Piaget's work, suggests that adults have a capacity for *dialectical logic*, if only we have the courage and encouragement to let go of our preoccupation with formal logic. A strong case could be made that the essence of the chaplain's role is to help people achieve dialectical thinking. Dialectical logic ends up with a question rather than an answer. It demands the ability to tolerate contradictions and by pondering the contradictions to discover more profound questions. The chaplain very much endeavours to keep alive a person's capacity to question and ponder and be at ease with the paradoxes that emerge as a result of honest thinking.

The capacity for dialectical logic is rooted in the very adult perception and experience that life is too complex and rich to be held within our thinking, and in allowing this awareness to entice and tease us, and thus energize the thinking process. Joyce's story (Story 6) in particular demonstrates this process. For her, the traditional formularies of the Christian faith no longer have purchase on her thinking, but are replaced by a sense of ever more closeness to God. Joyce, despite a lifetime of going to church and saying prayers, comments that she does not pray now as such, and says that now she is in the care home perhaps her thoughts are in some way like prayer – a steady communication with God, free of the expectations and embellishments that surrounded an earlier period of her faith.

The dialectical thought that Riegel considered to be the essence of maturity does not focus on right answers and formal reasoning, but rather involves the ability to hold together or integrate apparent contradictions and not to be troubled by these contradictions, but to allow them to provide a foundation for creativity and compassion. Riegel, like other developmental psychologists interested in 'post-formal thinking', notes that the features of mature adult thinking include an appreciation of the relativistic nature of knowledge, an acceptance of contradiction as a non-reducible component of life, and the integration of contradiction by embracing a larger and more inclusive frame of reference. This maturity of thought is a recurring achievement expressed in a number of the stories in Chapter 6 of this book.

The poet John Keats provides an elegant summary of dialectical logic when, in a letter to his brothers, he writes of our capacity for 'Negative Capability'. He describes this capability as, 'when man is capable of being in uncertainties, mysteries, doubts, without any irritable reaching after fact and reason'.[3] More down to earth still is the link between dialectical logic and wisdom, and the reminder that dialectical logic is not just for the clever; in fact Meeker (1981) suggests that the very opposite may be so:

> Unschooled people can acquire wisdom, and it is no more common to find wise people among professors than it is among carpenters, fishermen or housewives. Wherever it exists, wisdom shows itself as a perception of the relativity and relationship among things. It is an awareness of wholeness which does not lose sight of particularity or concreteness, or the intricacies of interrelationships. It is where the left and right hand brains come together in a union of logic and poetry and sensation, and where self-awareness is no longer at odds with awareness of the otherness of the world. (p. 62)

---

3 John Keats' letter to his brothers, 21 December 1817, writing from Hampstead.

In this etic understanding we find a meeting point with the emic, the 'insider' perception and understanding. This meeting point is poetry, and the discovery that more and different things can be understood through poetry than through prose. In our rightful concern for the spiritual well-being of those who are very old, the role and place of poetry needs to come to the fore. Poetry gives confidence that there is more to life than meets the eye. Poetry need not just be sombre or mellow, it can bring a smile or even laughter, and laughter is as Dante (and the sociologist Peter Berger (1969)) suggests, a rumour of angels. In referring to poetry, I might also be talking of hymns and singing, where reflectiveness and deep pleasure are also often combined.

Gratitude matters

Like the domains of cognitive and depth psychology, our Christian tradition also provides some etic insights that can meet the emic or world-view of the unbeliever. In particular, the practice of gratitude is transformational. Although my Sunday school teacher taught me to 'count my blessings and name them one by one', it is the positive psychologists who have most determinedly harnessed this practice to bring health to unhealthy minds. This double etic recognition indicates the validity and applicability of the practice of gratitude. Gratitude is more than a feeling, because it requires an active response. It involves three steps: the acknowledgement of goodness in one's life, recognizing the sources of this goodness and expressing thanks to these sources.

Just as the wider world undermines our confidence in the non-logical nature and mystery of life, so too the wider world undermines our practice of gratitude. The inclination to take things for granted, to have high expectations, and to assume that we've earned it and so deserved it: all these dent and reduce our inclination to be grateful and give thanks. I am reminded of the grace, uttered by Bart in *The Simpsons*, 'Dear God, we paid for all this stuff ourselves, so thanks for nothing.' This degrading of gratitude carries a cost, because gratitude is part of our psychological immune system in that it plays a part in how we cope with adversity. It is a phenomenon where etic insights and emic perceptions coalesce, and therefore it is legitimate for the caring practitioner to encourage the practice of gratitude by those who are very old. The example of Pearl's natural embrace of gratitude throughout her life (Story 2) demonstrates how a grateful attitude can transform even the most challenging and heartbreaking events that come with a long life.

As we become very old, our identity becomes more and more closely tied to significant life memories. We are who we are because of what we remember and they say that gratitude is the way the heart remembers. The recollection of gracious events such as kindnesses, cherished relationships, everyday blessings that come in unexpected ways, is not just about reminiscence; it carries the potential for *anamnesis* – the recollection of a grace-giving spirit.[4] For those for whom unbelief dominates, through the practice of gratitude it becomes possible to encourage the acknowledgement of the grace-giving current that runs through life, and open up the possibility that the recollection of past gracious events can provide a foundation for confidence that the future may likewise be enfolded by such grace-giving energy.

It is possible to be quite specific in encouraging both those who believe and those who don't to practise gratitude. There is scope to work with the very old to enable them to keep a gratitude journal of the gifts, graces, benefits and good things they may remember happening in the day. Writing each day magnifies and expands the positive impact of gratitude. Sometimes the list will seem impoverished, but as the focus on gratitude sharpens they will become more likely to notice blessings, and if they're really desperate, they can write 'nothing too bad happened today'! The practice of gratitude is not about the unrealistic optimism of Pollyanna because the practice of gratitude has to remember the bad. It is possible, although it needs appropriate skill, to work with people in response to the difficult things that have happened in

---

4 As well as the moment in eucharistic celebration when we remember Christ's invitation to 'do this in remembrance of me'.

their lives. The adversities of life are associated with strong emotions and become deeply etched in our memories. However, for the very old the message of gratitude can be rooted in the reality that they have coped with and got through all their worst sadness and losses and traumas. Just like Job, our gratitude has to bear witness to the suffering that has taken place. When suffering occurs at the hands of others, such gratitude takes on a defiant character, a vigorous determination to stay grateful in spite of what one has been through. It is this hard-won gratitude that is at the heart of resilience.

The practice of gratitude can be linked with the senses, encouraging both the person of faith and the person of no faith to be grateful for the functioning of their body. Fredric Luskin (2010, pp. 169–74) encourages an exercise he calls the 'Breath of Thanks'. He suggests that two or three times a day we bring our attention to our breathing and notice how our breath flows in and out without having to do anything, and after continuing to breathe this way for a short time, for each of the next five to eight exhalations we say the words 'thank you', silently, to remind ourselves of the gift of our breath and life.

I conclude with an example that brings together emic perception, etic understanding, and evangelistic fervour for the souls of those who are dying. A few years ago I gave a short lecture on the importance of gratitude in our lives and concluded with an etic insight from Meister Eckhart: 'If the only prayer you ever say in your entire life is thank you, it will be enough.' A woman came to me later, with tears in her eyes. She recounted how she and her husband had shared a vigil at the hospital bedside of her mother-in-law. She and her husband took their faith very seriously, and it was of concern to them that the old lady was dying without coming to a faith in Jesus as her Saviour. The hospital chaplain asked whether they would like to receive communion as the old lady drew close to death. They asked her, and she said no, but they said that they would like to receive the sacraments for themselves. When they shared the cup of wine, the woman told me how she put the small chalice to the lips of her dying mother-in-law and heard her say, 'thank you'; it was her dying breath.

Now, ten years on, and with the gracious etic message carried by Meister Eckhart enfolding her emic view of the teaching of the Church, she had had a glimpse of just how much grace there is in the world.

References

Becker, E., 1973, *The Denial of Death*, New York: Free Press.

Berger, P. L., 1969, *A Rumor of Angels*, New York: Doubleday.

Blazer, G. and Palmore, E., 1976, 'Religion and aging in a longitudinal panel', *Gerontologist* 16:1, pp. 82–5.

Hay, D. and Morisy, A., 1985, 'Secular society? Religious meanings: a contemporary paradox', *Review of Religious Research* 26:3, pp. 213–27.

Levin, J. S. and Chatters, L. M., 1998, 'Religion, health, and psychological well-being in older adults: findings from three national surveys', *Journal of Aging and Health* 10:4, pp. 504–31.

Luskin, F., 2010, *Forgive for Good*, New York: HarperCollins.

Meeker, J. W., 1981, 'Wisdom and wilderness', in Staude, J.-R. (ed.), *Wisdom and Age*, Berkeley, CA: Ross Books.

Rawls, J., 1993, *Political Liberation*, New York: Columbia University Press.

Riegel, Klaus F., 1976, 'The dialectics of human development', *American Psychologist* 31:10, pp. 689–700.

10

Remember the Lord your God!
Dementia and Faith

MARGARET GOODALL

When memory fails, love takes its place. (Goodall, 2012)

There is a challenge to both personhood and faith when dementia is encountered, for the person with dementia as well as for those who offer support. The aim of this chapter is to examine our understanding of dementia and the barriers to faith, and then to explore how a person's spirituality can be both supported and encouraged.

Dementia and faith

Our present understanding of dementia is that it involves irreversible brain cell death, and that the person will, over time, show deterioration in mental, and often physical, faculties so that 'if no other illness were to intervene, it would cause death' (Gidley and Shears, 1988, p. 18). But this does not happen until 'the individual has lost his memory, his use of language, his ability to dress or feed himself and his personality' (Dippel, 1996, p. 12). Dementia seems to strip away those human attributes that are valued most: the ability to think, to plan, to remember and to be an active part of society. A carer has written: 'Memory holds the whole of our past life and experience. Its loss is greater than the loss of any of our senses' (Gibbons, 1995, p. 3).

Dementia is not a simple disease that can be diagnosed and treated. It is a complex process affecting the body and brain, and the idea of self. One of the challenges to those who offer care is to find some way to affirm the person with dementia being in the world with some meaning in life, not just existing. Dementia calls into question how we understand what it means to be a person and affects not just the person with the diagnosis (or symptoms) but their circle of family and friends. For many the possibility of needing residential care with a diagnosis of dementia is one of the most dreaded aspects of growing older and can be more feared than death itself.

There has been a tendency to deny the depth of the questions raised by this disease and to think of a God who is outside and above the situation and not in it. For some there is the belief that they have been forgotten and abandoned by God; for others there is only the vague hope that in God all will be well in the end. However, Jon Stuckey, in his essay titled 'The Divine is not absent in Alzheimer's disease', notes the dilemma practitioners face and reminds us of the hope that faith can offer, stating that, 'Alzheimer's can steal memories; it can steal personalities, it can steal bodily functioning, but it must not be allowed to steal the human spirit' (Stuckey, 1995, p. 75).

Many ask why we bother to provide care to those who are lost in dementia. In our stories of encounters between the chaplains and residents in our care homes we have seen how, through caring relationships, spiritual support can be offered that can remind people who they are and nurture their spiritual lives as they are reconnected within the life of the people of God. Those who offer this type of care listen to inner promptings that connect them to the person, and a deep feeling that the person is still there.

Rather than concentrating on what the person is unable to do and be, the suggestion has been made that we might imagine the person with dementia as living with open trust and by faith alone, perhaps 'a more perfect way of being human' (Saunders, 2002, p. 17). It is this open and trusting nature that allows those who come to know the person, when they already have dementia, to make a meaningful relationship. But the person's response is likely to be inconsistent, and the way of approaching the person needs to be adapted to the moment. It is this uncertainty that worries family and visitors who rely on continuity of the self.

For some who watch and wait, it is as if the person is no longer living; the self has gone and we are just waiting for the body to catch up. What this says about their existence is that it is of less value than it was; the listener's only task is to remember for them the life in the world to come. There is nothing positive in this, only a prolonged dying that reinforces the fear and desolation that exists around the whole subject of dementia, even within the Church. The chaos of dementia, which many describe as a barrier to being within the love of God, is therefore compounded by a reluctance to engage with those whose experience of life is different. This emphasizes the feeling of abandonment for those who may already feel isolated in their dementia, as noted in Barbara's story (Story 15). This attitude of disregard has, in turn, an effect on us, as it limits both our understanding of the person and of the wideness of God's love.

Remember the Lord your God!

When we look closely at what it means to remember, it then becomes clear how difficult this is for someone with dementia. The definitions of 'to remember' include: to recall to the mind by an act or effort of memory; to think of again; to retain in the memory; to keep in mind; to remain aware of. All these are ways of thinking that rely on cognitive ability. However, another definition, 'to have (something) come into the mind again', reminds us that memory can also come unbidden, often cued in by the words or actions of another.

The traditional/historical command to 'remember' in order to be within the covenant love of God is not good news for those who remember things less clearly, and are not able to call things to mind without assistance. The Scriptures emphasize that God is with us, and that even in Sheol, the place of forgetfulness, God remembers us. Malcolm Goldsmith offers us the phrase 'remembered by God', which seems to encapsulate this 'Good News' for people with dementia, as it 'stresses the basic truth that we are remembered by God long before and long after we make any recognizable response to God' (Goldsmith, 1999, p. 131). This would support the views of carers who believe that you have to treat every single person as an individual by respecting them, and that the individual can therefore still be found. From visiting care homes I have found that those with dementia tend to assume that everyone knows them, so why would they also not assume that God knows and loves them? This is such a positive message that it could be that all that is needed is there, as 'nothing can separate us from the love of God' (Rom. 8.39). So the understanding that all are enfolded within God's love and remembered by God is a good starting point.

Scripture contains dire warnings of what the consequences will be if we forget what God has done, and to forget can mean to go our own way. And yet the prophet Isaiah reminds us that God has engraved our name on his hand (Isa. 49.16). God is more than our ability to think and remember.

Falling short

And yet . . . when memory fails there is a sense of being disconnected both from other people and from the faith that has held the person for so many years, offering comfort, challenge and connection. Remembering the question posed in Daphne's story (Story 12), we ask 'where does our help come from?' In dementia the ability to call to mind the steadfast love of God fails, and the person needs to rely on cues from others to remember for themselves.

Does this mean that they are lost to God, as some Christians of a more evangelical persuasion might assert? They are no longer able to bring to mind their faults and failings, so some would say that they are unable to receive forgiveness. Ada (Story 10) was in anguish because she believed that she was not good enough for God and wanted to be 'put right'. But how could this be when the experience of failing was all she remembered? The chaplain, in offering reassurance of God's continuing love for Ada, talked with her of the love and grace of God, which is greater than we will ever understand.

This idea of grace is especially important for those living with dementia as it takes the emphasis away from what we can or cannot do, to what God is able to do.

Grace

The doctrine of 'grace' is at the heart of Christian teaching, and while the emphasis is 'sometimes on God's initiative, sometimes on man's response, grace is always the dynamic, underlying reality' (Langford, 1998, p. 7). The founding father of the Methodist Church, John Wesley, wrote, God 'first loves us, and manifests himself unto us. While we were yet afar off, he calls us to himself, and shines upon our hearts' (Shier-Jones, 2005, p. 42).

This teaching has been re-emphasized in the words of the newest revision of the baptismal service in the Methodist Church, when the young child is baptized before any promises by the parents. 'God's Spirit is poured out on God's people in baptism, as a gift of prevenient grace, even though it is neither deserved, nor understood. As the text notes: "All this for you before you could know anything of it"' (Shier-Jones, 2005, p. 113). In infant baptism, this is *entirely* the action of God. Ann Morisy (2009, p. 98) reminds us of the power and life-giving significance of this 'undeserved merit', which does not depend on our actions, but is a free gift. This idea helped the early Methodists face the challenges of the times rather than having their spirits crushed; in a similar way, the offering of God's grace without condition can offer comfort to those who can simply rest in God's love.

Goldsmith (1999, p. 131) writes about the challenge that dementia poses to Christian theology, and reminds us that we are 'unconditionally accepted by God and unconditionally acceptable to God'. This positive note emphasizes that God's grace, love and mercy are not dependent on who we are or what we have done, but are there for us. God has taken all the initiatives; it is enough that the person just be as they are. This is prevenient grace.

It is this doctrine of grace that offers hope to those with dementia, as they become less able to reason their faith or confess as they call to mind their sins. Some might say that this inability has made them beyond the love of God, but the idea of prevenient grace puts the emphasis back on God as the source of value and personhood.

'Re-membering'

What people most fear about dementia is that they will not be known or understood and that others will put their behaviour and language (or lack of it) down to their 'condition' and make little effort to engage with them because there is no point. The fear and frustration of being alone and of not being understood is for many like a 'living death'. What is needed is a way to enable the person to be re-membered, to be put back together – a time when memories are re-kindled and the person's identity and faith are confirmed. And that can only happen through relationships. But in order to make possible such enabling relationships there needs to be a 'safe place in which the person can be themselves and not feel threatened' (Goodall and Reader, 1992, p. 145). This non-threatening space could offer the possibility of newness and change, while the person is held in a safety net through which they cannot fall and into which they can relax when they have exhausted themselves. This 'safe space' is necessary both for the person with dementia and for those caring for them, as this type of care demands much of the carer in terms of openness and self-awareness.

The 'safe place' could be a time when words are remembered together. Language is one way of linking ourselves with those around us, and saying words together offers a sense of community and belonging. For when memory fails so does the ability to bring words to mind, so other people are needed to offer the prompts and cues to enable the familiar words to be remembered and rehearsed.

Spiritual care and dementia

'Spirituality' is difficult to define and has a place in both secular and religious usage. In secular terms, it has come to mean anything beyond the merely material. In Christian terms, it means living as a Christian and involves the whole of life. What it means to each individual is a matter of temperament and background, as well as theology. Spirituality can be found in the sense of connection and inner strength, the comfort, love and peace that individuals derive from their relationship with self, others, nature and the transcendent: a sense of being 'more at home' in the world (Macquarrie, 1972).

There has always been a problem in trying to assess what it is that people with dementia need, and how spiritual care can affect their lives, as their world can seem closed to us. However, there are accounts, written by people who have dementia, which have opened up their world to us and which have suggested ways that connection can be made (Davis, 1993; Bryden, 2005).

The voice of those with dementia can give us many clues about how to nurture religious and spiritual care and what it means to the person. Christine Bryden writes through her own experience of dementia, and, while each person's journey of dementia will be different, her writing gives us an insight into what can seem puzzling and beyond exploration. To those who suggest that there is no way of reaching those with dementia she says:

I believe that people with dementia are making an important journey from cognition through emotion into spirituality. I've begun to realize that what really remains throughout this journey is what is really important. (Bryden, 2005, p. 159)

She reminds us that the underlying spirituality is:

not simply what religion we practise; it is what has given us meaning in our lives. Our garden, art, pets, the familiar ritual of religion. It is important to help us to reconnect with what has given us meaning as we journey deeper into the centre of our being, into our spirit. (p. 123)

Dementia is often described as the loss of self, which implies that, at some stage, the person ceases to be human (Goldsmith, 1999). And this can cause stigma that threatens spiritual identity. The identity of the one with dementia is often seen as resting not 'on what we know or remember of ourselves, but on being known by God' (Giddings, 2010, p. 3). Christine Bryden supports this, saying that 'this is silly . . . Exactly at what stage do I cease being me? My spiritual self is reflected in the divine and given meaning as a transcendent being' (Bryden, 2005, p. 152). If spirituality and identity are not diminished with dementia then people continue to have spiritual needs that we have a responsibility to seek to meet through our care.

At its core, spirituality is in some sense not about logic or abstraction or cognition at all. It is ultimately the ability to connect with someone or something outside oneself, and at the same time recognize that whatever happens there is a core that remains 'oneself' – a continuity of self (Mowat, 2004, p. 51). This is not something that can be conjured up, but an awareness of something, a sense of 'where did that come from?' It could be called a preconscious experience. For while in dementia reason and language ability decline, the feelings and emotions a person experiences do not. So in order to understand those with dementia, their spiritual needs could be grouped in a more concrete and person-centred way under five basic headings: to be connected, to be respected and appreciated, to be compassionate, to give and to share, and to have hope. All these are included within the larger themes of meaning and purpose, love and relatedness (MacKinlay, 2001).

The spiritual tasks of old age are not changed by dementia; they are just made more difficult to see. However, because of their need for help in all areas of life, those with dementia find meaning, purpose and love through contact with others.

Care is offered in response to a need, and spiritual need is something that aids the person to live fully in the present moment, that they might have life in all its fullness. It is something that needs to be searched for with intuition and imagination (Stanworth, 2004). But if we mean by spirituality the attempt to find meaning

lives, to recover our lost humanity, to contemplate cre-
and the possibility of value beyond death, or to marvel
at the connection of our own lives to the lives of others, then
these require the ability to process thoughts in an abstract way
(Jewell, 1999). In those with advanced stages of dementia, thinking becomes more concrete as the rational thinking parts of the
brain are lost. The world appears to be framed by their senses:
by what they can touch, see, hear, smell and taste. 'What if' questions baffle and, even for those with dementia who can still speak,
the capacity to initiate conversations or discuss abstract ideas is
lost (Goldsmith, 1999). It could be said that spiritual well-being
is the affirmation of life in a relationship with God, self, community and the environment (Ellor et al., 1987), and that good
spiritual care taps into the feelings and the memories that mean
that personhood is affirmed.

. . . yet this I call to mind

It can come as a surprise when someone with dementia is seen
joining in the familiar hymns, readings or prayers. And yet this
way of remembering is at the heart of our humanness, and it mir-
rors the way that we learn how to belong. Reciting the familiar,
without any sense of boredom, is one of the delights of being with
people who have dementia, as the joy, connection and comfort
are clear to see. What words to use needs some thought, especially
by those who may not have been brought up reading the Author-
ized Version of the Bible, using the traditional form of words
for the Lord's Prayer, or singing 'The Lord's my Shepherd' to
Crimond. These are examples of such words, which people of
faith have repeated so often, and which come to mind so readily.
It is understood that the emotional memory is deeply embedded
and can be accessed even when other memory fails. The way that
these words have been used, and felt, in public and private worship gives them a deeper layer of meaning so that their use is not
merely repetition for repetition's sake, but a reconnecting with a
deeply held faith.

One of the most well-loved psalms is Psalm 23, which begins, 'The Lord is my Shepherd'. It is a psalm of comfort and reassurance, and beloved of generations of people of faith. Lamentations 3.1–20 offers an example of someone who has had everything, body, mind and spirit, taken away and has become a laughing stock. The desolation seems unrelenting and although the passage was not written about someone with dementia there are echoes of the pain:

> He drove into my heart the arrows of his quiver;
> I have become a laughingstock for all peoples,
> the burden of their songs all day long.

> He has made my teeth grind on gravel,
> and made me cower in ashes;
> my soul is bereft of peace, I have forgotten what happiness is.
> (Lam. 3.13–14, 16–17)

Then come the words at verses 21–23, words of hope and faith that offer light into what seems an impossible situation:

> But this I call to mind, and therefore I have hope:
> The steadfast love of the LORD never ceases,
> his mercies never come to an end;
> they are new every morning; great is thy faithfulness.

But how does someone with dementia call this love of God to mind? Our stories suggest that it is through others offering encouragement and using the familiar words that enable them to feel held once more within the love of God.

In the New Testament, there are many stories about who is lost or found, and who is 'whole'. Those with dementia are said by some to be lost to the disease, as wholeness is only seen in terms of cognitive powers (Hudson, 2004, p. 95). However, if those with dementia are seen and valued for themselves, rather than pitied for what they have lost, then a relationship of support can be established because 'as cognition fades spirituality can flourish as a source of identity' (Dunn, 2004, p. 154).

Support through relationship

When a person's spiritual needs are met, the result is seen in the quality of relationship. Developing this type of support relationship enriches the experience of those offering care, so that it is like a meeting with old friends. Because of the importance of relationship, it has been suggested (Nolan et al., 2002) that 'person-centred care' should really be called 'relationship-based care'; people with dementia have to be 'understood in terms of relationship as that is the characteristic of all lives' (Hughes et al., 2005, p. 5).

In her reflection on Barbara's story (Story 15), the chaplain presents the common belief of those who visit that 'they won't . . . want the same sort of conversation . . . communication often becomes very difficult', and notes that 'visitors feel very inadequate and often give up, feeling their visit has no purpose'. The fear that there will be nothing to talk about and so no way of making a connection is a common one, and the idea that the person is 'happy in their own little world' and doesn't need visitors can be used as a valid excuse to do nothing. John Swinton writes about the importance of continuing to visit and suggests that 'if we don't take time to be present for one another, we will never see dementia for what it really is' (Swinton, 2012, p. 286). However, if a visitor is really ill at ease and uncomfortable with meeting the person with dementia and does not believe that the person can be reached, then it will be obvious to the person that the visitor does not want to be there. Insincerity can be detected. 'Throughout the course of the dementing illness, the individual remains sensitive to the attitudes of those around him' (Scrutton, 1989, p. 179). It is the accepting attitude of those who visit that can bring hope to the person, and the reassurance of a faith that can still be accessed even in dementia.

The basis of person-centred care is that others respond to the whole person. This is demanding both of attention and intuition. If spiritual care is effective the person will show a feeling of well-being, of being in control or simply not feeling anxious about their care or their situation (Lawrence, 2003). Christine Bryden

(2005, p. 99) says that because those like her who have dementia 'live with a depth of spirituality . . . rather than cognition, you can connect with us at a deep level through touch, eye contact, smiles'. Perhaps the main difficulty of putting this into practice is that people are not used to giving so much attention to another person. Attention and then reflection are potential vehicles for spiritual care, both in its offering and for the purpose of evaluation. This way of assessing need and effect is an offering of loving attention, which is at the heart of good care. A touch and a smile are proven ways of reaching the person: a coming alongside to share the experience of the moment.

Each person's journey with dementia is different as the disease interacts with the individual's life and experience, and no two people will respond in the same way. While therapeutic interventions, such as reminiscence therapy, reality orientation and validation therapy, have been developed to enable communication, it will often be trial and error as to which will be most effective. 'If there is one rule that can be applied consistently in dementia care, it is that there are no rules that can be applied universally' (Nolan et al., 2002, p. 193). It is in the richness of the relationships that develop that meaning can be found in a person's life, not in pre-scribed activities.

The quotation used at the beginning of this chapter reminds us that a person's life does not end with the onset of dementia. Being present in a relationship at that moment, which for many with dementia is all that is real, and imagining the needs of the person that will enable them to reconnect with their faith, and with the possibility of flourishing, is asking for a leap of imagination. We are asked to give significance to another dimension of life, other than the rational, and recognize the person as a human being made in the image of God and so deserving of our love and attention even as they are valued by God. Jesus has promised that he will not abandon us and will be with us always, so 'it is as our souls collide even in the midst of deep forgetting, that these promises are felt, touched, and lived into truth' (Swinton, 2012, p. 287).

References

Bryden, C., 2005, *Dancing with Dementia: My Story of Living Positively with Dementia*, London: Jessica Kingsley Publishers.

Davis, R., 1993, *My Journey into Alzheimer's Disease: Helpful Insights for Family and Friends*, Amersham: Scripture Press.

Dippel, R. L., 1996, 'The caregivers', in Dippel, R. L. and Hutton, T. (eds), *Caring for the Alzheimer Patient*, New York: Prometheus Books, pp. 11–27.

Dunn, D., 2004, 'Hearing the story: spiritual challenges for the ageing in an acute mental health unit', in Jewell, A. (ed.), *Ageing, Spirituality and Well-Being*, London: Jessica Kingsley Publishers, pp. 153–60.

Ellor, J. W., Stetner, J. and Spath, H., 1987, 'Ministry with the confused elderly', *Journal of Religion and Ageing* 4:2, pp. 21–33.

Gibbons, T., 1995, *Observations and Reflections of a Carer*, Darlington: Scarsdale Books.

Gidley, I. and Shears, R., 1988, *Alzheimer's: What It Is and How to Cope*, London: Unwin Hyman Ltd.

Giddings, P., 2010, 'Dementia and a Christian perspective', unpublished paper from the Church of England's Mission and Public Affairs Council.

Goldsmith, M., 1999, 'Dementia: a challenge to Christian theology and pastoral care', in Jewell, A. (ed.), *Spirituality and Ageing*, London: Jessica Kingsley Publishers, pp. 125–45.

Goodall, M. A., 2012, 'Imaginative Anticipation: Towards a Theology of Care for People with Dementia', unpublished Prof. Doc. thesis, Chester University, p. 111.

Goodall, M. A. and Reader, J., 1992, 'Creating spaces', in Ball, I., Goodall, M., Palmer, C. and Reader, J. (eds), *The Earth Beneath*, London: SPCK, pp. 133–57.

Hudson, R., 2004, 'Ageing and the Trinity: holey, wholly, holy?', in Jewell, A. (ed.), *Ageing, Spirituality and Well-Being*, London: Jessica Kingsley Publishers, pp. 86–100.

Hughes, J., Louw, S. J. and Sabat, S. R., 2005, 'Seeing whole', in Hughes, J., Louw, S. J. and Sabat, S. R. (eds), *Dementia: Mind, Meaning and the Person*, Oxford: Oxford University Press, pp. 1–39.

Jewell, A. (ed.), 1999, *Spirituality and Ageing*, London: Jessica Kingsley Publishers.

Langford, T. A., 1998, *Exploring Methodism: Methodist Theology*, Peterborough: Epworth Press.

Lawrence, R. M., 2003, 'Aspects of spirituality in dementia', *Dementia*, 2:3, pp. 393–402.

MacKinlay, E., 2001, *The Spiritual Dimension of Ageing*, London: Jessica Kingsley Publishers.

Macquarrie, J., 1972, *Faith of the People of God: A Lay Theology*, London: SCM Press.

Morisy, A., 2009, *Bothered and Bewildered: Enacting Hope in Troubled Times*, London: Continuum.

Mowat, H., 2004, 'Successful ageing and the spiritual journey', in Jewell, A. (ed.), *Ageing, Spirituality and Well-Being*, London: Jessica Kingsley Publishers, pp. 42–57.

Nolan, M., Ryan, T., Enderby, P. and Reid, D., 2002, 'Towards a more inclusive vision of dementia care practice and research', *Dementia* 1:2, pp. 193–211.

Saunders, J., 2002, *Dementia: Pastoral Theology and Pastoral Care*, Cambridge: Grove Books.

Scrutton, S., 1989, *Counselling Older People: Creative Response to Ageing*, London: Edward Arnold.

Shier-Jones, A., 2005, *A Work in Progress: Methodists Doing Theology*, Peterborough: Epworth Press.

Stanworth, R., 2004, *Recognizing Spiritual Needs in People who are Dying*, Oxford: Oxford University Press.

Stuckey, J. C., 1995, 'The divine is not absent in Alzheimer's disease', in Kimble, M. A. and McFadden, S. H. (eds), *Aging, Spirituality and Religion*, Minneapolis, MN: Fortress Press.

Swinton, J., 2012, *Dementia: Living in the Memories of God*, London: SCM Press.

11

An Ageing Church is not a Failing Church: Finding New Paradigms for Accompanying Older Pilgrims

LAWRENCE MOORE

Facing the challenge of the Fourth Age

A Church that does not know how to be old does not know how to be young. The demographic revolution that has seen life expectancy double over the past 150 years confronts the Christian Church with a set of challenges parallel to those that British society more widely finds itself facing: how does the Church meaningfully incorporate the oldest old into its life as the norm rather than the exception? Once the communal life of the Church is extended to include a significant number of those in the Fourth Age, the biographical and spiritual experiences that characterize this part of the Church can act retrospectively to alter the understanding of the whole Church's spiritual journey from infancy through adulthood to advanced old age and death. As James Woodward has written in Chapter 4, it is 'the challenge to befriend the elderly stranger within ourselves'. Or to put it slightly differently: old age defines youth; this is no less true of spiritual life and growth than it is of human development generally.

Unless and until that challenge is faced, the Fourth Age will remain both a mystery and a problem. However, the Church's instinctive strategies have been to avoid it and to mitigate its effects as far as possible. This is hardly surprising: it makes a quantum difference if, in early adulthood, we understand ourselves as being in the second of four life stages rather than of three. If the Fourth Age is not seen as a universal human experience, it can only be feared as the unnatural lot of an unfortunate few. We will treat it as something more akin to an illness than as a natural life stage to be embraced and understood. The oldest old will continually be strangers to us – the people we do not want or expect to become. Rather than seeing in them the mirror of our own future, they will be the 'freak to be feared'; the 'Other' to be kept outside the camp.

The corollary is that those of us in the earlier stages of life will similarly be strangers to ourselves until we understand ourselves as both faith pilgrims and life pilgrims en route to the Fourth Age. We will fear and resist any signs of its onset. Pastorally and in terms of spirituality and discipleship, we will have a diminished and truncated understanding of faith development.

My concern is that the Christian Church in the United Kingdom employs its own version of the 'resistance model' to extreme old age that we see in wider society, which operates by extending the Third Age 'indefinitely' through a strict regimen of 'diet, exercise and plastic surgery'. That is certainly true of my own United Reformed Church, whose average age is 65 – well above the national average and higher than any of the other mainline denominations. It seems ironic, on a cursory reading, that, instead of being at the forefront of exploring and excavating the positive resources for being an ageing church, we instead operate denominational psychologies that view age almost purely as 'problem'. In this, however, I suspect that the URC is not alone.

To take a representative example: although the numbers of children and young people in the United Reformed Church declined by 37 per cent over the period 2001–11 (i.e. faster than the overall rate of decline, which is 30 per cent), the United Reformed Church maintains a Youth and Children's Work Department in its central offices, and each of the 13 Synods employs a Children and Youth Development Officer (CYDO). By contrast, there is no 'official' systematic structure, allocation of resources or process for developing ministry and mission in ageing congregations, and no ongoing analysis and identification of the particular needs of the older members. The National Synod of Scotland has created a Special Categories Ministry post with special responsibility for Older People Ministry; this is the only dedicated full-time post within the URC that focuses on ministry to older people, and does so positively by developing more specialized, needs-centred ministry to this group (as opposed to 'solving the problem of being an ageing church').

This disproportionate allocation of resources makes much more sense if the only model for an ageing church that is moving into the Fourth Age is to extend the Third Age to breaking point. That this is the model being deployed is scarcely surprising: the Christian Church more widely (as well as the United Reformed Church in particular) is in genuinely new territory as it tries to assimilate the emergence of the oldest old in its communal life. The shift in its own self-understanding that is required has some parallels with the incorporation of the Gentiles into the early Church; the principal difference is that the 'strangers in our midst' are our own people, whose journey into the Fourth Age has involved them becoming strangers to themselves and to those of us who know and love them. These radical changes (made most clearly visible in those living with dementia) create unassimilated (or are they inassimilable?) discontinuities with the past. The 'diet, exercise and plastic surgery' model allows for the communal participation of an ageing population, according to the same 'rules' that have pertained since adulthood. These rules cope with, understand and respect the slowing down and gradual withdrawal from participation in some wider aspects of communal life. The changes of extreme old age, however, create a new situation in which oldest age is unrecognizable as meaningful participation any more.

The United Reformed Church: denominational psychologies of ageing

The problems of being an ageing Church are made particularly acute for the United Reformed Church because of its exceptionally sharp rate of decline in membership. The URC was formed in 1972 by a union of the Presbyterian and Congregational Churches (followed shortly afterwards by the Churches of Christ). The current membership is just under half of its 1972 level. By contrast, the denomination retains some 84 per cent of the church buildings it had at union. The URC is declining faster (in percentage terms) than any other UK church, and whereas there is evidence that the steady rate of decline among denominations is showing clear signs of slowing in many of them, this has not been true of the URC (Brierley, 2006). The decline has been sharpest among children and young people. At the same time, the increase in the age profile of the URC has been more pronounced than in other denominations, with around half of the URC membership being aged 65 and over (Brierley, 2006).

These statistics paint a sombre picture. The United Reformed Church is haemorrhaging children and young people at one end of the age range, and people to extreme old age and death at an increasing rate at the other end. The bulk of its active membership comprises Third Age retirees – people who tend to see their task as prolonging the life of the denomination through the church equivalent of 'diet, exercise and plastic surgery'. They are faced with the constantly increasing burden of sustaining buildings and systems that were constructed for a church with a membership of more than twice its present size – a membership that is now in apparently unstoppable terminal decline.

These concerns present themselves in two ways within the denominational mindset: as 'We need to get the young people in!' and 'We mustn't lose anyone else!' The first manifests itself in the disproportionate investment in ministry to young people at a denominational level (I use 'disproportionate' here in the strictly mathematical sense of measuring the size of the Youth and Children's Work departmental budget allocation against the size of that group within the URC); the second is a paranoia that manifests itself more destructively in a practice of rewarding the bad behaviour of members who will use the threat of leaving as a means of wielding power within the denomination's conciliar process of church government.

There is an unhealthy element of unreasonableness and drivenness in both of these patterns, which is why I am choosing to talk in terms of the URC's 'denominational psychologies of age-ing'. I am the Director of one of the Church's Resource Centres for Learning, which seeks to resource the URC's life-in-mission – among other ways, through the provision of a varied programme of courses and events. I have discovered, over 11 years of pro-gramme provision, that a course on 'Young People and the Church' will draw enthusiastic participants from across England, Scotland and Wales, whereas a course on 'Untapped Riches: The Spiritual Resources of an Ageing Church' will not attract enough interest to be viable.

This is a church that is acutely aware of its own finitude. It has become fixated with the prospect of the death of the denom-ination that is coterminous with the death of the current mem-bership. There is a positive sense in which the concentration of resources and initiatives on children and young people is quite properly mission-driven; the flip side is the conviction that the resources that the URC needs to guarantee its future lie with the young people who are absent from its congregations and stub-bornly resistant to every attempt to draw them in. The URC sees itself in the advanced stages of the institutional equivalent of the Third Age, with no intake of younger members and therefore with only the prospect of the Fourth Age ahead.

Ageing and old age are seen solely, and inescapably, in problem-atic terms. A church that is convinced that its most vital, necessary resources reside within its absent young people will be inevitably blind to the resources within its ageing membership. That sense of desperation is exacerbated by the fact that we experience the tran-sition of members from the Third to the Fourth Age as premature loss: we lose them as active, visible members of the Church. More problematically, they become strangers to us as their faculties and capacities diminish and fail.

Barbara's story (Story 15) illustrates the difficulty: her devel-oping dementia meant that she needed more and more time to process and respond to what people were saying to her. At the time when Barbara was wrestling with the fear that her dementia was a sign that God had abandoned her, her friends stopped visit-ing and phoning, because they could no longer have the type of conversations they had always had with her. As Barbara lost her purchase on the reality she had previously known and inhabited, her friends lost their purchase on the Barbara they had known. She became a stranger to them and they did not have the resources with which to cope with that transition.

In telling Barbara's story, her chaplain puts their finger on the nub of the issue: there is a reciprocity and interdependence binding us to one another within the Body of Christ (to which Paul refers in 1 Corinthians 12). Reflecting on Barbara's situation, the chaplain concludes, tellingly:

> Barbara's story shows us that when we are forced to let go of a sense of control or independence in our lives we need others to be the words for our continuing faith journey. People seem to feel very uncomfortable in the presence of those who are suffering with memory loss or dementia. Part of the problem seems to be an inability to cope with the fact that they no longer seem to be the person they were, and an assumption that they won't therefore want the same sort of conversation; and part that communication often becomes very difficult, or seems to be totally one-sided. Visitors feel very inadequate and often give up, feeling their visit has no purpose.

Barbara's visitors felt inadequate to the task of relating to Barbara in extreme old age. As she became a stranger to them, she became a symbol of their failure and an object of their fear. This is a common reaction: 'For God's sake, never let me get like that!' The story of Barbara and her visitors parallels the experience of the United Reformed Church: its members feel exposed by the transition of the membership into the Fourth Age, and inadequate. Like Barbara, the diminishment and eventual loss of former capacities can feel like an abandonment of the Church by God. Because many of the members lived through the URC's birth in 1972, its rapid decline and possible demise feels acutely like failure, reflected so eloquently and embodied in the 'descent' of its membership into extreme old age, senility and death.

Finding new paradigms for accompanying older pilgrims

I am not suggesting that the typical reaction of the United Reformed Church to the situations of its oldest members is to abandon them in care homes, unvisited and forgotten. General practice is for members to be allocated to elders, who have pastoral responsibility for those on their lists, who visit faithfully and actively keep the members and the church mutually informed of one another's lives. Congregations have their own 'inclusion rituals' for marking the continued presence of an absent member in the life of the Church. Typically, this might involve leaving their seat empty, as though they are only temporarily absent and can be expected to turn up at any moment – in much the way as Daphne's circuit kept her name on the Circuit Plan with the note, 'Not preaching this quarter' (Story 12).

Nevertheless, the pastoral care of the oldest old takes place within the 'diet, exercise and plastic surgery' model: each oldest member is treated like an exception to the rule that we die before we become 'prematurely lost' to the community. Those charged with their care are treated rather like specialists who are equipped for such exceptional duty; there is no sense that the whole Church might, as a matter of course, be made aware of and equipped for meeting the spiritual and pastoral needs of the oldest old, as they would those of people in the first three ages.

If the United Reformed Church has something distinctive to show us about the issues surrounding the oldest old in our churches, it is the close connection between old age and URC self-perception, self-understanding and self-confidence. The URC's self-understanding is expressed in its mission statement, committing the United Reformed Church to becoming 'God's people, transformed by the gospel, making a difference for Christ's sake'. In order to fulfil its mission, the Church recognizes its need to become 'viable and sustainable'. Faced with its demographic picture and the present trajectories, the URC is acutely aware that the search for a new paradigm of how to grow old as a church – for an account of human and faith development that is coterminous with the human lifespan – is, at the same time, a search for a paradigm in which the United Reformed Church itself has a future.

Finding new paradigms: some possible characteristics

How do we embrace (rather than resist) the Fourth Age – understand it in the context of the totality of human development and experience, to the point that we recognize in it our own biographies and futures? The difficulty of living through the current demographic revolution is that we are undergoing a radical shift in the experience of what it means to be a human being. The United Reformed Church, and I might suggest other mainstream denominations as well, needs to devote time and resources to the urgent search for a new paradigm that will emerge from the spiritual world of the Fourth Age. I want to pick out some possible characteristics that arise from an exploration of the stories.

The resources for the future lie in our present, ageing membership

The experiences of the chaplains in listening to their residents' stories show clearly that it is possible to learn how to cope positively and meaningfully with the transition into the Fourth Age. While Barbara's church friends gradually 'lost' her and no longer knew how to talk to her, Barbara's chaplain 'discovered' her and learned how to communicate with her. There are skills and techniques that can be learned by our present carers, who are already rich repositories of wisdom, experience and spiritual depth. Learning how to communicate in new ways opens us up to the sorts of transforming experiences to which the chaplains testify in the course of connecting with the residents (Story 12).

Sharing journeys: a model of pastoral care

The life of faith is most helpfully illuminated by the metaphor of a journey, or pilgrimage. The transition into the Fourth Age is a very particular journey, characterized by leaving the familiar, shared world and losing the security and comfort of those shared landmarks and memories. It can be a lonely and terrifying place. What the stories make clear is the pastoral importance and effectiveness of accompanying members on those journeys into extreme old age. Care needs to be consistent and committed: making connections and building trust is time-consuming, but hugely significant in helping the 'older pilgrims' to retain connections with that which has sustained them throughout their lives.

Carers can be not only the catalysts who keep individual memories alive for as long as possible, but also the repositories of the communal memories of church life, able to keep those connections with the church community alive, even when members are no longer able to be present at church.

Vitally, they are able to be conduits of God's healing and peace, as the chaplain movingly reminds us in the narrative of Ada's story (Story 10):

> Ada expressed her need to be put right with God before she dies and in so doing raised a number of issues for those caring for the spiritual needs of elderly residents in the final lap of their lives. In particular the conversation reveals the importance of creating a foundation for building loving and caring relationships with elderly people as soon as they enter the care home, and giving time to listen to their experiences so that it is not too late to gently offer new possibilities and ideas. While it is not possible to 'undo' damage, we are able, by using sensitive prayer, to allow God's healing to come into their situations and ask for God's peace, to take them beyond the hurt they may be experiencing.

Faith stories – the lifeblood of the Church

A theme in several of the stories is the way in which the residents of the homes connect with the chaplains through telling their faith stories; for some, this is their first experience of talking about faith. That experience would be generally typical of many church members in these islands. The URC in particular does not have a culture of talking about faith. I recall running a church weekend at the Windermere Centre in which I asked the members to divide into groups of three and each to spend no more than ten minutes telling the others why they continued to bother with Christian faith. At the end of the exercise, some of the members could hardly contain their excitement. 'That was amazing,' one enthused. 'I have known Jack for over 60 years. I know his golf handicap and the names, ages and careers of all his children. But until today, I have known absolutely nothing about what he believes! What an unbelievable privilege it's been to listen to him!'

A new paradigm will begin systematically to inculcate the importance of storytelling and sharing as a regular, unremarkable feature of church life so that churches live by the common faith testified to by its members.

Christian faith and the importance of 'being'

The United Reformed Church's notion of faith and disciple-ship is very 'activist' (cf. our vision of 'making a difference for Christ's sake'). The Fourth Age is the antithesis of the culture of 'diet, exercise and plastic surgery' (i.e. perpetual activity), because of the diminishment of faculties and abilities. Both the residents and the chaplains had to discover significance and pur-pose within 'being' rather than 'doing'. We have a very typically 'Third Age' spirituality, which derives meaning and value from achievement, so that we reflect uncritically our cultural assump-tions that 'value' is synonymous with 'usefulness' and 'produc-tivity'. Paying attention to the experiences and spirituality of the Fourth Age leads to the rediscovery of the truth that identity and human value reside in who we are – beloved children of God – and not in what we do or achieve. We need to allow these insights to transform our spirituality and enable us to practise a more rounded faith.

Facing finitude

Whereas medieval Christians were taught to pray for a slow death so as to have the opportunity to amend their lives, the contemporary paradigm of 'diet, exercise and plastic surgery' tries to put death 'out of sight, out of mind' until the last minute possible. The cultural anthropologist Ernest Becker concluded, in his Pulitzer Prize-winning *The Denial of Death* (1973), that the need to deny our mortality as human beings is the primary repression of humankind, which forms our individual characters and causes much of the evil in the world. Whatever its universal applicability, it is certainly a defining characteristic of our contemporary culture.

The oldest old, by contrast, have to spend time facing finitude and advancing death. The chaplains write movingly of helping people to prepare for death and come to terms with both their dying and their lives (see in particular Joan's story (Story 9)).

A paradigm derived from the spiritual insights and experiences of the oldest old will be authentically and importantly counter-cultural because it will encourage a spirituality that enables us faithfully to 'contemplate our own finitude'. We will learn the practice of 'letting go' – of abandoning the self to God in life as well as at the approach of death.

Conclusion

The challenge of the demographic shift has not been to find new ways of dealing with the very oldest people, but to find a paradigm that enables us to live as human beings with a much older future than we have hitherto envisaged. If we need to revise our pension provision in the light of a significantly lengthier retirement, we need similarly to revise our spirituality to embrace the Fourth Age.

The United Reformed Church is presently able to see an ageing church only in terms of failure, because it cannot see how to sustain the present into a Fourth Age. It is unable to recognize and access the potentially rich repository of spiritual resources in its Third Age population, because it can think of this group only in terms of inevitable 'decline and descent' into extreme old age and death.

I have argued that we need to learn how to grow old as a church, and that we do so by adopting a new paradigm that derives from insights into the spiritual worlds and experiences of the very old. The paradigm will equip us with an understanding of human faith development and spirituality that is coterminous with the human lifespan, with a serious account of old age and end of life issues, and with the means of progression from the Third to the Fourth Age.

The great fear of the United Reformed Church is of growing old, because we do not know how to do so positively and construct-ively. Rather than concentrate resources on developing a new paradigm, we divert them into trying to attract young people, in the mistaken belief that we can avoid the challenges of being an ageing church.

Part of our deep resistance to the Fourth Age is that it makes death 'prematurely present'. We need to learn to read this as a reminder of the Way of the cross: the pattern of Christian faith and discipleship is Easter-shaped. Death is inevitable, but, in the hands of the God who raises the dead, it becomes the gateway to Life. A new paradigm that enables the Church to discover how to grow old enables it to discover how to be young. As the Church loses its fear of dying, it will rediscover its courage to live.

References

Becker, E., 1973, *The Denial of Death*, New York: Free Press.

Brierley, P., 2006, *Pulling Out of the Nosedive. A Contemporary Picture of Churchgoing: What the 2005 English Church Census Reveals*, Lon-don: Christian Research.

12

Chaplaincy Among Older People: A Model for the Church's Ministry and Mission?

ANDREW NORRIS

The stories of older people that form the heart of this book have been captured through exchanges that have taken place between the chaplains in a variety of Methodist Homes (MHA) residential settings and the older people who live there. In this chapter, I want to examine the nature of this chaplaincy and the particular benefits that may arise from chaplaincy with older people in social care settings. The lessons that the wider Church can learn from these special opportunities of encounter, as part of developing its missiological task, are also explored.

The history of chaplaincy

The origins of the concept of chaplaincy are popularly traced to the sacrificial act of St Martin de Tours, a soldier who, around AD 337 in Amiens, France, noticed a poor man at the city gates, destitute and cold, to whom he gave half his torn-off cloak. This half cloak was heralded as a symbol of generous acts of service and the clerics who became its custodians came to be known as *capellians* (keepers of the *capella* = cloak) on French battlefields. They were, in effect, the first 'chaplains', exercising ministry in a particular (military) context, bringing spiritual nourishment and pastoral care to those who might otherwise have been denied it. From then on royal households, nobles, ambassadors and the like appointed their own chaplains, first to become the custodians of the sacred relics, which were sometimes preserved in royal chapels, but gradually to be those whose responsibility extended to cover spiritual jurisdiction. In this capacity, and as part of the educated class, they became not only the moral conscience of those to whom they ministered but also advisers and teachers. The appointments of chaplains by kings and the nobility led to their continued appointment in the military as well as other institutions such as hospitals, prisons, universities and schools, some of which took on a private 'religious' foundation as a result.

The two world wars were significant landmarks in the development of chaplaincy, when clergy were sent from their churches to be alongside the soldiers on the front line. On their return home from the front, the impact that the 'padres' had made meant that some people looked for easier access to spiritual support and guidance. This manifested itself in the development of a whole range of chaplaincies in a further variety of settings such as industry, airports and even shopping centres. As Jones (2010) points out, a number of common themes and distinctive features of chaplaincy emerge in tracing its evolution. First, it often reflects how acute need is addressed by practical help. Second, chaplaincy illustrates a reaching out to where people are, without their having to wait, ask or cry out. Third, the story of St Martin's gift of half a cloak also serves as a reminder that in meeting people at their point of need, chaplains make themselves vulnerable. It can also be seen as a move away from the expectation that religious and faith needs should primarily be associated with places of worship and the institutional church; they can take on a new pastoral relevance when addressed in the context of everyday life situations.

Characteristics of chaplaincy

Several reviews on the work of a chaplain (e.g. Jones, 2010; Legood, 1999) give testimony to the wide range of settings in which chaplaincy is now evident. What these reviews also reveal is the number of ways in which the role of the chaplain may express itself. In general terms, a chaplain is there to address the pastoral, spiritual and religious needs of those in a particular context. The fact that it is necessary to break down their task in such a way hints at the complex nature of that role. It is *pastoral* in the sense of helping to express person-centred care through listening, providing affirmation and comfort; *spiritual* in the sense of helping to understand each person's 'story', what gives them value, meaning and purpose, and finding a means of giving this expression; and *religious* in providing means of expressing spiritual needs through religious ritual, worship and fellowship.

The degree to which aspects of the chaplain's role will be recognized, understood and/or accepted will vary according to context. This means that the chaplain has to be cautious in making assumptions about how their role will be perceived or received. If not taken into account, some of these assumptions may well mitigate against the chaplain operating effectively. It is therefore important that the chaplain is available and accessible to those to whom they seek to minister in a way that indicates an openness and willingness to come alongside people at *their* invitation and timing, on *their* terms and/or at *their* point of need. This has been described as 'loitering with intent' (Campbell, 1985), akin to the concept of 'intentional presence' now being recognized in other disciplines (e.g. Holland, 2012).

Some of the qualities and skills necessary to facilitate this role of listening and accompanying people on their life's journey have already been described in Chapter 5. In the training resource, *Chaplaincy Everywhere* (The Methodist Church, 2012), the chaplain's role is referred to as 'negotiated presence', which means the precise function of the relationship that ensues cannot necessarily be either prescribed or predictable. It goes on to suggest that 'as chaplains get established as an authentic and reliable presence . . . relationships begin to develop and opportunities for pastoral care arise'.

It is only in the context of established relationships that spiritual need can be addressed since, as the stories in our book illustrate, the understanding of what gives meaning and purpose to a person's life is only gleaned through the process of gaining insight into another's life journey. As Cobb describes it:

> [C]haplains deal with the less tangible aspects of wellbeing through stories, narratives and dialogues, both of individuals and communities: precious stories of hope, spoken and unspoken narratives of suffering, and dialogues exploring what we might mean by health, life and death . . . it is the way we struggle to remember and find our identity as human beings. And it is in this search for meaning that the chaplain is a reminder of the spiritual dimension. (2005, p. 23)

This can be an end in itself, but it may also provide a platform for celebration, facilitating adaptation to circumstances, healing, resolution of conflict and grief, finding peace, and nurturing of growth.

Providing opportunities for exploring and expressing spirituality through religious worship and ritual is one of the most obvious tasks of the chaplain. But this is of greatest value when carried out in the context of having addressed pastoral and spiritual needs. It exploits both the 'sacramental presence' and the 'representative' function that chaplaincy reflects. It can be expressed just as much through the request or offering of a simple prayer of comfort in a specific pastoral situation as through organized fellowship/Bible study groups, services of worship or engaging in theological discussion and exploration of issues such as the creation of the universe, crises of faith, suffering and end of life. This will sometimes occur within the understanding of a particular denominational or faith context. Equally it may arise for those without any declared formal faith background at all. Gerkin (1997) recognizes the important role in developing relationships that is played by the dialogue between the particular life story of the individual and stories of the faith group communities and their beliefs and values. He describes the chaplain as being located in the space between the individual and the faith group she or he represents. Here, the chaplain endeavours to retain a balance between giving empathic attention to the story of the individual while being able to facilitate an open dialogue between that story and the story of the faith community. Sometimes the chaplain focuses more on helping the person to articulate their story, while at other times the chaplain may use a faith perspective in order to enrich and inform the dialogue. The model suggests that a chaplain may move between the stories of the individual and the faith community to facilitate effective and caring dialogue.

Threlfall-Holmes and Newitt (2011) describe the ambiguous position in which chaplains often find themselves, both organizationally and in relation to the individual, as examples of 'marginality' or 'liminality'. On an organizational level, as Legood (1999, pp. xi) suggests in his introduction to a book examining chaplaincy as sector ministry, the chaplain may be regarded as *of* an institution, being an integral part of the staff team, relating *to* it as a representative of the Church or operating *at* the institution where they exercise their ministry but are not necessarily bound by its values. Similarly, at an individual level, the chaplain must be seen as fully engaged with a person's story, but must also be able to retain a reflective distance in which they can represent and, where appropriate, offer an independent perspective or interpretation of the story they are being told. What is clear from these descriptions is that the way in which a chaplain is viewed will have implications for the way in which they can exercise their function. In the same book, Moody (1999), in his theological reflection on sector ministry, describes chaplaincy as a 'wilderness ministry' and explores in some depth the ramifications of this and other conceptualizations of the chaplain's role. As Threlfall-Holmes and Newitt point out, this feature of liminality is not exclusive to chaplaincy but is highlighted by the contexts in which chaplains find themselves.

Chaplaincy in social care settings with older people

One notable absence from all of these reviews of the exercise of chaplaincy in a variety of settings is any reference to chaplaincy work within the context of social care settings, and in relation to older people in particular. This is a significant omission, especially in light of the current changes in demography relating to age.

While it is not the only organization providing such care, MHA has pioneered the ministry of chaplaincy in the context of the social care of older people throughout its 70-year history. Over that time, the models of chaplaincy have evolved and developed so that, currently, there is dedicated chaplaincy time in each of its 150 residential, nursing and dementia care homes and independent living with care schemes. In a few cases chaplains are volunteers, but most are employed by the organization, suggesting that chaplaincy is seen as an essential aspect of the care that MHA provides.

In looking at some of the stories recounted in this book, it is possible to describe some of the particular features of chaplaincy in work with older people, to highlight how some of these characteristics manifest themselves in practice, and to show how they contribute to our understanding and promotion of faith development, both throughout the lifespan, and for the oldest old in particular. Those who find it necessary to move to a longer-term care setting are unlikely to do so until it is absolutely necessary. In the context of a chaplaincy model of ministry, however, such a move does present the opportunity for the formation of deeper, ongoing and longer-term relationships. The circumstances surrounding moving into a new home can also often provide a platform, willingness and desire to explore a whole raft of issues with which those nearing the end of their lives are confronted. The presence of a sympathetic and listening ear may literally be perceived as God-given!

In exploring the role of the chaplain in social care settings in more detail, it is helpful to focus on the three categories of issues that chaplains encounter when dealing with residents.

Pastoral issues

A core function in the role of any chaplain lies in listening to a person's story. Nowhere is this likely to be more important than in relation to older people, especially those to be found in a care setting. Not only do they have a greater lifespan represented by that story, but their presence in a care environment is likely to suggest that opportunities for adding to their formative experiences may have become more limited, although, of course, not necessarily totally absent. Indeed, it can be argued that the chaplain can play a major part in facilitating such opportunities, and in terms of acknowledging, affirming and valuing individuality, the presence of someone whose purpose is to give expression to a person's story can be invaluable.

In relating her own story, Sally (Story 11) describes how visits from her local vicars in training were essential in keeping her own faith alive. However, it was only when a dedicated chaplain for the home arrived that, for her, it felt like 'the icing on the cake'. In Joan's story (Story 9) we hear how it was only when the chaplain was able to give space and time to be with her that she felt enabled to share her life's journey. For Joan, in her early nineties, this marked the point at which she could then let go and, shortly after sharing her story, she died. As the chaplain reflects: 'Finding release from something that is bothering us can come through simply being able to tell someone else. It is not always necessary to do more.'

The need to resist the urge always to do something for someone, rather than just be alongside them and be ready to listen, is taken up in the chaplain's reflection in Nancy's story (Story 3). This requires patience and a trust that the right moment will be given when a person is ready to respond or move on in the next stage of their journey. Goodall (2011) describes this essential feature of the relationship between chaplain and resident as one of 'loving attention'.

It is sometimes suggested that a chaplain is in the 'opportunity business'; that is to say, they need to be available to exploit opportunities to share stories when they arise but, equally, to offer opportunities in a non-intrusive way, which may or may not sow seeds for future reaping. It's also interesting to note that Pearl's story (Story 2) might never have been told had she not been approached to express a view over whether someone else's willingness to share a story would be forthcoming.

In considering the significance of Edith's story (Story 8), the chaplain writes: 'It is a reflection of attentive ministry that relationships between home chaplains and residents deepen as minds meet, connections are made, reciprocity is shown and God works visibly in and through us.' The concept of reciprocity reflects both that chaplains find it a privilege to listen and share in someone else's story and that, in so doing, they themselves discover they are being ministered to. This is also seen in the stories of Mary (Story 1) and Pearl (Story 2).

Some people will require very little prompting to share their story, while for others it may be a matter of time and encouragement. So, in Arthur and Alice's story (Story 7) we can see how a synchronization of interests between the chaplain and the residents can prove fruitful. But there will also be those for whom verbal discourse is either difficult or impossible, particularly those living with dementia. In Ada's story (Story 10), we are reminded that connections may be made at a different level, where the details of events are forgotten but the emotions associated with the event can still be tapped into.

Spiritual issues

If pastoral concern is about acknowledging the importance of an individual's story, affirming it and providing understanding and support where necessary, then embracing a person's spiritual needs is concerned with recognizing how their story reflects what gives meaning and purpose in their life, and helping to find ways in which that spirituality can be expressed. Spiritual need also implies a desire or requirement for development, growth and change. This may be at the level of affirming a person's individuality and a sense of their worth and value. It may involve enhancing someone's quality of life, or addressing unresolved issues and conflicts that result from vulnerability, isolation or frailty, or working through bereavement and end-of-life issues. It may also mean exploring the dimension of belief and faith and, as we shall explore later, religious affiliation. None of these areas of spiritual need are exclusive to older people and their social care settings, but they will take on a particular degree of significance in these contexts. For instance, as ageing is a lifelong process, the opportunity to preserve hopes and dreams should always be kept alive even though they may have to be moderated and grounded in reality. These may be long-held ambitions, or horizons that only appear as the person matures and develops. Whichever is the case, it is important that these hopes and dreams are not only cultivated but also given an opportunity for expression, since the perception of some may be that, if a life is coming to its natural end, it therefore has limited value and worth. Chaplains are often uniquely placed to relate to people in these circumstances, to discern their needs and to provide forms of pastoral care. They can also nurture well-being, foster hope and support people through the transitions that accompany growing older.

Our stories illustrate some very powerful but varied ways in which chaplains in social care settings can help older people address spiritual needs. This is at its most obvious with those who can identify explicitly with a lifelong journey of faith. So, for instance, in Joyce's story (Story 6) we hear of a lifelong Methodist valuing the opportunity to discuss and explore issues of faith with the chaplain in a way she cannot with her friends because 'she does not want to introduce questions that may cause them to lose their faith'. The irony here is that the whole of her own faith journey, as described, reflects someone who has continually challenged belief and assumptions throughout her life, and shows how the continued opportunity to do this in her later life, with the chaplain as an accompanist, has been invaluable!

The mere presence and activity of the chaplain in organizing Bible study and fellowship groups, services of worship and opportunities to pray with people also provides those residents who have an active faith with a reminder of the sustaining presence of God in their midst. This is vividly reflected in the story of Daphne (Story 12), who, in the face of her difficulty relating to the present, found great solace in the words of familiar Scripture, prayers and hymns and in the comforting presence of the chaplain.

But the role of the chaplain is not confined only to those with a declared faith, as the story of Sidney (Story 4) poignantly illustrates. His time in residential care represents a period of exploration and spiritual growth in the context of a background of apparent atheism. This is achieved through an attitude of openness and invitation offered by the chaplain, and their sensitive and timely response to questions. Conversion was neither the object, nor necessarily the outcome, but rather spiritual growth reflected in reaching a place of peace.

Another feature of Sidney's story, also picked up in several other stories, including Joyce (Story 6) and Ada (Story 10), is the important role that chaplains in this context have in helping residents to address final wishes and end-of-life issues. As already described in Joan's story, for some this may simply be a matter of putting one's house in order so that they can let go. Some may need the opportunity to address issues such as fear of death, questions about the hereafter, final wishes, making funeral arrangements, and so on: areas which it is the particular privilege of chaplains working in social care settings to explore in the context of an ongoing relationship. Others, such as Ada (Story 10), might feel they need to put things right with God, which may involve religious rites such as confession and communion (discussed later). These are likely to become particularly legitimate areas of exploration in those contexts where death and how it is dealt with will become difficult to avoid. The chaplain therefore has a dual responsibility, not only for being personally available to individuals to share their concerns and insights, but also to help create an ethos and confidence within the care setting that makes this obviously acceptable.

Finally, if spirituality is concerned with affirmation of individuality, this should be no more so than in relation to acknowledging and giving opportunity for residents to express and utilize their own spiritual gifts and to continue to grow. Several examples of this emerge through our stories where individuals such as Mary (Story 1), Robert (Story 5) and Edith (Story 8) are given opportunities to encourage spiritual growth in others through the exercise of their own spiritual gifts – in effect as 'auxiliary chaplains'.

This is not only life-enhancing for the individuals involved but of considerable benefit to the well-being of others and to the ethos of the home.

Religious issues

Finally, in our exploration of the role of the chaplain in social care settings we must examine the importance of ensuring spiritual need has opportunity to be expressed through religious ritual, worship and fellowship. The stories of Mary (Story 1) and Sally (Story 11) illustrate that there is no doubt of the importance of being able to continue to be involved in acts of worship for those who have had a lifelong history of involvement in church life. However, Joyce's story (Story 6) also reminds us not to have preconceived ideas about what forms of worship may be acceptable to older people, as not only do they often have a broader concept of what constitutes inspiring worship, but more important to them is the fact that there is a continuing opportunity to avail themselves of any worship at all. This can be seen clearly in Winnie's story (Story 14), and I have already alluded to the importance of familiar words in Scripture, song and prayer especially for those living with dementia, particularly for Daphne (Story 12). But as Sidney (Story 4) reminds us, even for those without a declared faith, a Bible study, fellowship or meditation group may provide an important context for spiritual nurture and comfort.

Elizabeth's story (Story 13) shows us that even for those with an ambivalent attitude towards faith and the Church, opportunities for worship and exploring the Church's teachings may still be important. This story also highlights the role that the chaplain, lay or ordained, may have to carry as a representative of the Church, being perceived as one who holds authority and who is therefore conferred with the knowledge of their faith group, its doctrine and its guidance. It also means that, as in Elizabeth's story (Story 13), the chaplain may be required to absorb the person's ambivalence to the Church and the hurts they have experienced through it. The difference in a social care setting is that there is an increased likelihood that the chaplain will be present and available for a sufficiently continuous length of time to develop a conciliatory and positive relationship through which prejudice and past hurts can be healed. Ainsworth-Smith and Speck (1982) describe in some detail the role that sacramental rites such as confession, absolution, baptism and confirmation can play in bringing about healing and growth. It will often fall to the chaplain to make these available to residents in social care settings – whether in person or by ensuring there is someone appropriate available to do so. This also brings into play another role for the chaplain: making links to the wider church community for both individuals and the home as a whole, the importance of which is illustrated in Mary's (Story 1) and Sally's (Story 11) stories.

Chaplaincy as a model of ministry for mission

Because the focus of this book is on giving voice to the oldest old and seeking to explore the role of religious faith in their lives, I have concentrated on the role of the chaplain in coming alongside the residents of social care settings, and endeavoured to identify some of the characteristics that distinctively define and provide benefit to chaplaincy in these settings. These centre around opportunities that accrue from being alongside people who, generally speaking, are in a medium- or long-term care environment and with whom the possibility of developing ongoing relationships can occur. In turn, this can provide the bedrock upon which the establishment of trust and deeper exploration of spiritual issues can be built. Inevitably, older people are more likely to be facing issues of dependence, bereavement, loss and those associated with the end of their lives, and it is important that these are addressed. However, chaplaincy work in social care settings centres on residents who, although they may be physically or mentally frail, will not necessarily be in a crisis or acute situation. This means the issues explored are likely to be more relevant to the everyday, and existential in nature. The chaplain also has a wider brief in that their work brings them into contact with families, staff, volunteers and members of other faith communities that are associated with the care setting, for all of whom they may have an important function and purpose. They also have a significant role in helping to develop the community life in these settings.

Many of these aspects of ministry will be familiar to those engaged in the pastoral component of church-based ministry. But while the richness of pastoral contact between chaplain and resident, illustrated through our stories, will have echoes for those still actively engaged in this element of church life, they may also point to an area of need that a church, preoccupied by survival, administration and preservation of buildings, can find progressively more difficult to meet. Yet if a primary missiological task for the Church is to aid people in the exploration and progression of their spiritual journey, then this has to be an area of ministry that must regain its priority. The distinctiveness of chaplaincy as a model of ministry lies in ensuring it takes place within a particular context of the diversity of people's everyday life experience. The chaplain is an accompanist, companion and support in that context but has to be present in the ordinary so that he or she will be available and utilized in times of particular need. This model therefore offers much from which those engaged in the Church's pastoral ministry can learn. In an increasingly mobile, individualistic and sceptical society, no longer can the institutional church expect people to turn in its direction to spontaneously or instinctively seek support, guidance or answers to life questions.

Furthermore, as our stories illustrate, there is much that the Church can learn from the lifetime of experience, the accumulated wisdom and the extended journey of both personal and spiritual development – some rooted in the religious, much not – that older people bring with them. As Lawrence Moore describes in Chapter 11, 'we need to learn how to grow old as a church, and that we do so by adopting a new paradigm that derives from insights into the spiritual worlds and experiences of the very old'. The opportunities provided by coming alongside the oldest old are fertile ground for spiritual reflection, discovery and further growth – ground from which much spiritual fruit can be harvested through the time and attention that this model of chaplaincy can help to sow.

References

Ainsworth-Smith, I. and Speck, P., 1982, *Letting Go: Caring for the Dying and Bereaved*, London: SPCK, pp. 61–105.

Campbell, A. V., 1985, *Paid to Care? Limits of Professionalism in Pastoral Care*, London: SPCK.

Cobb, M. R., 2005, *The Hospital Chaplains' Handbook: A Guide for Good Practice*, Norwich: Canterbury Press.

Gerkin, C. V., 1997, *An Introduction to Pastoral Care*, Nashville, TN: Abingdon Press.

Goodall, M. A., 2011, 'Loving attention: chaplaincy as a model of spiritual care for those with dementia', in Jewell, A. (ed.), *Spirituality and Personhood in Dementia*, London: Jessica Kingsley Publishers, pp. 131–40.

Holland, J. A., 2012, 'What bedside nurses can teach nursing leaders', *American Nurse Today* 7:6 (June), http://americannurse today.com/article.aspx?id=9190.

Jones, R., 2010, 'Characteristics of chaplaincy: a Methodist understanding', *Epworth Review* 37:4, pp. 5–9.

Legood, G. (ed.), 1999, *Chaplaincy: The Church's Sector Ministries*, London: Cassell.

Moody, C., 1999, 'Spirituality and sector ministry', in Legood, G. (ed.), *Chaplaincy: The Church's Sector Ministries*, London: Cassell, pp. 15–24.

The Methodist Church, 2012, *Chaplaincy Everywhere: A Small Group Resource for Nurturing Engagement in God's Mission through Chaplaincy*, http://www.methodist.org.uk/chaplaincyeverywhere.

Threlfall-Holmes, M. and Newitt, M., 2011, *Being a Chaplain*, London: SPCK, pp. 103–40.

13

Lessons from Listening

MALCOLM JOHNSON *and* KEITH ALBANS

It might seem totally commonplace to some to direct so much attention to *listening* and in particular to listening to very old people. Yet it will be apparent by now that many in later life have no one to hear their concerns and recollections drawn from a long life. Even if they live with a partner or are looked after by a family member, there may be things they feel, want or need to tell, for whom family are not the appropriate audience. Those relatives may be too preoccupied by the tasks of caring, along with otherwise busy lives, to make time for deeper conversation. It may also be that addressing difficult issues from the past, identifying wishes for funeral arrangements or expressing anxieties about belief or death are matters to be positively avoided. It is often the case that talking about matters of deep concern is easier with an interested stranger.

The interested stranger may be someone you know you will never see or hear from again – perhaps a fellow traveller on a long train journey. But it may also be someone in our circle of living, whom you know to have special qualities of understanding, integrity and trustworthy discretion. Such dedicated listeners and accompanists may be a trusted friend, a colleague, a relative or a respected member of a church or organization. Clergy of all religions and denominations serve as pastors to their members and are often available to others in need. Their historic role as leaders of moral communities, as conductors of religious and public rituals, has greatly diminished in Britain as in other western countries.

These shifts in cultural practice have deprived communities of the recognized dignity of representatives of the churches and more particularly of the open access to clergy. In turn the availability of a listening ear for confessional tellings and the possibility of a redemptive blessing is further away from most citizens, most particularly the housebound elderly.

Contemporary civil society is greatly in need of new forms of ritual to mark the important transitions of life, both for individuals and for collective bodies. While churches of all denominations remain willing to offer hospitality and comfort, there are many people for whom entering a religious building is an alien experience. As Lawrence Moore points out in Chapter 11, the churches have yet to engage fully with the new populations of older people. He asks, 'How does the Church meaningfully incorporate the oldest old into its life as the norm, not the exception?' He too is drawn to the chaplaincy model which reaches out. Albert Jewell (Chapter 3) draws attention to research evidence that churches may exhaust willing older members in the tasks of church life without nurturing them spiritually, although he also relates evidence of well-conceived initiatives that help them in finding later-life reconciliation and peace. Alas sometimes this reconciliation is required to mend the hurts that churches have themselves inflicted as a result of fractured relationships and unchristian judgemental behaviour, as several of the stories in Part 2 powerfully illustrate.

In his chapter on the spiritual journey into old age, Keith Albans shows the importance of nurturing spiritual review and growth in the later years, signposting and valuing the landmarks along the way. In addressing the experience of very old age, he considers the diminishment that so often comes with failing health and frailty. But, in contrast, he highlights how the spiritual dimension of life can be seen as a counter to this feeling that life is on a downward path and emphasizes the role of accompanists in helping to rekindle new purpose and belief. In a complementary vein, in Chapter 4, James Woodward seeks to promote serious attention to life stories and enabling individuals to see their own life narrative as important and worthy. The growing movement in linking narratology with spiritual revelation is one in which he can claim a formative role.

Both Ann Morisy in Chapter 9 and Joanna Walker in Chapter 8 paint on a wider canvas. Ann's growing list of widely acclaimed books on living and believing draw as much on sociology as on theology. She uses a beguiling and instantly accessible language of expectation, aspiration and hope to empower believers and doubters alike to see the possibility of positive change both in individuals and in the world around us. Her enthusiasm for grace and gratitude, poetry and prayer, apply just as much to the old as the young.

Seeing the life journey as an exploration, to be a constant series of opportunities to learn, is central to Joanna Walker's work as an adult educator with a will to promote spiritual growth. She acknowledges that this is counter to the popular belief that old age is essentially about decline. Like Keith Albans she sees in the differing approaches of gerontology, psychotherapy and pastoral theology 'another aspect of the "second half" . . . [where] . . . other aspects of our personalities and of our gendered identities can be brought out in later life'.

There are clearly common themes in the diverse approaches of our authors. Central to their views about late old age is a conviction, drawn from their own studies and life experience, that the spiritual dimension of later life, though much neglected within churches and in wider society, is deeply important. Moreover, they are well aware that for most people the presence of a careful and responsible listener to act as an enabler of the life story to emerge and be valued, is essential.

Later-life ministry

As Andrew Norris describes in Chapter 12, chaplaincy is a later-life ministry that is based on relationship. In some forms of chaplaincy work the essential task is to fashion points of immediate contact, such as in hospitals where patients and their families may be brief visitors or there because of a life-threatening event.

Indeed, as 55 per cent of all UK deaths (and three-quarters of them are people over 75) currently take place in hospitals, the engagement is between strangers in distress and an unknown chaplain. The setting of a care home, supported living or retirement village provides a dwelling place for older residents. It is their home. Chaplains are part of the community, there to be available to all, residents, staff and families. Importantly they are apart from all yet available to all – not care providers, managers, nurses or chefs. This separateness and availability comes with open access to all who welcome it. Chaplains are trained to listen and interpret with pastoral care. They are obliged to maintain discretion, so those who speak with them and seek their nurture know they can do so in confidence. These are features of the ancient priestly role transformed into a twenty-first-century world of secular culture and private belief.

In Part 2, Margaret Goodall and Andrew Norris take us into the everyday world of chaplains and provide a context for 15 typical but powerful stories. The reader might perceive these as the result of a single encounter, but it is much more likely they developed over time, out of a growing relationship built on trust and empathy. In this respect their value is cumulative; closer to the extended exchanges between psychologist, counsellor or psychotherapist and their patients, than the emotion-filled encounters in busy hospitals and emergency units. But unlike the healthcare professionals, the chaplain is not there to attempt to remove identified pathologies by diagnosis and intervention. Engagement and listening are the central features.

Engaging with older people and the protected privacy of their past, takes patience and skill. As Andrew Norris reminds us in Chapter 12, the chaplain 'must be seen as fully engaged with a person's story, but must also be able to retain a reflective distance'. It is important to be clear about the rules of conduct and the 'marginality' that is required. After all, this work involves entering the personal worlds of other human beings. But it is not and must not become the exclusive province of a new professional group. There are many who have empathy, life experience and discretion, who know how to befriend and support.

Yet if there is to be – as we advocate – an expanded ministry to older people, it must be based on being exposed to the body of knowledge and to tried and tested approaches. Then there are the ethical issues that attend all privileged access to the private zones of individual lives.

The reader will have observed that our attention has been largely devoted to the frail but cognitively competent older person, who can relate their recollections, feelings and aspirations in a comprehensible fashion. Of course, much of what becomes a story will be made up of disconnected fragments and repeated but differing versions, even where clear minds are present. But for the expanding numbers with dementia, whose factual memories become unreliable and whose cognitive impairment is a deep frustration, the processes of hearing a story out of a period of accompanying requires a higher order of skill and tutored empathy.

Margaret Goodall, in Chapter 10, emphasizes 'the doctrine of grace', or as Malcolm Goldsmith (1999) articulates it, we are all 'remembered by God'. Behind these theological abstractions is a joint venture to create a place where the person can feel safe in the present and at ease with the past. This safe place can be a time when words or sounds or images are shared and their meanings celebrated. If spirituality is centrally about meaning, identity and belief, then there is an emergent body of practice that penetrates the disorder and frustration of cognitive decline, to sustain personhood. More experience, research and skill development in fashioning meaning within dementia is essential.

Struggles with faith, belief and the Church

Among the recurring themes in the Stories are the struggles with faith and belief. Many also speak about the damage the Church and its representatives have done. Derived from his four decades of studying the beliefs of a sample population of people now in late old age, Peter Coleman reports on their contemporary experiences of living: what they believe, how those religious convictions have changed, and what meaning they have in their lives. His data lend support to the theory of gradual secularization, while showing evidence of a stabilization of religious and spiritual belief among the older UK population, who, in turn, are more religious in attitude and interest than younger members (Coleman, 2011, p. 29). When interviewed in more detail about their beliefs, many of the study sample spoke of doubts about the basic tenets of the Christian faith. Concerns about God as a person, preferring to think of a powerful life force, the nature of a loving God and the doctrine of the Trinity also figured in their responses (p. 31). But for Coleman, as for many writers in this field, the presence of doubts and the continued struggle with belief is both normal and healthy.

These findings are reflected in older Americans as reported by Eisenhandler (2003). She writes of 'a grown up faith' which has shed a good deal of the Sunday school mythology and the churchly rules, along with the fears and guilts that formed the platform of their beliefs in childhood. Yet many are still rooted in the lives of their churches, see the Christian way as their route map of life and continue to pray.

Leading gerontologists, from very different societies, both active members of Christian denominations, provide strong evidence of failings in churches and faith communities which have damaged the lives of present or lapsed members. Some, as Eisenhandler reports, have grown through the experience of less than loving treatment and developed new faith foundations, either through another church or through their own synthesis of what beliefs are central to them. Others harbour their anger and resentment, without apology or recognition. Love and forgiveness are fundamental to Christian beliefs and practice, but not always present. As churches develop a theology of old age, they need to place redemption and mutual forgiveness at its heart.

The art and discipline of listening

Dylan Thomas's best known work, *Under Milk Wood*, was written for radio and was described as 'a play for voices'. The narrator opens the play with an elegiac invocation to the multitude of unseen listeners. He introduces the people of Llareggub through their dreams and creates some idea of what will be important to them when they are awake. For Dai Bread it is harems; Polly Garter loves babies; and Nogood Boyo dreams of 'Nothing'. The town as a whole has its own personality, which is divided along Freudian lines into a conscious world of daily activity narrated by the First Voice, and a subconscious world of intimate thoughts and feelings revealed by the Second Voice. The actor Richard Burton claimed, 'the entire thing is about religion, the idea of death and sex'. These important themes are central to our comprehension of the seen but unobserved undertow of other people's lives.

It is Spring, moonless night in the small town, starless and bible-black . . . And all the people of the lulled and dumbfound town are sleeping . . . Only your eyes are unclosed, to see the black and folded town fast, and slow, asleep. And you alone can hear the invisible starfall, the darkest-before-dawn minutely dew-grazed stir of the black, dab-filled sea . . . Listen. It is night moving in the streets, the processional salt slow musical wind in Coronation Street and Cockle Row, it is the grass growing on Llareggub Hill . . . Time passes. Listen. Time passes. Come closer now. Only you can hear the houses sleeping in the streets . . . Only you can hear and see, behind the eyes of the sleepers, the movements and countries and mazes and colours and dismays and rainbows and tunes and wishes and flight and fall and despairs and big seas of their dreams. From where you are, you can hear their dreams. (1962, pp. 1–3)

Thomas the poet is inviting us into his acutely observed world, where he sees and hears the hidden and unseen lives of the people of his fictional village by the sea. His invocation is to listen to the world and take delight in hearing the life-scripts of the saints and sinners, their hopes and fears. In their human frailties, he also finds humour and mischief in the doings and indignities of everyday life. Too often in our pursuit of meaning in the accounts of older people's lives, we can overlook the humour of past transgressions as well as in the recollection of warmly remembered anecdotes.

Just as poets and writers down the ages have portrayed the great stories of human affairs and biographers revealed the inner lives of the famous, there is a strong tradition in theology and in sociology of using life histories to illuminate the social fabric of past and current societies. In recent times there is emerging a new literature in this domain of pastoral theology which reflects both on the need to engage with the spiritual needs of older people and to understand the experience of old age. Notable among these would be James Woodward's *Valuing Age* (2008), Albert Jewell's early books *Ageing, Spirituality and Well-Being* (2004) and *Older People and the Church* (2001), Ann Morisy's *Bothered and Bewildered* (2009) and *Borrowing from the Future* (2011). The work of Elizabeth MacKinlay (2001, 2006) from Australia has been formative in this field. From the USA there is a wider literature, but two worthy of special mention, by leading gerontologists, are Robert Atchley's *Spirituality and Aging* (2009) and Harry Moody and David Carroll's *The Five Ages of the Soul* (1997).

In contemporary society there is a still expanding range of what are loosely termed 'listening therapies' – psychiatry, various forms of clinical psychology, counselling, psychotherapy and so on. Chaplaincy is not any of these. Its distinctive characteristic is pastoral rather than therapeutic treatment. So the listening is a form of shared exploration, where the teller does all or at least most of the talking. In this respect, the listening style portrayed in this volume is much closer to the listening of the oral historian. Over the past three decades an illuminating literature of older people's oral history accounts has meshed with the related field known as biographical studies. Here the researcher is also a listener to life stories, for the academic purposes of understanding the experiences of ageing. There is much in common with the chaplaincy enterprise.

The voice of the past

When Paul Thompson published his seminal book on oral history, *The Voice of the Past* (1978), it was widely disparaged by leading historians for whom history was to be observed through the lives and doings of the great and the powerful. Source material for such accounts of national fortunes was to be derived from documents written by the literate minority and through the study of art and artefacts which represented those past times. Thompson argued that history is made just as much by the so-called ordinary person living his or her life in the everyday circumstances, where they experience love, health, work, illness, joy, success, failure, belief, achievement and death. This thesis fitted the emancipatory social and political climate of the 1960s and 1970s and rapidly gained a respected place both in social science research and in the practice of social support professionals. It gave credence to the value of storytelling and began to find a place in a wide range of settings where valuing and learning from personal, as well as group, reminiscence could be seen as enabling greater self-esteem and facing up to relationship problems and depression. So what commenced as a methodology for developing 'bottom-up' history quickly sponsored an emergent set of practices that had wide application to older people.

A leading figure in the growing oral history movement was Joanna Bornat, whose early work at Help the Aged produced the first 'reminiscence packs' designed for use in care homes and day centres. The development of books, products and experience of how to use reminiscence techniques is reported in a series of publications, notably *Reminiscence Reviewed* (1994). Here we see the way listening to the past of older people in need of care has become widespread. Life-story books, visual reminders of the lives of those now old and attention to the cultural favourites of those years are now a welcome and affirming presence. But in an overview of reminiscence and oral history (Bornat, 2005) she cautions against uninstructed use of the resulting accounts of lives lived. Bornat draws attention to the way reminiscence work is sometimes used inappropriately in care home settings where staff attribute aversions or decided but difficult preferences to past traumas, when these judgements have no validity (2005, p. 320). Like all techniques and approaches, reminiscence work requires training both in evidence-based practice and, in particular, in the ground rules of interpretation.

Being heard and being valued

One key message of this present volume is that being taken seriously in very old age is an often ignored right. Slowly that right is being recognized by the agencies of society and within belief communities. This book is an attempt to authenticate the right of older people to be valued and to have the distinctive needs of life review, with all its implications, taken as an essential requirement of later life. But the book is not a theoretical treatise. It grew out of deep, profound experience and a rigorous distillation of what works. The years of development of spiritual nurturing, which is at the heart of chaplaincy, are reported not as a body of data or a series of charts mapping achievements against set parameters. Instead, we have provided a selection of stories along with interpretations, nested in the reflexive essays of leading explorers in this old but new venture of understanding and caring for the inner lives of the very old.

The other key message of this volume is that the value of listening to those in extreme old age is not for them alone. Their testimony to both the nature and the role of religious faith in the latter years of life has something profound to say to clergy, religious educators and church leaders alike. On the one hand, their stories serve as a reminder of the value of a faith unencumbered by many of the doctrinal and exegetical debates which have dominated church life for the past 40 years. On the other hand, they also warn of the lasting damage that can be done in the name of religion and that, in an ageing society, will be borne for very many years.

There are also missiological implications to be gleaned from listening. In many communities the experience of a 'cradle to grave' religious life, which many of our stories illustrate, is increasingly rare. Indeed, during the next 20 years or so the last generation of those for whom weekly attendance at Sunday school was common will enter old age. As has been argued by both Albert Jewell (Chapter 3) and Lawrence Moore (Chapter 11), the Church needs to rethink its mission strategy and take seriously the task of bringing more older people into Christian discipleship. If it is to do so, learning from today's oldest pilgrims as to how a personal religious faith and the community of faith can be a help in addressing the vicissitudes of ageing is a task worthy of serious consideration.

References

Atchley, R. C., 2009, *Spirituality and Aging*, Baltimore, MD: Johns Hopkins University Press.

Bornat, J., 1994, *Reminiscence Reviewed*, Buckingham: Open University Press.

Bornat, J., 2005, 'Listening to the past: reminiscence and oral history', in Johnson, M. L., Bengtson, V. L., Coleman, P. and Kirkwood, T. (eds), *Cambridge Handbook of Age and Ageing*, Cambridge: Cambridge University Press, pp. 316–22.

Coleman, P. G., 2011, *Belief and Ageing: Spiritual Pathways in Later Life*, Bristol: The Policy Press.

Eisenhandler, S. A., 2003, *Keeping the Faith in Later Life*, New York: Springer Publishing Co.

Goldsmith, M., 1999, 'Dementia: a challenge to Christian theology and pastoral care', in Jewell, A. (ed.), *Spirituality and Ageing*, London: Jessica Kingsley Publishers, pp. 125–45.

Jewell, A., 2001, *Older People and the Church*, London: Methodist Publishing.

Jewell, A. (ed.), 2004, *Ageing, Spirituality and Well-Being*, London: Jessica Kingsley Publishers.

MacKinlay, E., 2001, *The Spiritual Dimensions of Ageing*, London: Jessica Kingsley Publishers.

MacKinlay, E., 2006, *Spiritual Growth and Care in the Fourth Age of Life*, London: Jessica Kingsley Publishers.

Moody, H. R. and Carroll, D., 1997, *The Five Ages of the Soul: Charting the Spiritual Passages that Shape our Lives*, New York: Doubleday.

Morisy, A., 2009, *Bothered and Bewildered*, London: Continuum.

Morisy, A., 2011, *Borrowing from the Future: A Faith-Based Approach to Intergenerational Equity*, London: Continuum.

Thomas, D., 1962, *Under Milk Wood*, Letchworth: J. M. Dent & Sons Ltd.

Thompson, P., 1978, *The Voice of the Past*, Oxford: Oxford University Press, 3rd edn, 2000.

Woodward, J., 2008, *Valuing Age: Pastoral Ministry with Older People*, London: SPCK.

Index

abandonment 133, 141, 155, 176, 193
acceptance 25, 26, 72, 91, 140, 148, 156, 166, 169
accompanying 11, 18, 33, 75–6, 140, 194, 196, 202
Adamson, David 11–13
Albans, Keith 17, 45, 48, 215–16
Anglican Church 81, 101, 105, 107 *see also* Church of England
Atchley, Robert 221

Baltes, Margaret 11
baptism(s) 79, 81, 124–6, 178, 211
Baptist Church 38, 81, 112–13, 116, 124
Becker, Ernest 165–7, 198
Berger, Peter 170
blessing(s) 37, 55, 60, 83, 96, 106, 113, 140, 150, 170–1, 215
body 4, 8, 12, 34, 60–1, 67, 135, 141, 166, 172, 174, 176, 183, 193, 218, 223
Bornat, Joanna 222
Bryden, Christine 180–1, 184
Bunyan, Paul 7
burden 8, 29, 37, 39, 55, 103, 111, 115, 183, 191

Burton, Richard 220
Butler, Canon Michael 47
Butler, Robert 7–8, 10, 14, 17, 75

carer(s) 11, 13, 31–3, 52, 54, 94, 103, 125, 163, 174, 177, 179, 195–6
Carroll, David 221
chaplaincy 18, 34, 72, 74, 80, 92, 163, 200–5, 211–12, 215–16, 221, 223
chaplain(s) 17, 20, 34, 44, 71–5, 80–1, 85, 88, 104, 108, 110–12, 116, 119–20, 122–3, 127, 136–42, 146, 148, 152, 157, 163–5, 168, 172, 175, 178, 184, 193, 195–8, 200–12, 217
choice(s) 9, 61, 62, 105, 111, 124, 151
Church of England 38–42, 53, 86, 112 *see also* Anglican Church
clergy 137, 201, 214–15, 223
Cole, Thomas 7
Coleman, Peter 42, 152, 153, 218–19
comfort 12, 63, 82, 87–8, 92, 97, 99, 121, 123, 139, 177, 178, 180, 182–3, 196, 202–3, 210, 215

Methodist Homes 17, 20, 34,
71, 200
ministry 40–2, 44, 46–7, 88,
96, 104, 107–8, 134, 148,
189–91, 204–5, 207, 211–
12, 216, 218
Moody, Harry 221
Moore, Lawrence 212, 215, 224
Morisy, Ann 178, 216, 221
mortality 4, 5, 20, 64, 98, 198

narrative(s) 23, 26, 27, 34, 58,
97, 153, 196, 203
neglect 10, 14, 42, 52
New Churches 37
Newell, Philip 28
Norris, Andrew 18, 216–17
Nouwen, Henri 99, 146–7

Orthodox 37–8

pain 59–60, 78, 86, 94, 98,
102, 103, 119, 141, 209
biographical 17, 150
patience 73, 79–80, 206, 217
Paul, St 33, 79, 96–7, 114,
135, 193
peace 49–50, 84, 90, 92,
111–12, 115, 132, 134,
136, 142, 180, 183, 196,
203, 209, 215
Peberdy, Alyson 22
Pentecostal 37–8
Piaget 167–8
prayer(s) 30, 40, 44, 48, 49,
54, 72, 79, 82–4, 86–7, 95,
99, 102, 107, 110–14, 118,
121–2, 131, 134, 139, 142,
157, 168, 172, 182, 196,
203, 208, 210, 216
Presbyterian Church 190
privilege 20, 63, 73, 90, 127,
149, 197, 207, 209

purpose 18, 23, 25, 28–9, 34,
39, 49, 71–2, 74–5, 87, 116–
17, 123, 134, 149, 151–2,
159, 166, 181, 184–5, 193,
202–3, 206–7, 212, 215

Rank, Otto 166
Rawls, John 164
reflection(s) 4, 15, 40, 44, 64,
75, 104, 114, 116, 119, 132,
137, 148, 151, 154, 157,
163, 184–5, 204, 206
religion(s) 5, 22, 25, 42, 44,
61, 72, 79, 86, 89, 93,
152–3, 156, 166–7, 180,
214, 220, 223
resilience 151, 155, 164–5,
172
retirement 9, 40, 44, 47, 49,
63, 81, 94, 102, 132
Riegel, Klaus 168–9
Rohr, Richard 151
Roman Catholic(s) 38, 40, 93,
117
Roosevelt, Eleanor 59

Sarton, May 59–60
satisfaction 14, 43, 74, 95,
108, 148
Schachter-Shalomi, Rabbi
Zalman 21
Shakespeare 7
Shields, David 60–2
Sitwell, Edith 28
Snowdon, David 55
spirituality 22–3, 25, 28, 40,
42–3, 46, 72, 85, 100, 145,
152–6, 159, 174, 180–1,
183, 185, 189, 197–9, 207,
209, 218, 221
stranger(s) 13, 58, 188–90,
192–3, 214, 217
Stuckey, Jon 175